Nonfiction Books by Ken Cashion:

BALL TURRET GUNNER...Weather Bad/Flak Heavy

Soft Cover 8.5" x 11" ISBN 0-9771187-0-3
ISBN 978-0-9771187-0-0
Soft Cover 6"x9" ISBN 978-0-9985271-1-6

BERLIN GIRL...Her Story 1929 -1952

Soft Cover (1st Printing) ISBN 0-9771187-3-8
ISBN 978-0-9771187-3-1
Soft Cover (2nd Printing) ISBN 978-0-9771187-4-8
eBook (2nd Printing) ISBN 978-0-9771187-8-6

LONG CAPTIONS...Sixty-Six True Stories

Soft Cover ISBN 0-9771187-1-1
ISBN 978-0-9771187-1-7

LONG CAPTIONS – VOLUME ONE...Thirty-Three True Stories

Soft Cover ISBN 978-0-9985271-2-3

LONG CAPTIONS – VOLUME TWO...Thirty-Three True Stories

Soft Cover ISBN 978-0-9985271-3-0

MUSINGS FOR MUSIC LOVERS...With a Bit of History

Soft Cover ISBN 978-0-9771187-7-9
eBook ISBN 978-0-9771187-6-2

A SOCIAL HISTORY OF BRITAIN...From First Humans to the Creation of Great Britain

Soft Cover ISBN 978-0-9771187-2-4
eBook ISBN 10; 0-9771187-5-4
ISBN 978-0-9771187-5-5

AN AMERICAN'S TRAVEL JOURNAL OF BRITAIN... 23,000 Miles in the Left Lane

Soft Cover ISBN 978-0-9985271-0-9

SOLDER SLINGER...An Engineer's Journey from the Future to the Past

Soft Cover ISBN 978-0-9985271-5-4

RANDOM THOUGHTS FROM A VEERING MIND... A Journal of Whimsy

Soft Cover ISBN 978-0-9985271-4-7

A SOCIAL HISTORY OF THE UNITED STATES FROM 1945 TO 2018...With 20/20 Hindsight

Soft Cover ISBN 978-0-9985271-6-1

A SOCIAL HISTORY OF THE UNITED STATES FROM 1945 TO 2018

~~~

With 20/20 Hindsight

Dedicated –

To all those who, in their innocence, caused changes
&
To all those who, in their innocence, were the occasions of the changes.

Windmill Productions
Luddite Publishers
~~~

This book is nonfiction. All comments, observations, and reflections are the results of public circumstances as revealed to the author. Events and dates referenced in this book are a matter of public record. There may be some exaggeration, sarcasm, or satire, but this should be obvious; it is presented to humor or illuminate.

A serious attempt has been made to maintain other's sense of privacy; however, there are many commonalities in defining the human condition and few people are so unique as to lay claim for creating a generality.

Unless names are given, any similarity to persons living or dead is a coincidence.

The images/graphics are owned by the author or are in public domain.

Windmill Productions
Luddite Publishers

Available from Amazon.com and other retail outlets.

Cover: Designed and produced by the author.

ISBN 978-0-9985271-6-1

Table of Contents

Preface

This book is not a continuation of this author's *Random Thoughts From A Veering Mind – A Journal of Whimsy*, but it could seem so in a few places. There is considerably more research invested in this book, *A Social History of the United States from 1945 to 2018 – With 20/20 Hindsight*. Consequently, the reader would profit more by reading this book before *Random Thoughts*.

Acknowledgments

Because my nature demands it, I continue to write, but I get no new information about *how* to write. I have the mechanics of writing figured out, but I may still produce incorrect grammar and employ my creative spelling. Additionally, I may construct clumsy paragraphs. In one chapter there could be a paragraph that is a stream of consciousness, while the next chapter begins with, "It was a dark and stormy night..."

I simply organize my material, put my thoughts down in text as if I were speaking with someone, and then I do my research to make sure that what I was thinking and saying/writing was actually valid. Generally it is, but when it is not, I must adjust my thinking to be consistent with the research – not the reverse – i.e., not adjust the research to agree with my perceptions. Long ago I learned that when writing fiction, the author leads the reader; when writing nonfiction – as I write – the research leads the author.

Because I want my writing to appeal to a wide audience, I must rely on others to correct my manuscript so that it conforms to a proper writing convention.

I seem to have developed a staff – my proof readers. Without them this would be a much poorer work and the reader would struggle more and learn less.

I give all credit for success to my staff – my wife, Bettie, and our daughter Julia Baker. Their professional credentials have been presented in the previous nine books. However, by necessity, I am the last person in this book production process, therefore all blame eventually and justifiably comes to me – all credit goes to them.

There is considerable commonality in Bettie's and Julia's backgrounds, and this provides some wholesome double-checking in the proofing process; still, each of these ladies has her own talent and education. These were shaped by different training and then honed in different professional environments.

Bettie's professional experience as a government contract officer taught her to question details and to recognize inconsistencies that may appear with many pages separating them.

Julia has spent countless hours (years) assuring important people who were performing important work that what they had written was what they wanted to be conveyed to their readers – readers who were other important people doing important work. This occurred in national and international security documents in the United States and in Germany. These documents had to conform to several specific writing styles and formatting requirements.

Other people have already recognized each of these ladies for their proofing skills and work ethics and this is far beyond any acclaim that I can offer.

Through Political Correctness' influences, authors have been intimidated into employing grammatically incorrect procedures. However, this author will continue with the old convention (tradition) and use the masculine reference. It is for the reader to know that when there is a collective "he," a "she" could be involved as well. If the subject is likely to be predominantly feminine, then "she" will be used. This convention prevents the plural being associated with the singular item. I will also avoid "s/he" and "they" for the singular condition.

Still, I do pride myself on my innate ability to insert grammatical errors and literary *faux pas* at the last moment before printing – even after my proofers had made my writing perfect. I consider my carefree spelling and convoluted sentence structure as being sort of a gift.

However, this could be a gift which no one would want. Perhaps I should try harder to resist this generosity in the future.

Introduction

In the simplest terms, this was a very difficult book for me to write. I did nearly two years of constant research on many subjects about which I thought I was knowledgeable; or at least, basically understood. I found that it is very disconcerting to have a life-long conviction altered by the reality of history. With research leading the nonfiction writer, I was led to even more questions requiring even more research. The basic difficulty is determining what that reality of history is – and when talking about sociology – reality is sometimes almost impossible to recognize.

As this manuscript was progressing, I was remembering the overall literary interests of our current society and its dislike of nonfiction in general and of history in particular. Because of this, I saw that the citizens of the United States had turned their collective backs on the Renaissance.

The process of the Renaissance is ignored when people stop asking the question which defined the Renaissance – "Does this really make sense?"

The citizens, in time (suffering from faults they are yet to understand), ceased to recognize <u>nonsense</u>!

Too many people do not know how to ask the correct question to get the desired information. They simply believe in misleading sources of spectacular-sounding (though incomplete) stories.

Today, it does not matter about the truth of a statement because if it is an <u>unpopular subject</u>, the statement must therefore be incorrect and it is not to be considered. Rather than discuss the statement and analyze it for validity, the author or speaker is condemned for having even written or said it. This represents the antithesis of the Renaissance.

This type of disqualification of rhetoric was also the guiding principle of the Roman Catholic Church up until about 1500 – immediately before the Renaissance.

The more general a history is (and this one, being a social history, is very general) the more difficult it is to determine the relationships of the challenges to society and its responses to those challenges.

Please remember that in social studies it is about "challenge / response," or "stimulus / reaction" – it is never "cause / effect." Living beings function by challenge and response; machines function by cause and effect.

Because of my interest in history and my reading about human nature, I am very sensitive to context. Context is time and place. The most significant historical event to occur in my life was World War II, and I am usually agog at how disinterested the current young generations are about the event which shaped world maps and modern times.

The most significant historical event that occurred in most of the younger generations' lives was the dissolution of the Soviet Union; yet, these generations likely know little-to-nothing about it. And this most important time in their lives ended the most important time in mine. This was the unification of Germany. This closed the journals on World War II.

We should wonder why the young people are unaware of this.

Yet, I am aware that I never asked my grandfather, who was born in 1869, about the Spanish-American War (1898) when he had been 29 years old; or even World War I. I did not ask because these events were well "before my time." As a young person, I was as self-centered as most young people were and still are. I did not see the relevance of those things. This, of course, meant, "relevance to me." I had my own concerns.

Back then I was just an ignorant kid and I could hardly be expected to be any other way. I was 10 years old.

By the time I was 16, I understood that many things that had happened "before my time" were very relevant to me – indeed, I was a product of them. I was the legacy! I was curious about who/what had made me. Yet, times continued to change and most of our 17-year-olds do not think this way today. They all seem to be original, or so they think. This book addresses the justification for why they may think this.

My two years of research demonstrated how amazingly adept the citizens are at accepting buzzwords and cute-sounding terms. The citizens thrive on any change in language or idiom. Maybe these clever-sounding terms and words are interpreted to be wit; consequently, the citizens are less discriminating when hearing or reading them – and repeating them.

It is a myth that clever wordplay contributes to better communication. It is often more of a transitory and whimsical affectation than actually satisfying any real need of communication. When these new terms are created and introduced into common discourse, it gives the layperson the impression that the people were (or at least their generation was) in some manner the originator of the idea...even a very old and proven (and documented) idea. The layperson is just calling it something different...something new. The word is new – as is likely the speaker – but not necessarily the idea.

Seeing how easily the citizen accepts catch-words as "facts," I decided that I would have to go far back to some basic ideas and expose the reader to some actual, natural truths. These are not opinions. Nor are they observations. They are heavy with reality and based on history. They just are.

Some of current society's facts/truths are based predominantly on desire. This book is my effort to return some misunderstood concepts to their roots – the language – and thereby try to remove some misconceptions. This will make the point of this book more readily recognized.

There are simplistic ideas which some people now think are achievable even in the face of 40,000 years of history to the contrary – some of this history was most likely accurate markers for events going back even more years. Yet, many people believe that contrary, simplistic ideas are achievable because (a) they do not know history, or (b) they are incredibly arrogant, or perhaps (c) they are just sweetly naive.

To demonstrate just how simplistic some of these hypothetical models for society really are, it will be necessary to go back to some basics of social intercourse. Ignoring reality is the bedrock of current society and it is involved in all things. This is more than mere casual denial; it is endemic in the national psyche. Ignoring reality and nurturing denial is a form of other mental problems – no matter how satisfying denial may be.

Is this an implication that current American society is mentally handicapped? Perhaps this book will give a little information to help resolve this serious question.

A social history of the United States can be compared to a public horoscope. Unless there is one horoscope for women and a different one for men, then the very nature of each gender is being ignored.

So there is a social history book for everyone?

All ethnicities?

Which American is this book about?

The reader will decide.

If talking about social changes, there should be a book for each basic group of Americans.

*****

I was present during the critical 73 years of social history discussed in this book. I saw some of the changes and I was aware of many other things as they were occurring. But I did not understand how the changes were coming about. I was engrossed in my own family's activities and my responsibility to provide for them.

I did not have the time to create a sense of the angel's brain and to cultivate an extreme level of righteous indignation about all abuses – real or imagined. I did not have the resources to march the streets, parade, and rebel. Other people, however, did have the resources to do these things. I had to walk the streets to get work and support a family. Therefore, many of the changes I write about in this book, I observed – and this created a problem in the book's production.

How much information could I personally contribute to make a point about social history?

I wrestled with this question and I determined that from my birth until near-1955, I was a natural product of my time. I was a child of general history. Because I was typical, so much of my story would parallel those of many, many young people. And my parent's story would match that of many parents that I knew. We were all just responding to current stimuli and trying to get through the day as best we could.

Shortly after 1955, my history would still match that of many others, but I was no longer typical. I was not a celebrity; I was only different because I was so fortunate. I had ceased being a child of circumstance and had become more of a tool to create a new age.

While writing this book, I could still speak of personal observations of the general events occurring outside my window, but after 1955 I was only an observer – I was no longer an active participant in a universal social history – as one being involved with the public would be.

Only in recent years have I experienced enough to know that a lot of the changes were not good; indeed, some will likely cause the end of the United States. The states will remain; but united?

Not hardly.

*****

I was going to maintain a detailed record of all sources in my research, but in doing so I was filling many pages with dry references. Such pages are rarely viewed except by the philosophically disagreeable attempting to cast doubt on logical conclusions. Since with thought, these issues seem logical, I have not added a fourth-inch of reference pages to the thickness of this book.

What references there are indicate sources of material and these may not be verbatim. This is why there are only a few references for those readers desiring more information on the topic.

Besides – who, reading this book, does not have an iPhone present? Anything written in this book which appears to be provocative can be referenced very quickly.

Therefore, I suggest to the reader as I did to my students in college: "Do your own research. You will learn so much more than you expect."

Following convention I am using occasion brackets. These are for the me to comment directly to the reader, to suggest additional reading, or to indicate other's editorial interjections in quoted material.

*****

Knowing that the reader does not have 100% retention and immediate recall, there are occasions when a small amount of repetition will serve to refresh the reader's mind.

Additionally, I have been questioned about some of my comparisons in other books. I may not choose an obvious one. I find it more constructive to use a comparison that is more thought-provoking. This is a habit I do not choose to break, though it may be unpopular with some readers. Again, this is about context. If wanting to illuminate the life of a little known but influential person, I might select another influential person – a surprising one.

*****

So now, let's take our time...let's find a good place to sit...and for minimal distractions, find a place with very little noise, and once this is done, start through this book. I venture that the reader will gain a better understanding of where we came from, who and what we are, and how we got this way.

Where we might be going will be demonstrated by others.

I think the reader will be surprised.

Ken Cashion, August, 2019.

Prologue

In this book I have avoided as many statements as I could that required me to name political parties. This seemed constructive. The political polarization of the United States in 2018 is approaching that of pre-Nazi Germany. The political party is taking precedence over the welfare of the Nation because each party is convinced that only its party can define the way the entire Nation is to be governed, and this means all the time – on every issue. This sounds familiar.

Modern political parties in the United States do not need party flags, window banners, brass bands, hobnailed boots marching on the streets, armbands, nor torchlight parades. They have the media. The media is not as exciting as a drum corps marching in torchlight parades, but it is far more dangerous than such parades. Parades end.

I will use political party names only when I must to avoid confusion, but I will try to always identify the political philosophy involved. That stays constant by any party name. These will be socioeconomic definitions and terms to identify a manner by which a population may be governed.[1]

I would like to think that after serious thought, no reader would want to live in a nation with either philosophy applied constantly, and as this book is read, it will become obvious why.

Therefore, I am not at all suggesting a solution to any perceived problem. I am not advising any social change. Any change I could suggest is for the individual; not for society as a whole. Besides, the United States already has too many activists and revolutionaries. And the United States has far, far too many forums.

I am not so sure of myself as to desire to influence a nation in any significant manner. I am not a revolutionary. I am not even an activist. I am but a mere observer, researcher, and scribe.

1

Socioeconomics is the relationship of society and economics; i.e., how the people and money interact. Socioeconomic philosophy defines how society is to be organized and function while maintaining an awareness of wealth at any degree.

Section I – Societal Basics

The Nature of Nature – Defining the Terms

Introduction

Words change. The spellings change for convenience. The meanings change almost by momentary interest, and too often they change by political manipulation; but worse, they change because of ignorance. Ignorance is not stupidity. Today ignorance of most any point can be corrected in five minutes. However, if the information is not remembered, then knowledge is not attained, and the Void's name is "Ignorance."

Change is the constant about language because Ignorance, and its slap-stick child, Whimsy, seem to be not only ever-present, but the size of both are growing. New words are needed as new technologies become popular, but words are changing for century-old terms as if the old ones simply seem less appealing to a new generation.

Most things change as our society's desires change. As an example – even into the 1950s divorce was near scandalous and it was not worthy of polite public discourse. Both parties in the divorce were embarrassed at their public, legal admission that they could not work out their difficulties "like adults are supposed to." Or, just as embarrassing, there was the admission that their initial judgment and selection of a spouse had been so flawed. A part of their embarrassment was their having taken oaths before God, the court, and friends, and then the oaths were being broken.

Today, it is legislated that the public is to be more sensitive to others' ways of living; indeed, multiculturalism/cultural diversity is a National intent, and the government mandates that all federal employees will have sensitivity training. This is to increase sensitivity – not to reduce one's excessive sensitivity. But few voters are aware of what the words "multiculturalism" or "diversity" mean for the long-term.

Therefore, to consider the culture of humans and their societies, there should be a little research to see what humans are really supposed to be. This does not alter who each person wants to be – but society as a whole should be considered. Yet before new words and attitudes are adopted to live with on a daily basis, it would be constructive to know what these current terms really mean.

Lewis Carroll quoted Humpty Dumpty as having said, "When I use a word, it means just what I choose it to mean – neither more nor less." But Humpty Dumpty had a great fall and could not be put back together. The parallel between Humpty Dumpty and the United States is a striking one.

It is a fact: Humans are a carbon-based life-form on a carbon-based planet. This is where these current thoughts should start. This is not open to debate nor interpretation. Some things just are.

Humans are physically constructed of only chemicals. They must exhaust chemicals and take in more chemicals. The word "chemical" in modern marketing jargon indicates something to be avoided. As if "natural and free of chemicals" is always desired. But this is hard to achieve – it is impossible – we, being made of chemicals. An effort should be made to use this "chemical concept" properly.

In truth, a chemical is any substance consisting of matter. This means that it has mass and occupies space. This includes any liquid, solid, or gas. A chemical can be pure or a mixture of other chemicals.

Oxygen and nitrogen are naturally occurring gases (chemicals). Humans need them to breathe. Hydrogen and oxygen make up water. In the entire universe, hydrogen is the most prevalent gas – which is a chemical.

For a few million years, the amount of water on Earth has remained fixed. Its form, however, does change from liquid to solid (ice) to gas (water vapor - clouds). But the amount of water on the planet was fixed a long time ago – 4.6 billion years or so. So some things are not changing.

Humans need a constant intake of chemicals to maintain the healthy chemical balance of the body. Not just any chemical – many are bad for them. But certainly not all.

All the elemental chemicals in a human are worth about $4.50 on the market. However, the value of the organs, which are also made of chemicals, varies greatly.

Chapter 1 Definition of Society and Social Concerns

The base for the word "society" is Latin *societas* with origins in the concept of "friend" and "ally."

A society consists in many combinations, but primarily it is a group of people who are engaged in near-constant verbal discourse. They share a common territory, have a similar government, and they agree on the ideals in the preference of living conditions.

Members of a society can profit in a manner not readily available to the lone individual. Also, since verbal discourse is necessary, it is required that they have a common language, or all equally share multiple languages.

To facilitate the better understanding of the development of societies, a section is taken from *A Social History of Britain From First Humans to the Creation of Great Britain*; ISBN 978-0-9771187-2-4.):

> Much of the following might be unpopular with today's population, but unpopular or not, there are some commonalities in the development of societies. There are always exceptions, but in this case, the story is about the general groups, not the unusual.
>
> Primitive societies, if they are to move toward knowledge, wealth, and ordered freedom, must travel along the path of Aristocracy, Kingship, and Priesthood. The names of these divisions vary but these words describe the conditions.
>
> Theoretical models can be developed for a utopian world, but no evidence exists that this path has been traveled any other way.
>
> There may be idyllic primitive societies to which one might aspire, particularly in a current overly-hectic culture, but when the primitive society exists beside the civilized, in time, the migration is decidedly toward the more-civilized of the two.
>
> Primitive societies do not represent the ideal. However, such societies are sometimes romanticized by an already civilized mind.

Primitive tribe members may be relatively equal in poverty, but they can never gain a higher civilization and the freedom of the individual without traveling this narrow path to aristocracy or the priesthood, sometimes these being attained by the same individuals.

When men collectively are very poor, some few must be made rich if there is to be any accumulation of wealth for civilized communal application.

When men collectively are very ignorant, progress is only possible through the endowment of an educated few.

In such a world, organization can only begin through personal ascendancy and can only be rendered permanent through privilege.

In current times, these are all unsavory ideas, but modern judgment has been altered by local, cultural biases. Consequently, the idea of a more realistic and natural perception of societies may be missing now.

Education and religion were, in primitive times, inextricably bound to superstitions (irrational beliefs). Initial progress is realized only through the ascendancy of the priest over the layman.

In a current democratic and scientific age, such contemplations of the past may seem strange, but this cultural development is demonstrated to be a large part of early history.

In early days, social leadership and religion grew together as harmonious parts of a general whole. These became at the same time, exploiters and saviors of an otherwise helpless society.

(Concludes)

There are many ways of dividing society into smaller identifiers…the most basic is hunter and gatherer; then agricultural (primitive and advanced), then industrial (at some minor level), and on up.

Some anthropologists have proposed a society name for this current information age – the Virtual Society. This is a society which exists only online and the individual member has only an online identity – a pseudonym. There is a natural appeal in a large, complex population where the citizens can move through the "ins and outs" of the society and at all times maintain their anonymity.

There are also societies that exist at the members' prerogative and are controlled by their own concepts of their norms. These can function within a larger, more dominant society. This would be a "subculture" and the term is used generally for criminal activity – but the term can apply to many variants.

– Social Systems

Some societies can be based on a form of tyranny, as with a warlord and his tribe. The members of this society may or may not have a choice, but it is to the general welfare of the individual to integrate into this society (or possibly the individual may remove himself from it).

And there are the political societies where laws/policies define expected behavior.

Adjacent societies with equal resources may compete or complement each other, or one may be absorbed by the other.

There are combination of societies which form a larger body but are still to be considered a society – in some cases it could be called "Western Society." This defines a group of societies with common traits and desires. They may all have an accepted stable, democratic form of government, allow religious freedom, demonstrate capitalism, and have some form of military alliance with each member society. Additionally, their laws and members may be affected by a general Judeo-Christian teaching – as in the example – "Western Society."

There are different forms of societies and often their technology and available resources determine which path they might take at any given time.

– Cultures

Culture involves the language, religion, social habits, cuisine, and the arts.

In some cases, a large group of people considered themselves to be a common culture when all they shared were the language and religion. It can be assumed then that language and religion are the prime identifiers of culture.

– Mores

This word (pronounced "mo-r′ays") is from the Latin plural of *mor* and simply means "a society's general customs and expected behavior."

– Ethics

Tied to mores, ethics is the interpretation of morals, meaning, "what is good and bad behavior." This is usually absolute and does not vary for circumstances.

– Religion

Religion is a belief system involving the idea that the functions of the universe are subject to a controlling God(s) or Goddess(es). These principal identities have the superhuman capability to affect everything within their jurisdiction. Religions will generally have a structured set of rules for society's conduct and ceremonies/rituals. Such rules will often be incorporated into civil laws for that community.

– Country

A country is a defined area of real estate with the citizens having self-government and a geographical identity. Some countries can engage in treaties and alliances with other countries. They must have regulations for local and foreign trade and have a financial system recognized by other countries. These countries are defined as being sovereign states because no other country has power over them.

– Nation

There are many critical differences in a country and a nation.

A nation is a large population within a defined area that is connected by language, religion, history, and other common traits, including even identifying physical characteristics.

A country may contain a nation, and when it does, the whole is considered a nation, but a country can contain more than one nation. The most obvious examples in the United States are the indigenous people. They represent nations having defined territories within the United States. Though they are nations, they are not countries; however, most nations prefer their own countries and they will go to great lengths to acquire them.

There are some Nation-States because they are a country sharing all the characteristics defining a nation. The best example is Japan. The large majority of citizens there share the same ancestry, birth place, language, culture, and history.

Other Nation-States are North and South Korea.

– Civilization

A most simplistic definition of a civilization would be a complex society having urban development, division of labor, social classes, and a more complex means of communication, such as writing. Also required are means of protecting the citizen from much of the environment. This can be something as simple as organized buildings to shield citizens from the weather. In some cases, permanent buildings are required to meet the definition of "civilization."

<u>People who require any degree of multiculturalism or cultural diversity in the definition of "civilization" would have to disqualify Japan and South Korea as civilizations. This would be rather unlikely – it is impossible.</u>

– Organizing Societies

There will be more detailed information about how societies may be organized, but there is one consideration that needs to be recognized very early on. There are only two basic forms of socioeconomic philosophy in the United States. (Socioeconomic was defined on page xix.) These can be identified in very general terms, but understanding them is crucial in any discussion of the health and status of the United States today.

In one case, there are those people who want no changes to their lives. They are content. They would like to conserve the status quo.

These people are conservative independently of any political party names or alliances.

The antitheses of these are the people who want to continue to change society. They want to correct any and all wrongs as they perceive them. These people are liberal, and again, it matters not one whit what the political party names are nor with whom they are aligned. (A more detail explanation of Liberalism and Conservatism is at page 216 – 218.)

Chapter 2 Definition of Anthropology

Anthropology is simply the study of humans and their social systems. At one time this was an entertaining study with only the occasional controversy when an unidentified artifact was found or there was the announcement of the first opening of a spectacular burial chamber.

The database was much smaller back then (1912) and the only thing that appeared to have much importance was to find what was then called the "ape-man" – the "missing link." This would be that last bit of information that could be used to fill in that last gap in the continuous evolutionary trail of human development from ape to man – or so it was thought by academicians at the time. This was more than a mere academic desire; lawsuits were filed in 1925.

At the conversational and social level there have been many definitions of humans and animals and this is ignoring that humans are animal, but at one time it was said that only humans were tool-<u>using</u> animals. Then Jane Goodall produced evidence that this was not true. She showed animals using tools. But many people wanted to believe the "tool" was but a twig picked up locally.

So humans were by necessity then defined as a tool-<u>making</u> animal. Then Jane Goodall produced evidence that this was not true, either. She showed the animal modifying a twig to better serve the animal's needs – and thus the twig had became a tool and the animal had made it.

Now it is popularly thought that humans are animals with the gift for introspection, meditation, or insight. There is no evidence that animals sit around and reflect on their meaning in the cosmos or how they fit in with the grand scheme of things. Perhaps animals are not so pompous.

When upper primates appear bored and pick at their navels, perhaps they are not reflecting on the injustices of the universe, but rather they are just bored – or it feels good when they scratch their navel, itching or not.

It is possible that in this era of desired, constant distractions – distractions which prevent the quiet moments for introspection – that this represents the slow, back-evolution of humans to become more animal-like.

As more precise analytical instruments and procedures are developed, the databases become very cluttered. There seems to be more links than first thought and, consequently, more gaps are created amidst the confusing information.

– Species and How They Are Classified

This subject is about taxonomy. Taxonomy is an accepted way of putting order to the planet. This immediate topic is about biological taxonomy in general, and that of humans in particular.

Human taxonomy is part science and part social preference – meaning that the part which can be repeatedly demonstrated (science), and that part which is only currently popular with the most dynamic group of practitioners (social preference). Biological taxonomy is accepted in many places and has been taught many years.

The taxonomic process once had all living organisms divided into either of the top two categories, called "Kingdoms" – this would be either the Animal Kingdom or the Plant Kingdom. As analytical instrumentation and technique improved, there were issues with categorizing bacteria and fungi. These are living, but they are neither animal nor plant. And then, there is the single-cell life form which is not animal, plant, bacteria, nor fungi.

So this taxonomic process was modified to have six kingdoms – animals, plant, fungi, bacteria, single-cell, and then in 1969 there was a general catch-all kingdom technically called *Protista*.

The following information is based on the taxonomic classification of humans (*Homo*).

– Human Taxonomy

The taxonomic process for humans can be tested at various levels with a high degree of probability. It is predictability that meets the terms to qualify it as a science rather than a philosophy – and if this predictability is not there, the subject should be in the University Department of Humanities and not in the University Department of Science.

Science starts with supposition, then a theory is developed, then a hypothesis is developed in an attempt to explain the not-yet-explained. The hypothesis can be tested by documented, qualified tests to acquire data – qualified data.

Having other qualified people duplicate the test procedures and get the same results are paramount in defining science.

In the taxonomic process, the highest order and the first classification is: Kingdom. Since humans are not single-celled, a fungi, plant, etc., then humans are assigned to the Kingdom of Animals. This is the conclusion every time the question comes up.

Because humans have a dorsally located nervous system, they are grouped into the next order down. This analysis continues on down the list of categories with evermore exacting requirements.

The following words are the commonly accepted ones in the taxonomic process because it is by the agreement among the knowing that matters – and again, some of it meets the criteria of being a science.

The complete list follows:

Human Taxonomy

Kingdom:	*Animalia*	Animal
Phylum:	*Chordata*	Having a dorsally situated nervous system
Class:	*Mammalia*	Having the above characteristic plus having hair on skin and females with milk-producing glands
Order:	Primates	(Either they are *haplorhini* or *simiforne* primates)
Suborder:	*Haplorhini*	In the human's case they are *haplorhini* because they have all the above plus a dry nose; cannot produce vitamin C; have large brain-to-body ratio; well-developed vision; and are diurnal living – functioning by day or night.
Family:	*Hominidae*	They have all the above and share the characteristics of the Great Apes

At this point the ranking becomes rather confusing relative to history.

In all scientific discussions, Pluto should be remembered! For 76 years Pluto was a planet, then in 2006 it ceased to be one. There is interest now for it becoming a planet again. What is, can cease to exist by its description with a blink of a panel's eye.

The rule of science gets very shaky as new instrumentation is developed and it could be misused. Care should be taken in the following grouping.

Subfamily:	*Homininae*	(Having the above plus meeting too many other criteria to describe here.)
Tribe:	*Hominini*	(Groupings seem to depend on many current social preferences by the people identifying the class with little and/or changing evidence.)
Genus:	*Homo*	Humans in all their forms and in all the ages when they lived.
Type species	*Homo sapiens*	Intelligent humans in all their forms in all ages, of which, modern man is but one.
Species	*Homo sapiens*{1}	All the above plus some undetermined characteristics.
Subspecies{2}		

{1} Modern man is classified *Homo sapien*, but what about the other humans grouped in his Genus *Homo*? There have been many others, and some coexisted. As DNA sampling continues, there is increased excitement as more bones and teeth are found. All this work is producing more opinions and suppositions than facts. The detail and depth of this analysis is amazing, yet a scientist's opinion is not science no matter how excitedly it is presented in the media. The more socially popular the findings are, the more readily will funding be made available for follow-on research.

The prescribed relationship of Neanderthalensis (Neanderthal) and modern man, (Cro-Magnon), has see-sawed back and forth and it is always covered in the media. The articles will have witty, informative titles – "A Neanderthal Lives in Your House!" or "Did You Sleep With a Neanderthal Last Night?" That, and the equally intriguing first paragraphs might be all the general public will read.

– Specie Pairing

Taxonomic classification/ranking is important, but the understanding that only similar species can reproduce is paramount. The degree of similarity is generally not defined before the fact.

When slightly dissimilar species mate, that is, those from the same genus but different species (as defined in their taxonomic table) then they may or may not produce offspring. Yet dissimilar species can produce offspring.

The mule was used as a burden animal in 3000 BC Egypt; consequently, this use of the off-spring of dissembler species (the donkey and the horse) is well known. Mules continue to be produced. The only time that mules existed in nature (as opposed to being the products of controlled breeding) was when wild donkeys and wild horses shared the same territory. In these cases, the donkeys and horses were naturally in close proximity because they both fed on grass.

In nature, the sizes of the mule herds depended on the availability and sizes of donkeys and horses having adequate grasses.

The horse is specie *Equus ferus* and has 64 chromosomes; the donkey is specie *Equus Africanus* and has 62; the mule has 63. Therefore, dissimilar species can mate and reproduce. Both are of the same genus; *Equus,* and this is one order/category above specie on the taxonomic scale.

However, it is expected that the offspring of donkey and horse, the mule, will be sterile. Controlled breeding of captive animals is a very old activity. Mules have been produced for thousands of years, but in the last 450 years there have been only 60 documented cases of fertile mules – all female.

These fertile female's male offspring would be fertile; their female offspring would be sterile. The fertile male mule would sire a horse; not a mule – and not a donkey. When fertility occurred, and it was very rare, it reverted back to the original form in two generations.

This long discourse about a seemingly off-topic subject is necessary to gain some understanding of species, their groupings, and the following topics which are current and too popular – and unfounded.

The Neanderthal and Cro-Magnon occupied the same space and time so their mating must be assumed, and it should be expected that this did, on occasion produce offspring...but sterile off-spring. It is "assumed" because this is supposition and not science; the science is demonstrated in the repeatable donkey/horse breeding results.

The reader should keep this in mind when exposed to the excitement of yet another human bone with mixed Neanderthal and Cro-Magnon DNA. Logic tells us that the offspring was likely sterile or nearly so. The acceptance of the perpetuation of such fertile hybrids will require more than a few bones.

To assume Neanderthal and Cro-Magnon did not mate defies nature. To assume they produced a population of fertile hybrids defies demonstrated history.

{2} Many zoological taxonomy charts have a further breakdown of species into subspecies.

Some animals have many subspecie classifications. In animal taxonomy these are called "breeds" and these breeds are being constantly qualified by DNA analysis.

Breeds are defined as having common appearance and behavior or other characteristics which set them apart from others of the same species. Breeds are formed by intelligent design (captive breeding) or naturally (without the immediate influence of humans). It is assumed that there is no scientific measurement to define any breed, but there is an evaluation plan used by experts in that particular breed's discipline. This is by the consensus of experts in that particular field.

In human taxonomy, breed/race has no formal measurement or criteria, but it would be ranked following the species classification – these are "subspecies." Another definition is that race may be genetically common in individuals within the same species, but not populous enough to define another species. Unlike "breed" such terms as "race" are not to be governed by any measured criteria.

There have been attempts at breaking the classification of the human animal into more detail, but humans do not permit this.

Nearly the last academic attempt at this was by John Randal Baker, who died in 1984. He was a biologist, zoologist, and professor emeritus at the University of Oxford. His book, *Race* set forth his reasoning for subspecie classifications based on race – or rather subspecies defined as race.

However, no amount of study can overcome the continued stigma of the genocide attempt in WWII. Genocide continues today but the choice of words are often "ethnic cleansing." Though this term and action are as equally immoral and unethical, the word "genocide" carries the WWII connotation. There will likely be no literal data now involving race. It is an unpopular subject and suppressed by influential and vocal factions.

Note: The tiger has 5 subspecies; the lion 4; the cow 2; and the dog 37. *Homo sapiens*, in all their variations, and which populate the planet, have none. Modern humans do not have the intellectual freedom to even discuss this.

– Government Anthropological Ranking[2]

Independently of philosophic desires for a more perfect future, there is at least one group that is serious about defining race – the United States Government. Since academia cannot engage in any qualified measurements and studies, we can rely on the United States Office of Management and Budget (OMB) to clarify the question of race.

They want to know the American racial profile so they can adjust civic discourse as they see fit. To this end, the United States Census Bureau must use the OMB guidelines to acquire the desired racial profiles.

According to the United States Government, a person's race is determined to be White (-American), Black/African (-American), Native (-American), Asian (-American), or Pacific Islander (-American), by the following criteria:

White (-American) – Is a person having origins in any of the original peoples of Europe, the Middle East, or North Africa.

2

Much of the following is from United States Government resources.

(Technically, white is not a color nor is it a race, but to the government it is a "race." This race used to be "Caucasian," but using "C" to define "Caucasian" on government forms was awkward because some statisticians could think "C" meant "colored" – as the word is used by the "National Association for the Advancement of Colored People" – NAACP.)

Black or African (-American) – Is a person having origins in any of the black racial groups of Africa.

Native (-American) – Is a person having origins in any of the original peoples of North, Central, and South America <u>and who maintains tribal affiliation or community attachment</u>. [Underline is by the author for a better understanding of the race description.]

Asian (-American) – Is a person having origins in any of the original peoples of the Far East, Southeast Asia, or the Indian subcontinent including, for example, Cambodia, China, India, Japan, Korea, Malaysia, Pakistan, the Philippine Islands, Thailand, and Vietnam.

Native Hawaiian or Other Pacific Islander (-American) – Is a person having origins in any of the original peoples of Hawaii, Guam, Samoa, or other Pacific Islands.

Then OMB started permitting the reporting of more than one race because of the increase of mixed races. An individual's response to the race question is based on "self-identification." This was permitted in 2000. People could check more than one block/race if they preferred. It would be logical for the person who believes that we are all one race to check all blocks.

If ancestor origin is to be used in determining race, and if science is to be believed, then all humans came from Sub-Sahara Africa – at the current time (2019) this would be from Ethiopia. Consequently, all Americans are Afro-American – and all Germans are Afro-Germans, etc. Or if someone wants more accuracy, all people are Ethiope-somethings. Such is the problem with using popular whimsy in statistics.

The issue is: How can the government alter society if it is based on a subject which cannot be discussed – or defined? And liberal governments really do want to alter society.

Providing that there is just one race – the human race, then perhaps race should not be used in the census. (Humans are not a race, but that does not matter when it comes to common, clever word usage.)

As mentioned earlier, the United States government is the principal local organization dealing in multiracial/multicultural comparisons.

In lieu of races, a different word can be used – ethnicity – and while this seems a racial term, it is not. (But sometimes it is presented as if it were.) Words are mixed to avoid the appearance of discussing race. The best example might be that the government recognizes five groups – groups that could be called "races" in a more literate time. Within these groups (races) there can be any number of ethnicities. This basically means that culture can be included and this can be ancestry and language.

These words are tossed back and forth to the point that they appear as double-talk to avoid any real meaningful dialogue. When reading of the many races and ethnicities, it all appears to be nonsense and to be the fumbling efforts of bureaucrats to satisfy the varying desires of vocal minorities. In lieu of factual discussions of races as a taxonomic subspecies, the public is left with confusion which borders on humorous satire.

Ethnicity requires that a person have racial, cultural, and other ties in common. Race is biology. Ethnicity is custom. People are humans, but they can be many other things at the same time.

Someone could marry a person of another race (by the government's categories) and perhaps their children could then have a choice of race.

What race is a mixed race?

It is simply "mixed-race." That is a classification and an accepted one. But the government would like to know what races were mixed. This is genetics, not preference of association. Still, the government wants to adjust society to be fair – which is hardly possible with so many arbitrary categories. This fairness is achieved by government regulations so that one race will have an advantage over another...at some time...in some situations...in some manner.

This is very complicated – yet the government tries to do this.

One may choose to associate with some particular group with their unique language, food, music, and all the traits that define a people's preference for living. Religion can be included. Yet, race is biological, while ethnicity is sociological, and therefore, ethnicity can have many descriptions.

An Asian infant born to Asian parents can be moved from China to Germany and then grow up in Germany with adoptive German parents. As an adult he will still be Asian biologically, but culturally and in all other respects, he will be German. So German would be his ethnicity. This is how he identifies himself by his action and history. But no matter where he lives or how, his race will remain Asian. (But never forget Pluto.)

Section II – What the United States Society Was

Introduction

There is always a beginning, but in history, one person's beginning may be another's ending. History is that way. This section will deal first with events which came to an end in the mid-1940s. This will immediately prepare the reader for the more detailed subject of "from where did the current society come."

It is easy to select some high points in history. The following is a narrative of those significant events that affected nearly everyone – certainly Europe, their commonwealths, and Asia, as well as the citizens of the United States.

Chapter 1 How the Current United States Developed

– World War I

Basically, World War I was initiated by a Bosnian Serb. Today the United States citizen knows more about this region and their multicultural warring than he did when in June of 1914, a young Serb assassinated the heir to the Austria-Hungary throne, Archduke Franz Ferdinand and his wife. The resulting instability in the region inspired Russia to mobilize its army to take a large part of the always-desired area: the Balkans. (Events in 2018 demonstrated that this desire has not changed.)

During the post-assassination panic, in short order one crisis followed another until all the factions had lined up against each other. Starting with Germany, one side after another declared war, so by July of 1914 most all were involved in combat.

It is interesting that because of the intermarrying of European royalty, World War I was almost a family squabble – but one of horrific scale.

The United States tried to stay out of the European war, but May 7, 1915 a German submarine sank the British luxury liner, Lusitania, while it was bound from New York to Liverpool, England; among the near 2,000 deaths were 128 Americans.

Then in January 1917 Germany solicited Mexico to become a German ally against the United States [the *Zimmerman* note]. In return for Mexico's support, Germany would give Mexico the United State's areas of Arizona, New Mexico, and Texas.

By the time German submarines had sunk seven United States merchant ships, it became imprudent for the United States to continue to provide only passing, material support to Germany's foes. The United States went to war also, but it was in the spring of 1917; three years into the war.

When the shooting stopped on the 11th hour of the 11th day of the 11th month of 1918, there were 17.6 million people dead (9.9 million military and 7.7 million civilian). Poison gas had been used in such warfare for the first time when Germany used it against the British in Belgium.

World War I was over but by then something just as bad, or worse, was occurring.

– Influenza Pandemic

This was known locally as the Spanish Flu [*H1N1 influenza virus*] and between January 1918 and December 1920 it had infected 500 million people around the world. There were 50-to-100 million deaths; this was 3% to 5% of the world's population. (About four out of each 100 people on the planet died.)

Twenty-eight percent of the United States' population was infected; killing nearly 580,000.

The percentage of deaths was 10%-to-20% of the infected – the more familiar flu death percentage is 0.1%.

In barely 12 months, in the United States life expectancy was reduced by 12 years!

The pandemic had "arrived" in three waves. Those who survived their infection on one wave were immune to the next. This was called the "Spanish Flu" because initially only the deaths in Spain were being reported for fear of causing general panic elsewhere. The United States and other countries were downplaying it in hope of keeping the morale up as it was at the end of WWI. The virus did not originate in Spain; it was somehow influenced by a swine population in the East.

– Social Recovery: 1920s

As the war came to an end and the pandemic waned, people wanted to forget the bad times and enjoy themselves – nothing helps to forget, enjoy, or celebrate like alcohol. Drinking increased with the soldiers coming home and a general period of trying to cope in a rapidly changing world.

This drinking was not only disrupting family life, it was disrupting businesses with employees arriving for work in no condition to perform well. Problem drinking had been increasing for a long time and while prohibition was initially a women's movement, it was put into effect by men.

A prohibition of alcohol was a grass roots effort that became a religious quest. This was a complicated process dealing more with passion than politics. When it became political the problem became one of demographics: voters. The political division was not by party but by "drys" and "wets" and this was a good marker of rural and urban living. Those living in the rural districts were more likely to be "drys" than those in urban environments. And this was also a reflection of religious ardor. Some religions were more lenient toward moderate drinking than those religions being practiced in the rural areas.

This urban/rural split played the most significant part in the prohibition movement.

In 1880, 72% of the population was rural, but the urban areas were expanding because of immigration. In 1880, immigration was 455,000 per year.

From 1900 to 1930, the average immigration was 603,000 per year – for each of 30 years. There were a million immigrants in 1905 alone. That was the peak of this early period; in 1935 there were only 35,000 immigrants.

Many of these immigrants were staying in the cities and these were Jews, Germans, Italians, and other cultures for which drink was part of their social heritage. Indeed, German immigrants were the largest brewers, so during the United States' involvement of WWI, the "drys" made the Prohibition movement a patriotic one.

The 18th Amendment forbade the manufacture, transportation, importation, and sale of alcoholic drinks in the United States. It was not, however, illegal to consume it. The 18th Amendment passed June 29, 1919.

Since women did not get the right to vote until the 19th Amendment was passed in August of 1920, prohibition was men's (political) response – just as it was the men who gave women the right to vote.

Other nations had their own prohibition laws: Canada, Russia, Iceland, Norway, etc.

However, in the United States, the real problem began with the Volstead Act. This was introduced by Andrew Volstead in the House of Representatives and it was so stringent that it was vetoed by the president but it later carried and was passed. It set the limits and specifications of violations and penalties. The alcohol limits were set by the act at 0.5%.

It had been thought with good logic that the Prohibition amendment would exclude beer. Now even medicines were regulated, as were wines used in religious sacraments. They were permitted under some circumstances. Overnight everyone was in the pharmacy business and becoming a rabbi was by word of mouth. Family doctors were writing prescriptions by the handfuls to permit families to stock their "medicines."

The Volstead Act required a trial for anyone violating the act.

Prohibition was a federal law and the states and counties could not afford to enforce it, nor did many counties want to. So Prohibition was generally ignored, even in the areas that had pushed so hard for Prohibition.

In the cities, a fellow with a small amount of alcohol on him had to be arrested and stand trial. Juries rarely convicted. Of the first 4,000 arrests in New York, there were but six convictions, and none of these received a jail sentence. However, it loaded up federal courts with superfluous trials.

Prohibition was repealed by the 21st Amendment in December 1933. It had been a law that was poorly conceived and presented and it became unpopular and nearly impossible to enforce. And it was too easily violated with money changing hands at all levels in and out of government.

*****

Social freedom increased in the 20s and the young particularly enjoyed the many changes. Women were no longer passive and were learning to be assertive. The more outrageous they could be, the better. In general, the young ladies were called "Flappers."

The flirting ladies were called many things – "Vamps" being popular. This was in reference to a woman who could suck money out of a fellow's wallet as a vampire sucked blood.

With the loosening of established rules for public behavior, the women could pick and choose which social custom they preferred at the time. This changed sometimes hourly – home, school, work, public, church – a woman may have a different persona for each environment and this meant in behavior as well as in appearance.

"Gold Diggers" became a term and occupation for some of the ladies. Ladies could rise just so far in polite (moneyed) society by being promiscuous. Then promiscuity had to cease and it took flirting, baiting, promised pleasures, and general manipulation – and it also took restraint. There would be no "hanky-panky" until <u>after</u> the wedding.

Many women married so they could be divorced. Marriage was an investment; divorce was redeeming the investment.

Husbands never prospered in a divorce, the wives did; hence the reason for the term "Gold Diggers." Mental cruelty and incompatibility were the reasons for the fastest divorces, but the lady was expected to "try" the marriage for at least 90 days. In those days, assets were not at all divided equally. The ladies did well in these planned divorces. Besides property, they usually received a monthly alimony check. She, now being more affluent, could move in higher social circles and the next husband have more wealth than the first.

The "Anything Goes" attitude of liberal America came to a close near the end of the 1920s. Because the stocks had kept increasing in value, people who were ignorant of investments, money usage, and business, were borrowing money to buy stock. It appeared a sure-investment. They were making a lot of money. However, for many people this gain was only on paper. And the buying was driving up the price of stocks.

There had been a lot of stock speculation on the borrowed money, but employment had not increased and stock prices were well above their real value.

Because of bad weather, the agricultural business was starting to suffer. The farmers were borrowing money against their farm's value and they were having difficulties even paying the banks the interest.

Then in September 1929, the London stock market started to collapse.

There was an avalanche of stock selling in the United States and this drove the price of stock down. Fewer and fewer people were buying. They had no money. The banks needed the money back that they had loaned their customers to buy stock – the stock which was then rapidly falling in price. Those owing money could not wait for the stock price to go back up, and they had to sell at the lowering prices, further driving down the price.

In October 1929, the United States stock exchange was swamped with sell orders and it could not keep up. The economy went into a monetary abyss.

– Depression

The Crash was caused by a combination of several things, but one of the most important was the realization by so many individuals who did not understand the market and were being asked to provide the money they had borrowed to buy stock – the stock they could not sell.

Those who could sell their stock may have gotten only a small percentage of what they owed, and this meant that they lost what was used to buy the stock to start with. The selling price did not even cover the loan used to buy it. Some of the stock owners had originally paid less than 20% of the stock price. They had borrowed the other 80%. This stock could be used as collateral – assuming the price would increase. There were many tiers of speculation – from hairdressers to boardroom executives, as well as naive bank managers.

Their thinking had been that they would get the rest back when the stock went up and they would sell at a big profit – then they could buy even more stock; but they would still owe 80% of that price. This was too simple. But it was done over and over and not just by individuals in the United States and Europe.

Businesses failed because no one had money to buy their products. The workers were laid off because of the reduced sales. Unemployment went up to 25% and wages fell 42% for those who could find work; and these workers were happy to have any job at nearly any wage.

*****

[At this point in this historical review, the author will be making more direct and personal comments as he feels he is qualified to do so because he is speaking from experience and for a large number of people.

This story has progressed to the beginning of "his" era and rather than deal with a hypothetical home life of the American during this time, he will use some actual examples. Anecdotal evidence can be qualified when it is autobiographical. Tables and statistics can improve understanding, but occasionally, some points can be better made from the perspective of personal experience.

He maintains that he was that example from birth in 1934 until the mid-1950s. In the fifties, he ceased being typical because his fate started being governed by probability far outside of the average. But from 1934 through this period, he was a typical boy in a typical family in the United States.]

*****

During the Depression, I was a young child in Central Texas and my father was very proud and fortunate to have a job driving a dump truck for $1 a day. (In 2018 value this was $19.)

Bread was 12¢ a loaf and a quart of milk was 10¢. He, like other men of the day, took his responsibility to provide for his wife and two sons very seriously. This was the measure of a man and this ability defined who and what he was.

His average annual income was $315; this was 1/3rd less than the average yearly income in the United States.

*****

– Dust Bowl

Hard winds out of Canada started coming down through the farming states in the Midwest and these initiated dust storms. Long-term farming practices had depleted the fields of many nutrients and soil-stabilizing fibers so the winds took what loose top soil there was and scattered it downwind. This left behind a hard, infertile crust of land. Additionally, it was the beginning of a long drought. The climate was changing as it always does over the long term.

Winds continued to blow and sand dunes were moving across agricultural states where there were no longer any crops but just fields of straw and yellow stubs sticking up from a flat plain.

Family farms had no value, and worse, there were a lot of outstanding loans that had been taken in an effort to produce crops, but these were ever-dwindling crops in a failing economy. The banks took possession of over-financed, non-productive farms which no one wanted to buy. There were more failing banks. Many, many farms were going to auction for the total property – homes, furniture, and farm equipment included.

Near destitute farm families loaded what personal property that could be put in (and on) family cars and farm trucks. Belongings were piled high with spare tires and chairs and mattresses. The family climbed in (and on) and they left the worst of the areas in Oklahoma and Arkansas and headed for the produce fields and fruit orchards of Southern California.

Between Oklahoma and California were deserts and mountains. Many of the overloaded, poorly maintained farm vehicles, which were already old from years of abuse, failed along the way and the large families were marooned. They were forced by circumstances into tent cities with no work, little food, and bad sewage.

In the 1930s, Dust Bowl refugees were on the move and a quarter of a million arrived in California.

This was as desperate a situation for the farming communities as the stock market's crash had created for the cities.

The government tried various social programs and some worked – most did not – but the federal effort did bolster the peoples' spirits. There was some upswing in the job market when more oil was discovered and many of these migrants found work in the oilfields. The men had to travel far from home to find employment and then see that the money got back to their families – many families were now much too large for even good times.

Franklin Delano Roosevelt was president and in this fully national emergency, socialism was appealing and many socialist programs were started. These were supposed to be temporary but socialist programs generally are not. This will be a recurring theme.

Roosevelt was one of the more famous Liberal/Socialist United States presidents and he said, "The country needs, and unless I mistake its temper, the country demands bold, persistent experimentation. It is common sense to take a method and try it. If it fails, admit it frankly and try another. But above all, try something."

This trying is safer for a president having so little opposition that he served as president for over 12 years. Before he died in office, the presidential term had been reduced to two consecutive 4-year terms.

To follow his idea of trying something and, if it fails, trying something else, it can be seen that during his terms there were many deaths because of insufficient food, and this was while there were huge agricultural surpluses in areas outside of the Dust Bowl.

With this surplus, he created an economy of scarcity by having the government pay farmers to reduce production. They sold pregnant animals as well as the young to slaughter houses. Food was deliberately spoiled or burned rather than have it on the market and this was by federal policy handed down locally through nearly 99% of the farmers.

This created-scarcity resulted in both people and animals starving in various places and there were breadlines and soup kitchens for people in the cities and towns.

His program appeared to be successful because by the mid-thirties farm income was 50% higher than three years previously. The production was not up; just the prices – as were the incomes of the farmers with large acreage and agro-combines. It was not good for the small-time farmer who represented a much larger percentage of "farmers."

These small farms with the tenant farmers and sharecroppers were hurt the worst. This was mostly in the Southern States. Cotton was a southern crop and the government reduced the acreage dedicated to cotton by one-third. This hurt the people who were paid to farm those acres. At the best this reduced their incomes by 30%; at the worst, it could be by much more.

The black people suffered more than the white because the black people were nearer the borderline between food and famine.

This scarcity decreased the ability of the farmer to move to better fields and opportunity. He was then nearly bound to the previous fields which had the usable area for production reduced by 30%.

This reduction created the desired scarcity, and increased the price of what produce there was. This increased income aided the economy, but not for those standing in breadlines and at the doors of soup kitchens. They did not profit by this artificial scarcity.

Blacks, expecting less, became the preferred tenant farmers for the larger land owners. The white farmers had to move on.

Some of the farm owners and sharecroppers could not start the long trek to California so they migrated to the cities where they could use the soup kitchens and breadlines.

One may wonder how such a presidential experiment could be admitted to be in error and something else tried. The farmer's crops would not be growing in the fields the next morning, nor would wasted livestock be back in their pens and pastures with their young.

Just saying, "Oops!" hardly seemed sufficient restitution for those who were ruined and living in squalid tent cities.

*****

During these Depression days, our family was not middle class. We were not poor – I do not think. I am aware of my wife's childhood – her family was poor. When the five members of her family live in a 10x20-foot, oilfield tool shed and the three children slept on the porch – that defines poor. These sheds were made so they could be slid onto the bed of a short truck and moved to the next oilfield.

Their most important possessions were a treadle sewing machine and a cow; "Baby." The cloth from Baby's feed bags provided the material for the children's clothes and these were produced on the treadle sewing machine. They were living in arid South Texas...there was little public grazing land for Baby.

I thought everyone had the same supper – white gravy on toast, small pieces of crisp, fried bacon, sliced onion, sliced tomato, and iced tea. I never went hungry nor did I go to bed dirty, and I always had enough clothes to protect me from the weather.

My wife's family had plenty of cornbread mashed up in a glass of Baby's milk.

We had a little more food than they and lived better, though we did not know them at the time. My dad left his dump truck job of a dollar a day in Central Texas to move his family of four, 400 miles to the recently developed South Texas oilfields. His brother from Central Texas had found a job there and had written him about the work.

Oilfield work was a hard, dangerous occupation, but the pay was better. We were still not quite middle class, but I could have one small present on birthdays. The present came from the toy counter at a distant five and dime store. Christmas presents were another flannel bathrobe and a new can of wooden Tinker Toys. (Tinker Toys were the Legos for the children of my generation.)

My mother made most of our clothes. She was a good seamstress and the clothes were nice and fit well. And we had electricity. My wife's family had kerosene lamps and then gas lighting through 1948. I knew them then and I remember when they got electricity.

– Social Recovery: World War II

Recovery came from an unlikely place by an unfortunate situation.

The Treaty of Versailles from back in 1919 put a legal end to WWI, but the terms of the treaty were very harsh and these punished Germany for many years. There was a peace-time land-grab by the WWI victors as territory changed hands, borders were moved, and governments switched alliances.

The restrictions of the Treaty of Versailles were holding the German economy back and this stagnation seriously hurt all aspects of their industry. The middle class was very rapidly joining the poor because of hyperinflation. In 1923 the American dollar had been worth 4,210,500,000,000 German marks. This was primarily because of WWI and the Treaty of Versailles. One might wonder how Germany could suffer through such inflation.

Germany, too, had been caught in the Depression. The American financial market affected many countries because their markets depended on American industrial strength.

Then there arose a leader who proposed the first positive message that Germany had heard in a long time. He was for change. And he would change many things. Even before WWI, the German citizen had been without any tangible opportunity because of the conservative aristocratic families, nepotism, and ethnic favoritism.

The new leader would change the traditional ways of government and business when promotions had been based on family name and the region of birth. He would promote qualified individuals no matter who they were or where in Germany their family lived.

This idea of leaving the past behind was a revolutionary idea of change, and was a liberal movement by definition.

This new upstart's influence and popularity grew, and for good reason – he was a superb orator, and by this date the radio had become the principal home entertainment. He was intriguing, but certainly not a man of mystery. He had written a book about what he thought was wrong with Germany and how he thought it could be changed.

Furthermore, he said the biggest change would be that he would ignore the Treaty of Versailles and rearm Germany.

He also expanded the electrification of the country, increased rail mileage, and put in virtually modern auto through-ways in Germany. People were being put to work with a promise of a wonderful future. Pride was returning to Germany because of just one man. His liberal political party came to power because of the changes made to nearly everything. For too long, the nation had been stagnated by a conservative government which had been resisting all change. (The definitions of two basic socioeconomic philosophies are on pages 216 – 218.)

With the popular support of the German people his political party gained sufficient votes that he was named Chancellor. Then, utilizing a provision in a legal emergency act, he simply took legal dictatorial control of the nation. He was the supreme leader of the German people. He had promised change and he had delivered.

Now he could legally ignore any law and create a new one.

Later, after his political party had successfully made its changes in both government and German society, the party became satisfied with its success and therefore became conservative and oppressive. In this way they could maintain the control that their changes had gained them. This practice is not that uncommon. Changing traditional policies always has risks.

Adolph Hitler and the Nazi party had become a force that would influence the world from their rise to power in 1933 to the reunification of East and West Germany in 1990. The division of Germany at the end of WWII (1945) was a result of the actions Hitler had put in motion in 1933.

His influence exists today in many forms and places...all as very bad examples of the raw extent of the inhumanity a political party can bring to a nation and inflict on the world.

He wanted to recover the territory that Germany had before the Treaty of Versailles. These were places where a large number of the citizens spoke German. He did this with no opposition. The ease with which this occurred encouraged him to be more bold.

Many people in the world admired him – their politicians did as well. The rest of Europe was doing nothing about him nor his actions. The other countries were dealing with their own Depressions.

Germany gained a tremendous amount of land.

Then Germany invaded Poland. This attack was hardly more than subterfuge and a shallow play of world politics, but Poland had a mutual defense treaty with Britain and France.

World War II had begun. It was September 1, 1939.

The United States tried to stay out of another European war, but with repeated German successes, the United States started supporting Britain with material – as they had done in WWI.

Japan had a massive army and navy and they invaded most countries on the southwest Pacific Rim. They needed the oil of that region to power their ships and war machines, but the United States had put an oil embargo against them. On December 7, 1941, while the United States was negotiating with Japan for a peaceful settlement of that embargo, Japan bombed the American territory of the Hawaiian Islands, killing 2,400. The United States was at war.

Germany and Japan had a mutual defense treaty. Now everyone (seemingly) was involved in World War II. Even neutral nations were choosing which side to be "neutral" with.

Japan continued to systematically, and with little difficulty, take over all countries on the Western Pacific Rim.

*****

The Depression went away almost overnight with the full mobilization of United States industry to produce war material. Dust Bowl refugees then found work, but not in the fields and orchards of California as much as in California's aircraft factories. Soup kitchen lines in the East became employment lines at ship yards.

In 1940, the population of the United States was 132 million – the lowest growth thus far in the 20th Century – this, too, because of the Depression.

So from the poison gases and muddy, bloody trenches of Belgium in World War I, to the indiscriminate death from the Influenza Pandemic, to the "anything-goes" celebrating of the Roaring Twenties, then the collapse of the economy and a dust-filled Depression, and finally to four years of World War II – this was the history of many – including the citizens of the United States.

The military history of WWII is complex, but it can be found in many forms for easy dissemination; consequently, there will be no detail provided here. However, the changes to United States society will by necessity be discussed.

*****

In 1941, I started school in the first grade in the South Texas oilfields, but then we had to move 500 miles to the West Texas oilfields where the family was miserable. We had gotten used to living closer to middle class, but in West Texas, we were certainly lower than that.

Because of my mother's pride and my father's love for her, we moved 450 miles back to Central Texas where their families were. Between living in South Texas in 1941 and Central Texas in 1943, I had gone to six different schools while in only three grades of elementary school.

A borrowed, or recently purchased, very-used cattle trailer would be hooked to our 1936 Ford and everything we owned piled in and on it and we would move again. We were not exactly Dust Bowl refugees, but we could certainly identify with them.

I remember just twice eating in a cheap roadside café and thinking that was where the middle class got to eat. At one of these cafés, I ate only donuts.

Our meals on the road were generally eaten under a tree by a two-lane blacktop. These were common picnic places for fellow travelers. We would all honk, yell, and wave as we passed. The windows would be down and we might be doing as much as 50 mph.

These roadside meals were sandwiches – two slices of bread, a smear of mustard, and a slice of bologna, and all washed down with a swig of milk. Generally, we had a few sweet onions. We said all food tasted better when on the road and under a tree. It might also have been because we were hungry – and bored from riding. Dad would stretch out on the grass beside the car and take a nap. Then he would get up, fill the car's radiator, and we would move on – and on.

I recognize a lot of the Depression- and Dust Bowl-era photographs because the people in the pictures look like us.

Just outside of Waco, in Central Texas, my dad got a good-paying job on a military airbase which was training bomber pilots. He was a fire department crew chief. Finally! We were middle class!! But just barely!

– During World War II

Now that we were middle class, we lived in a neighborhood of rapidly constructed tract houses where all were built, many at one time, using one of eight floor plans. There were perhaps 600 of these houses making up our subdivision.

I walked a mile straight down our street to school. All kids ate from their lunch sacks at their desks.

We had a lot of moms and kids on our street but few men. The dads were in service somewhere.

We made our own toys and invented our own games. We got a lot of exercise because we played outside and walked to school. Later, I had a beat-up bicycle that I had assembled from various used parts I had traded for. Because of the bike, with bike friends I had increased my range of wandering. If we would not suffer physically from being outside, that was where we were sent by our moms. If we got thirsty, we could drink from anyone's outside faucet.

I was nine years old and in the 3rd grade. It was 1943.

Naturally, we played war games. I liked playing a German because I was really good at dying.

[Again, such a personal account is not unique to me. I was doing what most kids my age were doing, so I represented a really large statistical population over most of the United States.]

We collected scrap to donate to the war effort and we bought Defense Stamps at school. The stamps I bought were a dime each. I would aim to buy one on each Friday but sometimes I could not. There were different priced stamps and a Defense Stamp book filled with more expensive stamps could be traded for a War Bond. The face value of the bond was $19 ($283 in 2018 dollars), but after 10 years the bond would have matured and be would be worth $25 ($375 also 2018 dollars). I never got a bond because I generally lost my book before it was even half-full.

Movies would have the lights come up so that there could be cash donations to the war effort. There were filmed reports, newsreels, on the progress of the war at each movie showing. Often the newsreels were more interesting than the movies.

We kids went to the movies maybe three times a month – always Saturday matinees and generally a double-feature; both Westerns. With magazines and the ever-popular radio, we were kept as informed as the censors allowed.

During this time, it was the war that occupied our lives. I had a ration book. Most everything was rationed and I would tear stamps from my ration book for my mom. I remember using the little fiber ration tokens which were sometimes given as change when using the stamps.

I turned in pencil stubs to buy a new pencil because the lead in lead pencils was needed to make bullets. The fact that there was no lead in lead pencils was irrelevant. The intent of the effort was to keep the war on our minds and that we had to sacrifice to win the war. We also had to turn in a depleted toothpaste tube to buy a new full one. The tube was of a lead/tin alloy.

At our house, when we had canned food, it was my job to pull the paper label off the can, take the can and top to the sink and wash them. Then I would cut the bottom from the can and slip both the top and bottom into the can. And then came the best part – put it on the floor and stomp on it until it was smashed flat. This would hold the top and bottom inside and have it occupy the least space. These went into a sack or box which would be delivered to a war scrap pile. Recycling is an old idea.

The radio was the chief family entertainment. In the afternoon, when the homemaker (mother) would be able to rest a bit – or while ironing – there were all the soap operas on the radio. These were so named because they were sponsored by detergent companies. I heard these with my mom during bad weather. In good weather, I was somewhere in the neighborhood – and not always close enough to the house to hear my mom yell for me to come to supper. This was because I had ranged a little far for my mom's comfort and I would be so informed of this.

Week nights there were the mystery and detective radio stories, and the variety shows were on Saturday nights. These appealed to the men and on weekends there were the many adventure programs for the kids. Just as detergents were marketed to the women during the radio dramas, there were cigarette commercials aimed at the men during the detective stories and variety shows.

After hearing a few hundred cigarette commercials telling me how many doctors smoked some specific brand of cigarettes and the doctors declaring that there was not a "cough in a carload," I decided that someone must have doubts about the pure pleasures of smoking. Not in these commercials were the public comments that... "They are called 'coffin nails.' Every cigarette was 'another nail in your coffin.'" In print the "coffin nails" were sometimes "coughin' nails."

Cigarettes were included in the service men's C-ration meal packs. And free cigarettes were provided even in the veterans hospitals where the soldiers were recovering from war wounds.

The R.J.Reynold's Tobacco Company advertised on the radio that they wanted the service men to know that they had not been forgotten, and then the current, chosen hospitals which were receiving free Camel cigarettes were named. On one radio recording I have, it was announced that the tobacco company had "sent more than 191 million cigarettes to these healing, wounded veterans."

Many men may not have smoked before they went in service, but they did when they came out.

I would be sent in stores to buy my aunt's cigarettes and I always got "Wings" cigarettes because they had a colored picture of an airplane in the pack.

On occasion I could also get a pack of cigarettes for me – a pack of candy cigarettes. These came in the same sized and colored packs as the real ones. The candy sticks were white and the dimensions of real cigarettes – they even had a little red color on the tip to simulate the cigarette's glowing ember. They were peppermint candies. As we sucked on the end, the "embers" got closer to our mouths. They were partially porous so we could suck air through them and that increased the flavor. We, however, could eat our "cigarette butts."

The only thing marketed to us kids were breakfast cereals, and this was during the children's radio programs. When we knew that our mom was going to the grocery store, we might ask for some Wheaties ("The Breakfast of Champions!"). We all wanted to be champions and we knew it took a lot of work (and cereal), but for us to ask for any clothing by a name brand was not at all likely. We might need some pants. We would have never asked for "Levis" or "Wranglers." We got what was cheap and on sale and glad to have them.

Jeans/denims/dungarees were work clothes and we kids did not work. We did, however, go to church and needed nice, long pants. As these wore, they would also be outgrown, and they would be replaced with new, and then the worn ones became "school clothes." But we were outgrowing most clothes before they could be worn out. This generated a lot of "hand-me-downs" and these did not exist only in the family. Mothers stayed aware of which neighbor kids were growing and their ages. It was understood by us that we did not comment if we saw "our" clothes on someone else.

We had church clothes, school clothes, and play clothes. Khakis were what the lower-middle class boys wore to school (but not church, nor did we play in them). The social classes a little above this wore dress slacks to school – though showing a little wear.

The kids in a social class below us were wearing bib overalls. I never owned a pair. My mom had taste – and pride – so I would never have bib overalls...like farmers wore. I envied those bibbed kids when it was summer. Such open, loose overalls without a shirt must have been wonderful! And all those pockets!! I was too often in wool because, as my mom explained, "Wool wears so well and always looks nice!"

We mostly wore "tennies" (tennis shoes) and these were the high-topped fabric sort. Our color choices were black or black. However, in decent weather we were barefooted and this was most of the time. We just wanted to be comfortable. However, this was not possible in un-air-conditioned churches in the summer while wearing wool.

But when going barefooted, we had a lot of stumped toes when our feet came down wrong at the wrong place. Sometimes the tips of the toes were only skinned a little and we would have a douse of Mercurochrome on them – which we kids called "monkey blood." But sometimes the toenail would be torn and this really hurt. The prescribed pharmaceutical procedure was to get a strip from an old bed sheet, wrap it around the offended toe and then saturate the wad of cotton cloth with coal-oil/kerosene. This was soothing and kept infections down.

If it was summer and six kids were outside without shoes, at least one kid would have an oily (dirty) bandage around his big toe.

Girls were more particular about what they wore, but it was not to make the boys interested in them. We knew how our gender subcultures went –"What are little girls made of? Sugar and spice and everything nice! That is what little girls are made of." The girls would often remind us boys of this.

The boys avoided the girls. They were silly and just got in the way of our important business.

"What are little boys made of? – Snips and snails and puppy dog tails! – That is what little boys are made of." If we had cared, we could have been indignant at such a sexist slight.

Sundays were for church. This was where I interfaced with adults other than those who lived on our street or were in our schools.

I learned many things in church – like dancing was sinful as was most anything else that seemed fun. If it made someone laugh, question it; it was most likely evil.

But mostly I found that the lessons I learned on the 3rd grade school yard had been well established a long time before. We knew we were to be nice to everyone. We were to be truthful, but support our friends. We were to leave other people's property alone. This seemed at the time to be simply fair behavior. And we had a strong sense of fairness.

I had already learned that desired things were not going to be dropped in my lap. I would have to wait for them – work for them – in some cases, struggle for them. I had to plan ahead and nothing came easy. (Pouting got the wrong kind of attention. Whinning got nothing – sometimes not even supper.)

The simple principles of child rearing were – "A child is to be seen and not heard," and "Spare the rod, and you spoil the child." These two were paramount and it taught us to remember our places in society.

We were never told, "Adults are talking now, Dear." Or, "Use your inside voice, Dear." I was never called "Dear." I had a name.

A dad might snap his fingers to get our attention and then with his head, motion to the door. We left. Such semaphore signals served to produce a quiet and respectful home life. We were kids with kids' interests. We were not "small adults."

When adult guests visited, we would be introduced and we would shake hands, and say, "Sir" and "Ma'am." We would politely answer the expected questions. The visitor always wanted to know our age and what grade we were in, and we honestly answered the question, "Do you like your school?" These were not meant to be essay questions and we were not to expound on the subject – "Yes, Sir/Ma'am" was all that was necessary and that was all we were to offer.

Then (thankfully) we would be excused from adult company.

In our neighborhood, every kid played in the streets. We were rarely inside and, unfortunately, every parent knew every kid. Any adult would be quick to chastise us for any antisocial behavior. Back then, it was only called "misbehaving" and they would do everything but smack us on the seat. (Aunts, uncles, and grandparents could, however, give us a swat.)

Our greater fear was that our parents would learn of another adult chastising us! Then we would really be punished! Our misbehaving reflected very poorly on our mothers for being bad homemakers, and on our dads because it appeared that they were not controlling their kids. This reinforcement of social mores and ethics had a far-reaching effect. We kids tried really hard to behave, and considering our opportunities to do mischief, we were for the most part well-behaved.

"Corporal punishment" was not a term then. We knew that a corporal was just above a private and below a sergeant, and there was no other "corporal" in anyone's language that we knew. "Spare the rod and spoil the child" was current, however. I remember being "unspoilt" several times. I had an aunt half a block down the street and I was there so much, she would readily give me "corporal punishment." If I were lucky, she would not tell my mom. (I certainly was not going to mention it.)

From experience, we tried hard to behave so there would be no problems reported to our parents. We were not to intrude on the peace of our neighbors. Their peace was sacred.

"Time outs" and "go to your room" were so silly that our parents would have never said this to imply it was punishment because it would have never been perceived as such. We enjoyed being in our rooms! We had an old, reject radio with a scratchy speaker but it could still get two stations, and there were our comic books and toys. We had to keep our room neat. We could not leave them to go outside until the rooms passed inspection.

What we really wanted to avoid was discomfort or pain. We understood that there would be times when we would hurt and those times taught us to try to avoid them. We would become more clever as we aged and "get away with more," or we could, with adequate inspiration, modify our behavior and still have lots of fun and independence without fear of "pain."

[Again, the reader should remember that when there is a "we," it could mean tens of thousands of young people like myself. I was not at all unique.]

Between church and the 3rd grade play ground, I learned that I did not make fun of people because if I did, some older brother might bust me in the mouth. (Note: "Avoid pain.") And we learned that there were some things we were good at and some things we were not.

If we dropped the baseball when it was thrown to us; if we let it roll between our legs when hit our direction; and we never managed to make the bat and ball come in contact; then it was no surprise that when dividing up for baseball teams, we were selected last. Even we would not have selected ourselves for a team!

A baseball game materialized when someone produced a ball and bat. Some kids had gloves. The worst thing that could happen then would be an adult come along to organize things for us. We understood our rules. They evolved as social things should; by slow change to correct demonstrated problems.

We had a lot of games and some were brutal, but we survived and were the stronger for playing them. One such game caused me to break half of a permanent front tooth off. It was an accident. It was tough luck. This was not corrected until my parents got it fixed when I was ready to leave high school and home. This was a matter of prioritizing expenses.

Scores were kept in all games. It would be silly to play a game with no scores. With no scores there would be no winners or losers. (Theoretically.) In any game, one side lost; one side won. If it bothered us to lose, then we should try harder next time.

In time, we did get better, faster, and stronger. And most importantly, we learned determination, and to recognize the rewards of dedication and hard work – and not necessarily ours.

*****

In education, the principal challenge was to not fail. "Learning" would be nice, but mostly we just needed to pass. It was humiliating to be held back a grade. We would be big and the rest of the kids would be smaller. It would be embarrassing. Because of this, we tried harder and harder to pass...or rather, to not fail. There was a stigma for failing. I never knew a kid to fail twice.

Yet some kids did fail. They could not do the work in the allotted time. In another year they could – and they would be much more inspired to work and learn. For the kids who gave up...well, too bad. We knew what a quitter was. We kept trying harder to avoid being one of those. We had tutors. They were called "parents." Plural. And we did not want the teacher to tell them that we needed to study more.

We lived in the Waco, Texas, area from 1943 to 1945 – a couple of the "war years." We went by rail into downtown Waco to shop. This was fast by a street car that went maybe 20 miles with just a few stops.

I was always taken to the courthouse where the jail was, but fortunately I was left in the basement, which contained the county library. My mom could take a long time shopping and all that time I was wonderfully surrounded by books. I read everything – the more science the better. The librarians knew me. I was polite and I was cute, and I appeared smarter than I actually was. And I had a long time to select the maximum number of books I could check out and take home with me.

Hours spent in that county library were some of the happiest of my life! My day would always improve as soon as I could smell those books – and I believed that I could smell them from the street sidewalk.

I have two remembered smells from those days – the books – and chlorine.

Also in Waco, the YMCA gave free swimming lessons in an indoor pool. I was sent to these and I hated them. All boys swam nude. It was said for health reasons. If concerned for health, one would not get in that pool. The greatest health danger was the extreme chlorine. Eyes watered and turned red...and this was in the dressing room before even going to the pool area. The "swim course" was five consecutive days for about two hours each day. Every time we were there our eyes burned and our noses hurt all the way back home.

I felt that I was the most naked kid in the county! I was that modest.

I finally managed to splash across the pool and got a swimming certificate – we called them "drowning papers."

Fortunately, the only swimming distinction was "swimmers" and "sinkers."

On any competition list we knew that there was a top and a bottom – good guys and bad guys. I tried not to be on the bottom; some tried to be at the top. When they got up there, they deserved it!

The recognition of reality made us accepting of our accomplishments and taught us to cope with our shortcomings.

Chapter 2 The United States Society: 1945 - 1991

Introduction

For American society at home during WWII, the men went to fight and someone at home had to make the war material. We hated our enemies. We knew it was not just a little problem with communication. We wanted them all dead! They wanted us dead! We were killing each other. This is what war was about.

On March 9, 1945, United States bombers dropped incendiary bombs on Tokyo. Japan had 50% of its war material production scattered throughout the city – amidst commercial and residential areas. This was a plan to eliminate the industries as being mass bombing targets. This single, fire bombing mission left 120,000 dead and over one million homeless. This is the most destructive bombing raid in human history. Japan's resolve to continue the war was reaffirmed.

We saw all the posters of Japanese soldiers and emblazoned across some were the words "Save your Scrap! Kill a Jap!" Every one collected scrap metal.

And there were posters of a grinning Hitler and a sinking American ship that read, "Loose Lips Sink Ships" – spies were in many places and U-boats seemed everywhere. There were ships torpedoed in the Gulf of Mexico just off the Texas coast. Clever word usage has always been a superb motivator and it continues excessively today.

The women had left the homes en masse and gone into the workforce; many directly into building armaments. They were good workers; they were inspired workers! Many had husbands, brothers, uncles, and sweethearts in service, and these women learned that there were other things available to them besides being a homemaker. They were enjoying their independence. They were making money, contributing to the defense of America, and they learned that they had personal worth beyond the home. This pride can be a rather heady, new experience. The men did not like it that so many women were in what had been "their" work places. But they understood that it was necessary.

This was Culture Shock for the men, as well as for the women.

During many centuries leading up to 1945, women were supposed to be protected and cared for. Their job was to raise the family and be a good homemaker. Those women would beam when a lady friend would compliment her – "Oh, Roberta! Your husband and children always look so nice and your children are so well-behaved and your house is so neat and pretty. And the way you cook and sew! You are certainly a great homemaker!"

Roberta would glow at the ultimate compliment – she knew that other women recognized that she was a good homemaker. This meant that she had been elevated in her community, as well as in her husband's eyes. She had about the most important job in the world and it was very difficult to do it well, particularly in the lower-income families.

At the time, the upper class was way, way up there! The middle class was way down, and only comfortable. All the rest of society was lower class trying very hard to move up. This has to do with income. But in WWII everyone was in the same condition; at war against numerous and powerful enemies.

The men knew whose wives worked. This was less important during the war, but not good between the wars. The husband was to be a good provider just as his wife was striving to be a good homemaker. The man with the working wife knew that the other men thought he was not doing a very good job or his wife would not have to work to help support the family. Her working reflected badly on him and this hurt his pride.

But during WWII, the families' young men might be halfway around the globe fighting and the father was not. He was working in a factory – with a lot of women. For the Depression Era mature men, this was difficult to accept. The men wanted to do more, but could not. This was psychological emasculation.

While the young men were fighting, they were looking forward to getting back to a peace-time America, getting a job, marrying their high school sweetheart, then getting a car and little house, and starting a family. They were looking forward to the life from which the women were learning to enjoy being away.

– The War Ends

In May, 1945, Germany surrendered and there was no more fighting in Europe, but the United States and some Allies were still at war with the Japanese in the Pacific and Asia.

In July, 1945, the bomb that was to end the war was successfully tested at Alamogordo, New Mexico.

Also in 1945, President Roosevelt, who had been president since 1933 and served for three consecutive terms (12 years) died in office during his 4th term. The Vice-President, Harry Truman, became president. Truman authorized the dropping of the atomic bomb on Hiroshima, Japan.

It was dropped August 6, 1945. Approximately 85,000 Japanese died. (As well as 20 Allied prisoners of war; 12 of whom were American.) More Japanese died later from radiation effects.

I remember hearing the announcement on the radio that the bomb was dropped on Hiroshima. I was visiting with a lot of relatives and I heard their shouting and clapping at the good news that in a matter of days the war would be over and loved ones would be coming home.

It was unbelievable!

Just one bomb?

At the same time, they heard of the death and destruction in Japan.

'Tough!' they might have fleetingly thought... if they thought of it at all.

They remembered December 7th and Pearl Harbor.

There was no response from the Japanese relative to the bombing of Hiroshima.

Three days later a second atomic bomb was dropped on Nagasaki, Japan. This killed approximately 60,000.

Japan sued for peace.

August 15, 1945, Japan surrendered.

*****

Now that the war was over, the factories started to switch from making tanks and planes back to producing cars, washers, fridges, and all the things that been worn out during the war, as well as other things the GIs had been fighting for.

The GIs got home and they could hardly recognize their sweethearts. The girls were dressed about the same as when the men had been sent off to war, but their attitudes were different. They were not reserved, shy, or coy. They were active in conversation and knew many things that the guys thought only guys should know. The GIs were seeing the first modern American woman.

Culture shock!

For the men, having their cigarettes lit by a smoking woman was very off-putting.

And there was the brutal realization that though she had promised to wait, nights did get long and lonely at home, as well as they had when he was on leave in Paris. Both had found company, distraction, and comfort where they could.

Culture shock!

The ladies could go when and where they wanted. These women could take care of themselves and did not need a man to protect them. Indeed, she might still be working at the factory while he was looking for work – and worse – looking for a place to live.

The military was no longer housing these men and in many cases the girls were still living with their family. Not all military factories could be immediately converted to home-consumption products.

Now the girl and boy wanted to marry – as soon as they could find him a job and them a place to live. One solution, but one that was not all that popular, was that the ladies could leave their factory jobs and the returning vets take those jobs – this would free the lady to start her home life and family. A lot of ladies had mixed emotions about this.

But many were getting married and starting families. Between mid-1945 and early 1947, over 10.5 million men returned to the United States. As veterans, they needed work and housing. They felt that they had offered their lives for the United States and now they wanted to just be a citizen with a house, job, car, and family – the American dream.

Finding a place to live was difficult.

Before the war a construction company, Levitt and Sons, had been building upper, middle-class communities on Long Island, New York. The head of the firm's son, William Levitt, had served with the Seabees in WWII. The Seabees were the Navy "Construction Battalion" and they were trained in the rapid construction of airstrips, forward bases, shipping docks, and all the infrastructure a dynamic military requires, and particularly, one in an island-hopping war.

While performing these operations, William Levitt learned how to rapidly put up temporary buildings for the military. He knew that when the war was over, the service men would be needing immediate housing, and that of the cheaper sort.

When William returned from the war, he served as president of Levitt and Sons, and he adopted a very utilitarian manner of home construction. He, with his younger brother Alfred, produced homes rapidly and en masse. The construction procedure would follow the same as used by the military.

The Levitt company bought large sections of farmland on Long Island and started constructing 6,000 homes.

This approach produced 30 homes a day – a one-floor house with an unfinished attic. The building material arrived on the construction sites already cut to length and the company employed anyone who could do the work – union member or not. The company received a waiver to use concrete slabs for foundations because this would contribute to the fast-building of sturdy houses.

There were early union problems, but Levitt paid their workers so well, with incentives, that they often earned twice the union scale for that labor. The company was buying in such mass that they could buy all they needed directly from the manufacturers – this cut out the costs of the middle men – the wholesalers.

Levitt's construction of thousands of houses, and building many at the same time, allowed the houses to be sold with kitchens fully furnished with modern appliances. Often included in the house price was furniture with a TV in the living room. Occasional special sales included fully stocked kitchen cabinets with food in the refrigerator.

Schools and stores were built as part of the planned community.

This house cost $8,000 ($85K in 2018 dollars). With the aid of other programs, the move-in could be as low as $400 ($4K in 2018 dollars).

Levitt's original intention was to build rentals, but as his production costs went down, this quickly changed to outright ownership on a 30-year mortgage with low down-payment and monthly payments the same as if the house was being rented.

The Levitt company was providing "The American Dream" – fast, move-in-ready, and with a low down-payment.

After the first Levittown in New York, other Levittowns were built – the second in Pennsylvania. Five others followed over the years.

Many other companies adopted Levitt's construction model – all to improve the home-buying experience for the citizen.

Levitt had to follow the Federal Housing Administration's regulations which required the developers to specify the racial makeup of their home-buyers. <u>The FHA did not offer mortgages to integrated housing developments</u>. This was an FHA business decision based on experience. It had nothing to do with the FHA's nor the Levitt brother's social preferences.

The military from whence so many potential buyers were coming had also been segregated. The government had Levittown specified as "Caucasian only." In this way, every potential buyer would know what the social makeup of the community would be.

Levitt and Sons would end up building over 140,000 quality homes. (In 2018, many are still occupied.)

*****

With the end of the war, my dad was laid off from the airbase fire department and he got a job driving a long-distance freight truck. He was on the road a lot. We had to move to East Waco and into a slummy little house that was not only on the wrong side of the tracks, it was on the wrong side of two tracks. Many black people lived around us. We were back to toast and white gravy. There was one positive thing for me – I was much closer to the county library!

I still had a lot of kids to play with and this was my first time to play with black kids. They liked me because I could build such good kites from apple boxes and the newspaper comic pages. Flour and water paste was the kid's glue of choice, but this had to dry overnight. On more than one occasion, during the night the mice managed to eat away all the paste and paste-soaked paper – leaving in the morning nothing that looked like it had ever been a kite.

I would spend hours lying in the field behind our house enjoying the sun. Lying in the tall weeds, I was shielded from the cold wind. This is also where we flew our kites. I would gather up all the various wads of discarded tangles of kite string. With my patience, I could unravel miles of this string and firmly reattach the ends and roll it on short sections of broom sticks. I gave these away or swapped them – the kids appreciated this. Most everything we kids (of any color) played with, we had to build, restore, modify, and/or swap for.

I had a good idea that we might be a lot further down the social ladder than we had ever been. We might even have been upper, low class – everyone else around us was. But I was assured by my parents that it was only a temporary setback. My mom told me, "We are not poor. We just do not have much money right now."

I hoped so. I was ready for some more middle class – at any level.

We moved to three other places for just a couple of months at a time and then we returned to South Texas with my dad working in the oilfields again.

I was in the sixth grade (12 years old) but I had some cousins in the same school which made it seem familiar. I had a few close friends and we flew model airplanes and ran little rocket cars. My friends and I were interested in science; science became a hobby because we were a curious bunch of kids.

And being curious, I started noticing girls. Most of them were a lot of noise and bother, but some were not so bad.

By the time we were in high school, we had a home life that we understood was to be temporary, but now of a different sort. It would be over when we became adults. This would be at 18 or 19 years old. This seemed then to be a long, long time into the future. It was not.

Additionally, now I had a steady girl friend.

It was understood that the children would get a better education than the parents and they would, in-turn make more money and live better. We understood that it took our parents a long time to get to the standard of living they enjoyed, and in which we were being raised, so we would have to work just as hard as they had for us to match their standard of living.

We never expected to start our own homes at the same level which our parents had worked many years to achieve.

We, with our parents, had seen days not nearly as good, so we knew that we, too, could work through the bad ones and do more on our own. We were resilient. Our role models were our parents.

I have photographs of what we all looked like then. Few of the kids were heavy, and almost none were fat. We were active outside and did not have all the food stuffs of later years. We may not have run as much then, but we walked anywhere we wanted to go. Living out of town on an oil-lease, I had a lot opportunity to walk – but I never refused a ride by a passing motorist.

I remember one fat boy in all my 12 years of elementary and high school. I remember one fat girl. In 12 years!

We could leave the high school campus to eat if we wanted (no permission needed) and across the busy highway from the school was a little hamburger joint that fed students who wanted something other than in a bag from home or something served in the institutional school cafeteria.

Hamburgers then were commonly no more than 4" across and a little over an 1" thick – including the bun. This, with a small pack of chips, and an 8-ounce soda was the standard fare. When the weather was very hot, I thought the walk from school to the joint and back pretty well took care of any "energy" I might have gained by eating there.

For a while, I got my lunch in return for using my lunch period to rack up the returnable drink bottles, with each case destined for one of the four bottlers that delivered the drinks.

We were an agreeable bunch of kids. In <u>all</u> those school photographs, there are smiling, confident kids. The girls dressed nice and their hair was properly done, or perhaps in pin-curls with scarves around their heads. This would likely be on Fridays and they had a date that night. There were no surly kids posturing with threatening attitudes and antisocial gestures.

Our parents expected more of us and they thought we would amount to something. We tried hard to please them. The height of our rebelliousness was in wanting to be alone. In the cactus and mesquite country of South Texas it was easy to be alone. We had a rapidly approaching future and we had to decide a lot of things. No one was doing our thinking for us. I remember no school career counselor. Then, counselors were called "parents."

As was generally the case, most socializing occurred in school or in church. There were 53 students in our 8th grade class and of these, six were Mexicans. This is how they referred to themselves so that is what we called them. We were 50 miles from the Mexican border so there were a lot of Mexicans living in the town and local area.

We made little distinction in the Mexicans in our class, other than they usually sat together. I do not know if we gave race much thought, but we knew that birds of a feather flocked together. That seemed natural. (And it is observed in nature.)

Like "spare the rod and spoil the child" and "a child is to be seen and not heard," we learned many social lessons by simple homilies.

Though we would not say it, we intuitively knew that a witty saying proved nothing – it was like a joke. And we knew that some wit was not even correct, yet we got the point of it anyway.

There were three guys in our school who would always fight and almost always with each other– two were brothers. If some kid yelled, "FIGHT!" we just kept on with our business – we had a good idea who it was and did not care about the outcome.

When we graduated from high school, there were 36 in the class; 3 Mexicans – girls. Many young people had left school to work in the oilfields and some had left to get married. I had a couple of summer jobs and one was in the oilfields.

There was a lot of hunting in our county and I would expect that every household had a gun. It was common for men to go to the coffee shop in their pickups with their deer rifles in the racks behind the seats and in front of the rear window. This was sort of showing off good rifles with telescopic sights. It was hot in the South Texas sun so the pickup windows would be down some – the truck door might not have even been locked.

In the 8 years I lived there, I remember no particular theft in our town and only two murders – one man was killed with a pistol and it had been assumed that would happen eventually. We knew to leave other people's property alone and wives were considered valuable property – to leave alone.

The other victim owed a lot of money to a local shop. He would not pay his bill and the shop owner was going out of business if the bill did not get paid. The victim really should not have ridiculed the shop owner as a bad business man for giving him so much credit. The shop owner beat the victim to death with a piece of iron pipe, which was the closest weapon at hand. It was lying in the back of an oilfield pickup near where they had been standing and arguing. This happened on the main street of town and this made it seem even worse than it was.

We were not particularly naive. We lived in one of the most corrupt counties in Texas. It was so crooked that our county and town were featured in a *Life* magazine article as well as in many newspapers. Indeed, the crooked election in our county and the adjacent one took the election result from the legitimate winner and gave it to his competitor.[3]

The good part of this is that it increased our attention in one of the most boring school courses ever invented to plague young students: "Civics." Our teachers would jest about the local politics and use it as an example of (bad) government.

[To repeat, the events recalled here are typical of what was being experienced by many young people across the country, and therefore, though personal, the comments provide some sociological insight into that time in America.]

All high school students had their own lockers in the hall. They did not take their books back and forth to home and school bent over like Sherpas with heavy humps on their backs. The boys were assigned lockers near the floor and the girls had the lockers above the boys'. The campus was spread out and this necessitated that there be enough time to exchange books and still get to the next class on time.

There had to be water fountain and restroom time between the classes, as well.

When our next class was next door to the previous class in the main building, we had time to loll in the hall at our lockers and visit. If there were "hall monitors," I do not remember any.

There was never a search of a student. It someone had cigarettes (forbidden), he would have been smart and left them off campus. There was no student parking area because so few students brought cars to school. Everyone parked just anywhere they could find.

But the students were learning and getting a good education by the diligence of superb teachers who could rightfully be called "educators." What I learned in high school got me jobs, and these fed and housed me later while I was in advanced school.

No one in school caused any serious problem that a teacher could not resolve – male or female.

---

[3] This is known as the "Ballot Box 13 Scandal." Instead of Coke Stevenson going to Washington, D.C. as a Texas Senator, Lyndon Johnson did.

In the 12 years I was in school, I never saw a policeman on campus. I never saw a police car on school property nor even parked where we generally went during lunch.

If there was trouble around town, the sheriff would be called and no one wanted that. He liked staying out on his ranch and did not want to have to come to town because someone was acting stupid. This would mean that he arrived in a bad mood. He might be seen at a football game on Friday nights, but he was there to see the game anyway.

There were a lot of deputies (many, many), but they had political business to take care of for the county so we did not see much of them.

For real trouble, we had the Texas Rangers. No one wanted them to be called either. They were peace officers and their job was to restore the peace. How they went about this was simple and sometimes rudely efficient. The same troublemaker would not cause trouble again. He would not want to deal with the Rangers anymore. The Rangers were very well respected and the troublemaker understood that he had caused the trouble and was made sorry. There were other things that he could have done and he would strive to do things differently next time.

The Texas Rangers had started in 1823 while Texas was a Republic (before becoming a state). They were responsible for maintaining the peace for the 45 years before the United States' Fourteenth Amendment was ratified. This amendment defined "due process of law."

The Rangers had their own effective system for maintaining the peace.

*****

With the men and women having gotten married after the war and setting up housekeeping, they were moving into tract housing developments. Thank goodness for Levittown and similar housing developments.

These young families had babies.

Lots of them.

At the start of the Depression in 1930, there were 2.62 million births in the United States and in the middle of the Depression in 1935 there were 2.38 million – 240,000 fewer. This seems logical considering national events.

Just before WWII, in 1940, there were 2.56 million babies born which was 180,000 more than 1930. In the last year of WWII (1945) there were 2.86 million – 300,000 more than 1940.

In just five years, in 1950, with the now-settled WWII families, there were 3.63 million births – 770,000 more than 1945.

The moms and dads were young people and maybe their moms were not just next door anymore because the nation had become so mobile. Now new dads and moms were holding their first born and wondering, 'Now what? How do we raise a baby?'

In 1946 a book appeared to be just what they needed. Noted pediatrician Dr. Benjamin Spock produced his book, "The Common Sense Book of Baby and Child Care." This was touted to be a modern guide for modern parents – and everyone wanted to be modern – and use common sense in the process.

The extended families were no longer living near each other, but living states apart. Yet young mothers were talking with other young mothers; their mothers and grandmothers were far away and these experienced and trusted adults were not readily accessible.

The young couples were on their own. They were healthy and enthused, and for their young family, they certainly wanted the best – whatever that was.

Spock's book was their answer and his book created a new United States. No one anticipated this. Social change is often this way.

[There will be several passing comments about Dr. Spock and then a detailed discussion of his contribution to American society in Section IV.]

– The Iron Curtain: 1950s

This was a term coined by the British leader Winston Churchill to explain the condition in which the world found itself after WWII. The Soviets back-pedaled on many of their signed agreements and they became the definitions of "obstructionist" and "opportunist."

The Soviets would use the expediency of the moment to justify any action.

They put up walls to keep people in the Soviet Zones in East Europe as well as in East Berlin. Too many people had been leaving because of their preference for more freedom and less Political Correctness.

In the 1950s the idea of strict Political Correctness had returned to East Germany and other eastern European countries by the Communist Bloc – just as Political Correctness had been in the same areas in the early 1940 days of Nazi Germany.

The Communists had a stated and published mission to revolutionize the world to be governed by Communism. They were doing what they could to fulfill this mission. Those countries not desiring a Communist political system would need to do what they could to avoid it. It would often come in the form of revolt – first in the streets and then in the following wars. These conflicts generally involved Soviet forces in Europe, and Communist China in Asia. Sometimes they were successful.

Those citizens not following their brand of Political Correctness would be "re-educated." Similar things would be happening in Communist China in the Cultural Revolution. Political Correctness was the term for an old idea formerly called "brain washing." To ask if anything about Political Correctness made sense was considered politically incorrect and was an offense against the state and public. The citizens were told what to think and if it was questioned, it could become very bad for the curious. Those who did question any of it were re-educated – sometimes for months – and then, being more enlightened, they would be returned to their community and in the future enthusiastically support the Party Line.

As opportunity permitted, the stated Communist goal of world-wide Communist Revolution was proceeding according to their plan. There was the great start of Russia becoming the Soviet Union, and then in the 1950s having Eastern Europe well-established with Communist governments.

In midyear, 1950, Communist North Korea, supported by Communist China and the Soviet Union, invaded non-Communist

South Korea. At the request of South Korea, the United Nations sent troops from 21 countries. The United States provided over 90% of the total forces to protect South Korea from uninvited Communist dominion. United States citizens were back in combat just a little more than 4.5 years after the end of WWII.

Two days after the North Korean invasion, South Vietnam requested United States support against Communist North Vietnam's invasion of non-Communist South Vietnam – North Vietnam was supported by Communist China.

In mid-1953 North and South Korea signed a cease fire. This ended the shooting but there was no peace brokerage, so in 2018, they were still at war but not always fighting.

*****

Between the 1940 and the 1950 United States censuses, there was an increase of births by 14% and this would be the first generation raised according to Dr. Spock's little book. This era was called the "Fabulous Fifties."

One of the justifiable reasons for this name was that at the end of WWII, the United States was the only industrialized nation with their infrastructure not only undamaged by war, but having their industry in full production. No matter what the United States made or grew; the world needed it.[4]

*****

Like many young people of the early 1950s, when we got out of high school, we were supposed to be on our own. We were not to be living at home as if we were still some little kid. We would have been embarrassed to continue living at home and being supported by our father.

4

Britain maintained food rationing until 1954 – nine years after the end of WWII! Their manufacturing capability had been that damaged. They had 14 years of rationing anything that had contributed to the war – gas, tires, meat, sugar ... everything, was in short supply. By contrast, the United States had nearly full industrial production from 1943 on.

All this applied to me when I got out of high school – going to an advanced school or not. "If not," then it generally meant in the military and going to a military school.

If in advanced schooling, it was preferred that it be far enough from family so the kid could learn to be an adult and make his own decisions – also, it would need to be in a town where he could find work to help pay for his follow-up education which was in support of his chosen career. Public transportation was a near-necessity since a car did not come with high school graduation. Responsibility did.

Graduation prom vehicles were the family car – just washed and swept out. We were used to school busses, bicycles, and walking. That is how we had been getting to school for 12 years so we continued to use what we could when we went away to school in another town.

I had left South Texas for technical school in Chicago and when I was not in school, I was delivering packages around Chicago in a company van and working in a couple of factories using machine tools. This was for about 5 hours a day; the rest of the day was in school or transit. Because of my training in high school Industrial Arts in South Texas, the Chicago school had no difficulty finding work for me.

I know now that I could not have finished school in Chicago if I had owned a car. I could not have handled the added responsibility of a car. Between work, school, and marriage, I needed the time on public transportation to study or sleep. And again, I was being independent; i.e., not depending on parents.

We had to have a place of our own – shared with others or not. Where we were raised ceased to be "home." That was where our parents still lived, but now we lived somewhere else. The old town was still our "home town" but we knew that we would have to make our own home and it would be only as good as we could afford. Consequently, in Chicago, my bed filled most of my first room. To open a chest of drawers, I had to lay on the bed. But it was my room and I was paying for it and whatever food I ate. Additionally, I was paying for my transportation.

Later, I got more room but mostly because there was a Murphy bed that folded into the wall. If someone was visiting, the bed was let down and a small table was slid to the bed so someone could sit on the bed and be at the table. The bath and kitchen were down the hall. The floor tenants were to keep them clean. We divided up the duties as necessary.

The only available phone was three flights down by the stairs. I do not remember calling anyone. I wrote short letters by hand.

I did not feel abandoned. I had me! It was challenging and exhilarating – and with that came a lot of satisfaction and self-confidence. And with all the new experiences, I was aware then that this was coming on a day-by-day basis. I was raised in South Texas, but I have said that I grew up in Chicago – in 90 days. I had been only three months into my 19th year when I had gotten on a bus and moved from South Texas to Chicago.

Later, I was married there to my high school sweetheart from South Texas. She got a job also. Like many young people, I had established a family and now needed to establish a career for a better income. This always starts with education in a field of endeavor for which someone would pay me to execute.

*****

There were a lot of mixed emotions in America's growing families. During this time men were going in and out of uniform because of the continuing Communist business with world conflicts. But as the men were settling back into the happier business of family life, they would have preferred to turn back the clock and put war out of their minds.

War had interrupted their lives and they wanted to have continuity of the preferred social conditions while having closure of the negative. This is simply the appreciation of tradition. And it is Conservative thinking, but at the same time they had to recognize all the changes in society. These changes were liberal by definition, in that they were sudden, serious changes and most everything was now different. This is distracting whether the individual agrees or disagrees with the changes. Stress recognizes no values – good or bad – it is still stress.

Of comfort in the confusion of child rearing was Dr. Spock's axiom, "You know more than you think." The world had become much more complicated – the fathers had experienced a world of fear and doubt of the most serious kind, and the mothers had learned to cope with new challenges, and now it was uplifting to be assured that they both knew more than they thought.

They wanted to return to common sense and the way America had been, but without the economic hardships. And they also had the desire for new and more modern things. They wanted to look ahead to a new future.

With Dr. Spock, they made it.

*****

We had our first child in 1955 and we bought Dr. Spock's book. However, many of his recommendations were contrary to how I thought a child should be raised – which was basically, how I was raised – in the traditional manner. When he was discussing medicine, I naturally trusted his expertise, but if I knew more than I thought, then maybe I knew more than Dr. Spock thought I knew. Some of what he suggested actually seemed counterproductive to producing a well-rounded, confident young person ready to step into the adult world.

My thinking was not that unique and this will play heavily in what I saw the nation becoming in the next years. I was relying on the examples of my parents. This was simply tradition – which, by definition meant "in the old way."

But parents with Dr. Spock's book wanted to be modern. Many disregarded "tradition" as being "old fashioned" (true) and they wanted to be modern and at the same time, apply common sense. The idea did not occur to these parents that "common sense" and "modern" could occasionally be mutually exclusive, or that "tradition"and "common sense" are often supporting terms.

I had followed the dictates of my parents and now that I was 21, it seemed to have worked OK. I was working in the Nuclear Engineering Department of a major aerospace company and providing for a wife and infant daughter. (A son would arrive a while later, then another daughter, and lastly another son.)

[This is the point in this long story where I can no longer be counted as an example of public issues and responses. I was raised by parents who believed, like most other parents then, that we as children were not part of the adult world. We were not asked to contribute our childish fantasies to adult conversation nor were we to disrupt the adults in their affairs. We were taught that our time would come and we should learn the rules of adult behavior not by involvement but by observation – and behavior reinforcement. We children had learned that things went better for us when the important people around us were pleased with us.

But from 1955-on, I became an anomaly. I became more of an observer and historian of popular society than a participant. I had to concentrate on the business of becoming a responsible, producing adult and I was aided by good fortune that was well outside the normal bounds of possibilities.

In other words, I was no longer typical.]

Now the child was spending more time with TV than with his mom and dad. And this was during the child's most formative years. In the 1950s, almost all children were still living with both mom and dad.

TV did not cause the situations for which it is so easily blamed, but it did contribute to them in a significant manner. Today, it is amusing to remember that initially every home was to have a TV because of its "educational value." Some parents saw through this sham; not enough did, however.

TV became the opiate of the tired or busy parent. The modern child-rearing habit became one of just setting the child down in front of the TV. The child became a new market and TV made the most of it.

– Public Demonstrations: 1960s

Freud had postulated that there was a "narcissistic phase" in infancy. It went by other names but it was understood that with proper parenting this self-absorbed phase would be replaced by a growing sense of social adaptation and then maturity. However, with Dr. Spock's teaching, that is not what happened. This omission was not by his design but the first generation of these children occurred in the late '40s and the second generation in the '70s.

The first generation of children became adults in the '60s and they had a new persona because of the way they were raised. The population had gained 18% of what it was in 1950.

One can consider that the polarization of the nation over the Vietnam war had a lot to do with our involvement in a bad war. It was a bad war because war is the business of the military after the politicians' diplomatic efforts have failed. In this case, the politicians never admitted their failures and there were volumes of political "rules of engagement" in the war. These rules interfere with the execution of a war by the military.

The politicians would stay involved at a near-hourly rate during this war – even defining which targets could and could not be bombed at any given time. The media, in their belief that "Americans have a right to know" (Modern Myth) was telling of these war changes in almost real time on satellite news. Consequently, the opposition could know which targets to protect or move.

There was too much political posturing while TV production companies presented the war being fought in the background of the evening meals across America. Vietnam was a televised war being shown to a peaceful, nonviolent people in the comfort of their homes. Nothing could have been more out of context nor more difficult to understand. But it sold advertisements on TV and in newspapers. Selling is the responsibility of the media. Singularly.

The post-Dr. Spock children were growing up with Peter Max, cartoons, unicorns, ever-present rainbows, and fields of year-round flowers. Everything would be "fantabulous" if a mythical boat would just come take them all away. It was a psychedelic age of altered reality– with or without LSD. And such fantasies were not just those of pre-kindergarten children.

It has been said by the Sixties generation that if someone could remember the Sixties, they were not there. Many people remember the Sixties – and with little pride. The United States was not very united in the Sixties.

All that the young people needed was love and all problems were just a little matter of communication. "If the other guy could just understand how we feel, I am sure he would love us back."

This is both sweetly innocent...and dangerous. It precludes the idea that there are evil people in the world and that on occasion even well-meaning people can do a lot of social damage.

This "Sixties thinking," not surprisingly was at a very juvenile level and showed little awareness of cultures. Some cultures want some other cultures dead. <u>There is no communication problem</u>. They have been communicating with each other (and killing each other) for hundreds of years.

Knowing that the parents now used TV as a baby sitter, the TV producers started marketing to the children and educating them on product recognition. TV had finally become educational – but not in the manner others had expected.

Teaching a child what to desire could be a problem if the child had no money, but the child could get it – and easier than working for it. They just had to function within their home equality system and that which was denied would appear.

To them "No" was but an automatic, momentary, knee jerk response. It could be changed to "Yes" with just a little effort.

TV grew up with their child market until older children would kill (literally) for that special pair of $140 sneakers.

*****

There was the continued global effort by Communism to spread their preference of government. They were using revolution and blood rather than popular votes in a peaceful election. The young Americans declared that they would rather be "Red than Dead." This showed a very limited imagination as if "red or dead" were the only choices. But "Better Red than Dead" appeals because it sounds so cute. No one asked if it made sense. The Renaissance was a long time ago. The reverse: "Better Dead than Red" was equally catchy... and as intellectually limiting.

The young, antiwar enthusiasts had unrealistic aspirations caused by liberal educations. And the most intense of these people were the activists – "towering in the confidence of twenty-one." (Samuel Johnson, 1758.)

*****

The Sixties were a decade of lawlessness, but not all young people were in the streets. Some were quietly working to change the world a different way. Rather than react, they acted. In 1960 the United States launched the first weather satellite and 12 days later launched the first navigation satellite. Such navigation satellites were the beginning of a satellite global positioning system – GPS.

Early in 1962, John Glenn was the first American to orbit earth. The Soviets had made their first manned orbital flight a year earlier. The Soviets and the United States were in a space race to the moon. This was a bloodless Communism/Free Enterprise confrontation.

Near Christmas, 1968, Frank Borman, James Lovell, and William Anders were the first to leave the gravity of a celestial body and travel in space to the moon. They orbited the moon 10 times before returning to Earth. They read to the world from the Bible. American Political Correctness had not been invented, yet.

The 20th of July, 1969, Neil Armstrong and Buzz Aldrin walked on the lunar surface. Mike Collins stayed with the Command Module orbiting the moon. The first person on the moon was an engineer.

The Soviets, having lost the lunar landing race, then started developing systems to put heavy items in earth orbit, a task at which they excelled.

The modern computer world began on November 21, 1969, when ARPA-net was put into operation. ARPA-net, in short order became the "Internet." It was invented by the Advanced Research Projects Agency at the United States Department of Defense – financed by tax payers.

There were many young people locked in the hope of a better future and they were striving to provide it with science and engineering, and they were mostly separated from what was taking place on the streets. They were focused on the stars.

The United States was changing – in 1959 even the American flag changed from 48 to 49 stars with Alaska becoming a state. Hawaii became a state later that year to create the 50-star flag. To many Americans the new flags looked strange. The flag had 48 stars since 1912.

The next year, the Communists continued with their Global Communist policy and Communist Cuba nationalized a lot of American businesses. The United States severed relations with Cuba.

There were American military advisors in South Vietnam assisting the South Vietnam military in planning their war with invading Communist North Vietnam and their armed and inspired locals. Falling by the wayside in national reporting in 1962, was President Kennedy saying that the American military advisors would return fire if fired on. Before this, the advisor's authorized response was if caught in a firefight to cower.

In the fall of 1962, Cuba was back in the news when it was determined that the Soviets were placing offensive missiles in Cuba. It would be foolish for these not to have nuclear warheads. Even their medium-range missiles could put a nuclear warhead anywhere in an arc from Washington, D.C. to Houston, Texas. President Kennedy authorized a naval and air blockade of Cuba. This was as close as the United States had come to the Soviet Cold War becoming a Nuclear Hot War.

The Soviet Premier Khrushchev understood both the seriousness of the issue and the resolve of the United States. The Soviet Union removed the missiles from Cuba. The Premier had assumed that the United States would quickly neutralize the missiles in Cuba and during the same salvo, fire on the Soviet Union. They were convinced that the United States not only could do this but the United States would do this. The ability to strongly strike back is a good deterrent; the conviction to do so reenforces that deterrent.

Late the next year, Kennedy was assassinated.

There had been a foiled, mismanaged attempt by the CIA to invade Cuba.

The Civil Rights Amendment was passed in 1964, and as most revolutionary social changes do, it confused the populace.

In 1965, black leader Malcolm X was killed by black supporters of a black religious group.

In 1966, the black Watts district of Los Angles rioted and this resulted in a five-day siege with burning buildings. Thirty-four people were killed; the property loss was in excess of $200 million. This was an early black riot. Rioting without looting and personal property loss is unlikely.

One year later, black rioting and looting continued in United States cities. There were 159 such riots.

For five days of July, 1967, Newark, New Jersey, had black riots and 26 people were killed, 1,500 injured, and 1,000 were arrested.

On the 23rd of the same month, Detroit blacks rioted in their districts and 40 were killed, 2,000 arrested, and 5,000 blacks were left homeless. Over 12,500 federal troops and National Guard stopped the rioting.

In April of 1968, black leader Martin Luther King was assassinated by a white man in Memphis, Tennessee.

In 1969, presidential candidate Robert Kennedy was assassinated by a Jordanian in Los Angeles, California.

In July of 1969, the United States started withdrawing their forces from Vietnam. The war would continue for six more years until the end of April 1975 when the Communist North Vietnam gained control of South Vietnam to have a complete Communist Vietnam. There had been a maximum of 543,000 United States troops in Vietnam during this miss-managed war.

– More Civil Unrest: 1970 - 1991

For the first time the national census showed over 200 million people living in the United States. This was a 13.4% increase. It only took 50 years for the United States population to double.

In mid-1971, the Supreme Court ruled that newspapers could publish classified (secret) military documents and how they got this information was irrelevant. This continued the "American's have a right to know" premise, which means that the "world has a right to know." Sedition and spies were then protected by the Supreme Court.

Late in 1971, Texas Instruments introduced the microprocessor on a silicon chip – Intel did the same. It was not known which preceded the other. This chip was first used in handheld calculators performing just mathematical calculations, but these led to full-capability data processing computers.

In early 1972, President Nixon went to China for eight days on a journey for peace and this began the normalization of relations between the United States and China. Nixon was the first United States president to visit China while in office.

Later the same year, Nixon made the first trip of a United States president to Moscow. The week-long meeting led to a reduction of long-range missiles and a brief time later, the United States announced the on-going sale of American wheat to the Soviet Union.

In November, President Nixon handily won his next term.

Also in 1972, men were arrested for breaking into the Democratic National Committee headquarters in the Watergate building in Washington D.C. In the aftermath of the break-in, Nixon was incriminated. In the summer of 1974, Nixon resigned rather than face impeachment hearings. He was replaced by Vice President Gerald Ford who pardoned him. Nixon was the first United States president to resign from office. He was neither impeached nor removed from office. [Impeachment is tantamount to an indictment and comes from the House of Representatives. The charges are then considered in the Senate. If found guilty, the individual is removed from office.]

In December of 1972, the last lunar landing was completed. The lunar crew was Eugene Cernan and Harrison Schmitt. Ronald Evans remained on the Command Module in lunar orbit.

Early in 1973, the Supreme Court ruled that a woman could arbitrarily abort a healthy baby up to six months into the pregnancy.

Later in 1973, OPEC members of the Arab nations banned oil imports to the United States because of the United States' material support of Israel in an Arab-Israeli war. This petroleum crisis for the United States would last until March of 1974.

In mid-1976, a United States space probe landed on Mars and transmitted back the first color photographs of the Martian surface.

Late in 1976, Jimmy Carter narrowly defeated Gerald Ford for the presidency.

Also at that time, the computer company, Microsoft, was founded by Bill Gates and Paul Allen.

In the summer of 1977, there was an electrical outage in New York City for 25 hours. This provided thieves the opportunity to engage in massive looting. They took it.

In 1978 there was a meeting in the United States between the Israeli Prime Minister Menachem Begin and the Egyptian President Anwar Sadat and in 12 days a peace accord was drafted and signed. For this, they jointly received the Nobel Peace Prize. (Sadat was subsequently assassinated by the Muslim Brotherhood for making any deal with Israel, a state which the Brotherhood did not recognize.)

March of 1979, the United States had its worst nuclear power plant failure at Three-Mile Island. This was immediately reported in the media as being a catastrophe. After five days the reactor was under control. Though this was the worst United States nuclear accident, there were no deaths nor were there any injuries thus making it a rather benign "catastrophe."

In November of 1979, 3,000 Irani students broke into the American Embassy in Tehran and 63 Americans were taken hostage.

The next year, President Carter placed an embargo on grain and technology to the Soviet Union for their invasion of Afghanistan.

Also in 1980, the population of the United States reached 226.5 million for an 11% increase since 1970. One state, California, had nearly 24 million people, meaning that one out of ten people in the United States lived in California.

In the summer of 1980, Mt. St. Helens volcano in Washington state erupted killing 57 people and causing an economic loss of $3 billion. This eruption was <u>500 times</u> the power of the atom bomb dropped on Hiroshima in 1945.

In the fall of 1980, Ronald Reagan beat incumbent Jimmy Carter by a landslide after Carter's one term as president. Reagan had 489 to 40 electoral college votes and had an 8 million popular vote difference. This voter margin describes a mandate government.

[If only popular votes counted, Los Angeles County, California, could outvote the combined votes of 10 states, and it could outvote any one of 44 states. The electoral college was established to give a broader base of choice in federal politics.]

Early in 1981, the inauguration of Ronald Reagan was followed by the release of the 52 Americans still held hostage in Iran. They had been hostages for 444 days. Iran had their American bank assets released.

In the spring of 1981, President Ronald Reagan survived an assassination attempt when he recovered from a gunshot wound in his chest.

A month later the Space Shuttle made its first launch and returned to land two days later, making it the first reusable manned spacecraft.

In the summer of 1981, Reagan made the largest tax cut in history, reducing the public's taxes by $750 billion over the next five years.

Also that summer, the federal-employee air traffic controllers' union asked for a pay increase of $770 million a year with the threat of a strike to shut down all civilian air travel. The FAA offered $40 million; the union walked out. They wanted $10,000-a-year pay increases for 13,000 controllers, and a reduction in work hours from 40 to 32 hours a week. Reagan warned that as federal employees they could not strike and if they did not return to work, they would be fired.

They did not return and Reagan fired 11,000 air traffic controllers. To increase the number of applications for new traffic controllers, Reagan put a life-time ban on rehiring any traffic controller who had not come to work when his shift had started. Near 7,000 flights were canceled during the summer traveling peak. Reagan brought in military flight controllers and put non-union traffic controller supervisors to work. The union was being fined $1 million per day. The union was decertified that fall. All freight had continued flying, and civilian air travel started picking up as the FAA hired new traffic controllers.

Early in 1982, AT&T settled its United States Justice Department lawsuit by breaking up 222 of its subsidiaries. The Justice Department said that AT&T had committed no crime, but it had gained a monopoly in telephonic communication. They had simply been too successful.

Also early in 1982, Congress ended mandatory school busing as a means to force racial integration.

Late in 1982, the unemployment rate gained the highest level since 1940. 11 million people were unemployed.

In the summer of 1983, Reagan signed legislation to rescue the Social Security System from bankruptcy. Congress had been spending the social security set-aside-funds with the intentions of paying it back. They had not.

In the fall of 1983, a terrorist truck bomb killed 241 United States Marine peace keepers in Beriut, Lebanon. Another bomb destroyed a French barracks two miles away killing 58. The terrorists were members of a Lebanese political group.

Also in the fall, at the request of the Organization of Eastern Caribbean States, the United States invaded Grenada to depose a Communist regime which had come to power illegally. Additionally, Communist Cuban military and construction workers had come to Grenada and were building a 2-mile-long, heavily reinforced runway for large military aircraft. This far exceeded any requirements of a small, tourist destination. Many countries and the UN objected to the United States involvement.

In November 1984, President Reagan won reelection and increased his previous Electoral College vote margin to 523 to 13.

A year later, in 1985, the president met with the Soviet Union Premiere, Mikhail Gorbachev with a positive response by both parties. The United Kingdom Prime Minister Margaret Thatcher had previously met with the Premiere and announced that their meeting showed a change in Soviet posture. Thatcher and Reagan had many conversations over their periods in office.

Also in November, Microsoft released their first public version of a computer utility program called "Windows."

Early in 1986, the Space Shuttle Challenger exploded shortly after launch, killing all seven crew members. The temperature of the launch equipment was out of bounds for a safe launch – engineers called for a "no go." Their revelations and recommendations were overruled by mission management and Challenger was launched anyway. Those in charge were trying to avoid the bad publicity that a launch cancellation would have caused.

The Shuttle crew was: Shuttle Pilot – Michael Smith, an engineer, who had tried in the 73 seconds they lived after the explosion to restore electrical power to the Shuttle. This would have given him flight control. Additionally, there was Commander Richard Scobee, an engineer, who had flown a previous Shuttle in orbit and returned; Ronald McNair, a physicist for payload; Ellison Onosucki, an engineer for payload; Christa McAuliffe, a social studies high school teacher; Gregory Jarvis, an engineer for payload; and Judith Resnik, a brilliant, experienced engineer and pilot.

Since race and gender are such issues with the United States Government (which funds NASA), the seven crew members consisted of one black man, two white women (one, the first Jew to space), an Asian, and three white men. The racial makeup of crews is of paramount importance to those in the government who desire to be re-elected. [This information is provided because current history emphasizes it.]

Later in 1986, the United States and the Soviet Union agreed to limit deployment of medium-range missiles. Many of these missiles had been deployed in Western Germany and were a threat to the Soviet Union. There were no Soviet countermeasures for these missiles any more than there would have been for their missiles previously installed in Cuba. The missile of interest to the Soviets was the United States Pershing missile designed and manufactured by the Martin Company. Over 100 Pershings were stationed near the Soviet Bloc border.

In the fall of 1987, the New York Stock Exchange lost 22.6% of its value – the largest drop in one day. World investments would mirror this decline. This was not the result of any change in world industrial strength. It was the result of "automated sales."

Computers had been programmed to sell certain stocks when a specified profit for that stock had been realized. When that value was reached, the stock was automatically sold by the computer. Should many computers receive the "sell" order, this in turn, would momentarily reduce the price of those stocks.

Some other computers were set to sell a stock when the increase of price started to decline or the stock price went below a preset value. The first round of computerized selling caused the stock price to decline, and this in turn caused the loss-margin computers to automatically sell. One computer system was driving the other – "avalanche" selling. This threat has been partially normalized in that now there is timed selling with a top-selling rate.

Later in 1987, the United States and Soviets agreed to dismantle Intermediate Range Missiles; the United States would dismantle 1,752 Intermediate Range Missiles and the Soviets would dismantle 859. All had ranges of 300 to 3,400 miles and these included the Pershings deployed in West Germany.

In the summer of 1988, the United States approved 1.4 million applications for legal entry into the United States. They were already in the United States illegally. More than 980,000 of the criminals were from Mexico. [This is a true statement but is deemed harsh, so they are now called "undocumented workers." Therefore – John Dillinger did not rob banks. He made "undocumented withdrawals."]

In November 1988, George H. W. Bush became president with 426 Electoral College votes to 111 for the opposition.

In December of 1988, a bomb exploded on a Pan Am airliner flying from Britain to the United States, killing 270 people. The debris landed in Scotland. A high-ranking Libyan, al-Megrahi, was convicted and given life in prison. This defines another multicultural terrorist attack. (In the summer of 2009, al-Megrahi was released after serving 8.5 years. He was released on compassionate grounds because he had prostate cancer. He was returned to Libya and received as a celebrity with much fanfare. He lived until May 2012 when he died in his home. The home had been built for and given to him as a gift from a grateful people. In Libya he is considered a national hero.)

In 1989, economic reports indicated a 3.8% growth rate, the largest in 4 years with unemployment at 5.3% – a low for 14 years.

In the fall of 1989, the Soviets announced an opening in the Berlin Wall and German citizens were allowed to travel freely between East and West Germany for the first time in 28 years. Citizens on both sides of the wall started dismantling it.

East Germany's soldiers took off their uniforms and went home. This could be the first time in history that a well-equipped, first-class military had their soldiers immediately become civilians. The Berlin

Wall came down and nearly overnight the Soviets lost control of half of Berlin and half of Germany. Then in succession the Soviet Bloc ceased to exist in Eastern Europe.

This was not a military result. It was based on economics – socioeconomics.

In the summer of 1990, President George H. W. Bush and Soviet Premiere Gorbachev agreed to stop production of chemical weapons and destroy the current inventory. The things that a lot of adults thought could never happen were happening – and happening quickly. For those people who understood their history, these were wonderful days. For the other people, it was just another piece of paper amid more presidential posturing. It is unfortunate that they could not enjoy the wondrous world changes.

Also, in the summer of 1990, Iraq invaded its neighbor, Kuwait. The UN gave Iraq six months – until mid-January 1991 – to withdraw, otherwise there would be UN intervention. This meant that for nearly six months, the Iraqis could do as they pleased in Kuwait. They did.

On October 3, 1990, the Republic of East Germany ceased to exist. (Thus Germany was restored to the unity of 1945 when Germany surrendered in WWII. Therefore, WWII started with Germany's invasion of Poland September 1, 1939 and the result of that invasion was concluded October 3, 1990; 51 years later.)

In December 1991, the Soviet Union ceased to exist. It had been formed in December 1922.

[Soviet Nyet.]

Chapter 3 The United States Society: 1991 - 2018
Introduction

The end of the Soviet Bloc in Eastern Europe was an event which the world should mark on all calendars. It was that profound. But the greater a social change, the greater are the challenges and opportunities – and not all challenges are met with the best responses.

With social change, rarely can one back up from a liberal one to a less-liberal one; at least not without its being caused by a catastrophe. One such catastrophe was a world economic depression and huge inflation. Many who had money became poor and many who were poor became destitute.

When the United States society was conservative (during WWI) their dress and manners, and even their religion, were a reflection of daily life. For most women, dresses were long with hems down and necklines up. Men would wear suits and hats, and even when on the beach, gentlemen in three-piece suits are seen in old photographs "lounging" on the sand.

Married ladies' hair was up when in public, and the gentlemen did not remove their jackets in the professional environment. The lesser-paid male employees might remove their jackets, but not unbutton sleeves, collars, or vests. Only family members saw their father in shirt sleeves. If a guest arrived, the father excused himself and reappeared "properly" dressed for company – even for informal company.

Things became more liberal in the 1920s. Skirts got shorter than the many strands of beads around the ladies' necks. More female skin was seen in public during this time than any time in Western Europe since the year 1000, and in American society, ever. Evening dresses were beaded and light colored or of silk so they would shimmer in light. Long hair went away. Not put up; cut.

Young ladies, in particular, became outrageous (meaning being out of context with the norms) and their behavior was designed to gain attention by distracting others.

In general, the young public became more active and with less of their parents' decorum. Social customs were changing rapidly. Men would dress in a more feminine manner in bright colors and general flare. It was at this time that women started wearing men's trousers, and then these started being tailored for women.

A popular song in 1926 was:

> "Masculine Women and Feminine Men...
> You can't tell the rooster from the hen.
> It is all the rage today – Hey! Hey!
> Mom has a turtle neck to the chin –
> Dad's got a girdle holding him in.
> It is all the rage today – I'll say!

You try to steal kiss from your girl in the hall,
And you find you're kissing her brother, Paul...," etc.

Then the Depression – many thought that God was punishing them for the un-Godly ways of the 20s. Hems went back down, hair became just hair that required basic maintenance and was put up out of the way.

The whole Depression period saw a return to a general conservative society in America.

Western Europe had also become very liberal in the good times, and then with the following hard times, it, too, was turning back to being conservative.

At this time neither Europe nor America was into "victimization." "Victimization" is when the unfortunate individual's first thought is 'This is not fair!' and the second is, 'Who did this to me?!' But this was not the way it was thought back then. Then they accepted the results of bad fortune.

*****

With the end of the 1990s and the dissolution of the Soviet Union, the world was not necessarily a safer place. About the only time some multicultural societies were at peace was when a lot of Christians and Atheists were a threat to them. When these threats eased, the multiple cultures could resume their centuries-old, multicultural warring. [Reminder – the predominant measure of culture is language and religion.]

The surging of religious terrorists has ebbed and flowed many times in history. The invasion of African Moors/Muslims into Western Europe in the 700s was significant. The Western European Christian crusades and their following forces helped move the Moors from Spain back to their homeland. This started in 718 and ended in 1492.

Such an Islamic outward surge is taking place today. However, of the two cultures, Islam and Christianity, only one has remained constant. It is not the Christians. The early Crusaders wanted a status quo and would kill to maintain/restore it, but now there is a more modern political convention and the Christian Crusaders with their convictions have gone away. And they are not likely to return. (Not without a catastrophe.)

The dissolution of the Soviet Union only created an opportunity. Multiculturalists established the stage on which modern America and Western Europe will be governed for the long term.

– Post-1991

In the 1990 census there had been over 248 million people in the United States and this was near a 10% increase over 1980. But it was a smaller increase over the 1940 census and there were charges by political factions of counting irregularities, particularly in the (not) counting of homeless people. Counting these homeless voters was important to some political party because it would determine the number of legislators, the divisions of voting precincts, and the like. The homeless are rarely conservative. They do not want their status quo to continue. They want change. And they know which political party is always for change.

This concern for the homeless was politically motivated rather than for any humanitarian reasons. Homelessness is for the most part an urban problem. This puts a high-density, potential voting population in smaller areas.

"Homelessness" is an interesting term because it means so much. Home/land ownership is important.

At the beginning of the nation, voting rights were based on property ownership because of the idea that those owning property were the people with the most invested in the business of the nation and therefore it would be they who would have the most to lose from the installation of bad government. This idea has not been disproved.

There were many European laws and traditions maintained by the early European settlers in America. At the time of the founding of the nation, as in Britain, married women could not own property in their name; consequently, this was a reason that they could not vote.

Much later there were the Federal Homestead Acts starting in 1862. These established the procedure by which anyone having never taken up arms against the United States could apply.

This would give them the right to homestead some of the 270 million acres of public land.

In these acts, almost 10% of the total area of the United States was given free to over 1.5 million homesteaders. Women, as well as immigrants who had applied for citizenship, were eligible. [Do not confuse the immigration acts of the past with the current hoards of illegal aliens sneaking into the United States. This, too, will be discussed later.]

Blacks were encouraged to apply for homesteads and this could be the reason that in 1900, 14% of United States farm owners were black. This homesteading necessitated a change in many ownership laws since the women were now responsible for a lot of land. With this change in land ownership laws, the voting laws for women had to change as well. (This was the sequence of literal events without addressing ethical issues.)

*****

It was early 1990 when the Soviet Communist Party started losing its monopoly of power in Eastern Europe. Since the Berlin Wall was down and citizens in the Communist Bloc became more mobile, the movement was decidedly toward the West. The Cold War was ending – as was its attending Political Correctness in Eastern Europe.

It was not ended by bullets in a hot war but by economics in a cold one. In less than a week the plans were established for the reunification of East and West Germany. President Ronald Reagan and Premiere Mikhail Gorbachev had in many ways been instrumental to this end.

This was the most important social event to occur on the planet in a long time. Those born after 1945 can easily say that so far, this was the most important event in their lives, but... it appears that someone would have to tell them this because they are not likely to hear much literal history in public schools nor are they likely to do much reading of history on their own. Exceptions exist as they always do, but general statistics support this assessment.

*****

As 1991 was beginning, the UN had to decide what to do about Iraq's invasion, occupation, and pilfering in Kuwait. The Iraqi abused the Kuwaiti people and their resources by removing everything Iraq could use from Kuwait to Iraq. The UN basically had told Iraq that they had six months to enjoy Kuwait, but then the UN would "act."

In Mid-January the United States Congress authorized United States military support in Operation Desert Storm to liberate Kuwait from Iraq, compliant with UN directives.

Four days later bombing began against Iraqi forces in Kuwait. Iraq responded by launching eight Scud missiles into Israel. Israel was a non-combatant country in this conflict. It was Iraq's desire to bring Israel into the war; this would cause Arab support to turn against the United States. Again, this area is known for its centuries-old, multicultural conflicts.

Scud missiles still have a very important part in the modern history of the United States and the Middle East. Some of the specifications of the missiles should be understood. These Russian-made "old-world" missiles have a range of 430 miles. This removes the missile from a tactical battlefield support weapon classification and places it in the intermediate-range, strategic weapons class.

The Scud can carry a nuclear warhead with an 80-kiloton yield. This warhead is five times more powerful than the atomic bomb dropped on Hiroshima. This is hardly some overgrown artillery shell as depicted by the media.

The warhead can also carry more than 2,000 pounds of chemicals or high-explosives. The Scuds are still very popular in many countries and it is certainly a Weapon of Mass Destruction (WMD). Its warhead determines how massive the destruction would be.

In Operation Desert Storm/Kuwaiti War, Iraq launched 88 Scuds; 46 into Saudi Arabia and 42 into Israel, one killing 28 United States service men. Israel understood Iraq's intentions and did not retaliate as Iraq had hoped.

At the end of the Kuwaiti war, the UN recorded that Iraq still had 62 Scuds (WMD) and 19 Scud transporter/launchers. [This should be remembered because it becomes much more important later.]

By the war's end, the Iraqis had become very efficient with their Scuds. They had reduced the Scud set-up, launch, and hide times to just 30 minutes – the missile would have been launched and the transporter/launcher hidden back out of sight under an overpass. Coalition forces had overflights of remote sensing aircraft that showed the Scud launchers looked like any large truck.

During the previous Iraq - Iran war, Iraq had launched 189 Scuds against Iran. In the Afghan Civil War, Soviet technicians helped Afghans with 438 Scud launches. After 1992, the Soviet aides left and there were far fewer Scud launches. There were up to <u>2,000</u> Scud launches in Afghanistan. The Russian-built Scuds and launchers were/are located many places over the Middle East.

*****

In February 1991, the Operation Desert Storm/Kuwaiti War ended one day after Iraq withdrew its forces from Kuwait. While leaving, Iraqis set fire to Kuwait's oilfields. A cease fire was accepted by Iraq with the condition that they (Iraq) disarm.

The only thing the UN was concentrating on was the exit of Iraqi forces from Kuwait. When that occurred, the operations were concluded. For the United States to have stayed and done anything to anyone after this time would have been in violation of the authority which had justified the United States even being there. The operation was completed when the UN said it was.

In April 1991, Iraq agreed with the UN resolution calling for the destruction and removal of the entire Iraqi chemical and biological weapons stockpile plus any ballistic missiles with a range greater than 95 miles. Iraq also agreed to withdraw their support of international terrorism.

By the Iraqi Army's own reports, Iraq had three chemical weapons programs. They had used chemical warfare in 1980 against Iran. These attacks were directed against medical facilities and tens of thousands died; combatants and noncombatants alike.

Later in 1988, the Iraqis made the largest chemical attack in history against civilians, the Iraqis' own people, the Kurds. Five thousand died from mustard gas and "some type" of nerve gas. High levels of cancer and birth defects continue in the area in 2018.

In early March 1991, there was a popular, though disorganized uprising in southern Iraq. The Iraqi military used mustard gas, phosgene, and the nerve gas, sarin. Many thousands died.

Iraq's chemical and biological industry had expanded rapidly until they were testing biological weapons such as anthrax and botulinum toxins in the Iraqi desert.

Iraq reported that their mustard gas was 90-to-95% pure. This is very concentrated and well exceeds that used in WWI. However, the Iraqis were having trouble producing an effective nerve gas. What they did produce was only 50%-to-60% pure. They tried producing another nerve gas but it was only 18%-to-41% pure and they learned that this was insufficient for putting in weapons against combatants; however, it would and did serve well against noncombatants.

Iraq had documented and demonstrated their use of a chemical weapons program several times, and their ownership and use of such weapons are undisputed. That they had a delivery system (Scud - WMD) was demonstrated, though dropping chemical canisters from aircraft served as well when used against noncombatants.

The media's premise that the president of the United States "lied" others into a war is not true. Even the UN was reporting to the president that Iraq still had Scuds - WMDs. The lie was manufactured by the United States media. Additionally, the United States is not the only country with a biased media.

Multicultural conflicts continued into late 1991, and the UN proposed a resolution to establish peacekeeping forces in Yugoslavia. Three months later it was approved.

This Yugoslavia conflict was purely a multifaceted, multicultural confrontation between ethnic groups which had made up Yugoslavia. Yugoslavia was a federation of six republics in a large part of Southeast Europe – a region with a history of ethnic conflict.

These republics, with the borders for the most part defining ethnic and historical lines, were Bosnia/Herzegovina, Croatia, Macedonia, Montenegro, Serbia, and Slovenia. Within the republic of Serbia, two separate provinces were established: Kosovo and Vojvodina.

The once-nation of Yugoslavia split along ethnic lines, but unfortunately there were areas having mixed ethnic groups. This defines a multicultural country...one practicing cultural diversity.

This diversity occurred primarily in the Yugoslavian areas of Bosnia/Herzegovina, Croatia, and Kosovo. In the past, each republic had its complaints heard at the federal level and tensions were resolved there. This was when Marshall Josip Tito was president of Yugoslavia for life (from 1943 to 1980), but when he died, the weakened federal government had growing difficulties in an effort to resolve the number of ethnic complaints coming from regional rivalries in the six republics.

The Albanians of Kosovo demanded that their autonomous province be granted republic status. The Serbs of Kosovo resisted this movement, as well as disallowing any republic conflicts being resolved at the federal level.

In 1989, Slobodan Miloševic had come to power in Serbia and by populist movements gained political control over Kosovo, Vojvodina, and Montenegro. Slovenia and Croats in Croatia resisted Miloševic's consolidation of authority, he being a Serb.

In the face of increased ethnic disagreements, the government of Yugoslavia was peacefully dissolved at the first of 1990.

Between the summer of 1991 and spring of 1992, four republics declared their national independence, leaving just Serbia and Montenegro remaining as a federation. However, the condition of ethnic Serbs outside Serbia and Montenegro, and that of ethnic Croats outside Croatia, remained unsettled.

Yet, in 1997, Miloševic became president of the Federal Republic of Yugoslavia. This was a reduced Yugoslavia from the time of Tito.

There was a string of inter-ethnic (multicultural) conflicts and the Yugoslav Wars were the results. This was first in Croatia and then, more intensely, in multi-ethnic Bosnia and Herzegovina.

The UN deployed near 40,000 peacekeeping forces to the most volatile areas. They were welcomed by most all of the various groups who had been persecuted by their own uniformed and partisan "liberation" fighters. These UN peacekeepers were from 43 countries; among them there were 167 fatalities.

The United States did what it could to enforce the "no fly" zones to keep the fighting at ground level since not all factions had air power.

Ethnic cleansing (genocide) was not new to this area and this practice was being repeated.

A previous administration had dictated that one-third of the Serbian minority was to be killed, one-third expelled, and the remaining one-third converted to Catholicism and assimilated as Croats.

Serbians killed over 8,000 Croats. These were concentrated, civilian murders. At the same time Bosnia and Herzegovina were persecuting non-Serbs.

Few events in modern history can better demonstrate the powers of, and the conflicts from, cultural diversity and multiculturalism. There were no communication problems. All factions knew the others very well. This was an example of what can happen to a country when it fosters multiple nations within its borders. This was no exception and should serve as a long-term example.

*****

Early in 1992, the leader of a "new" Russia (the Soviet Union had ceased to exist), Boris Yeltsin said that Russia would no longer target the United States with nuclear weapons.

November 1992, Bill Clinton won the United States presidency.

Some extremist organizations continued in the United States. The leader of a religious compound in Waco, TX, had been charged with federal arms violations. Initial efforts to serve warrants at the compound had resulted in the deaths of four federal agents. After a stand-off of 51 days, federal officials raided the compound. During the raid, the religious faction set fire to their own compound and 75 members of their sect, including their leader, died. During the raid, some scompound deaths were by suicide and some were murders committed by sect members against fellow sect members.

In mid-1993, it was disclosed that Iraq had arranged an assassination attempt on former president George H. W. Bush to occur during his April 1993 visit to Kuwait. As a response to this information, President Clinton ordered a cruise missile attack on the Iraqi intelligence headquarters in Baghdad. (The word "assassin" comes into the language from the practices of a Muslim cult.)

Early in 1994, the North American Free Trade Agreement (NAFTA) went into effect. This created a free-trade zone between Canada, the United States, and Mexico.

A year later, President Bill Clinton invoked the Presidential Emergency Powers Act to give a $20 billion loan to Mexico to make up for the exchange rate correction between the Mexican peso and American dollar. Since this Act precludes legislative oversight or debate, it has been difficult to track what amount Mexico owes the United States at any given time, or what amount they are paying back.

It could appear that this emergency was the result of having no one consider the exchange rates when NAFTA was signed. Or possibly, it had been considered, but to bring it up in Congress might have caused problems with the agreement being ratified.

Mid-1994, the bodies of Nicole Simpson and Ronald Goldman were found outside her condominium in California. Her ex-husband and father of their two children was the sports star, O. J. Simpson. He was arrested and charged with the murders.

In September of 1994, Iraq started positioning its troops at the Kuwaiti border again. The UN Security Council stated that Iraq must withdraw its troops from the Kuwait border and cooperate with weapons inspectors. The United States reaction was to deploy some of its forces to Kuwait. Then Iraq started withdrawing its troops.

In the spring of 1995, two United States terrorists detonated a truck bomb outside a federal building in Oklahoma City, killing 186 people. The bomb was made from diesel fuel and fertilizer. The principal person causing the blast was executed June 2001; the accomplice was sentenced to life in prison.

In the fall of 1995, O. J. Simpson was acquitted of the murders of his ex-wife, Nicole Simpson, and of Ronald Goldman. The Simpson case was one of the highest profile murder cases in the nation's history, and one in which the audience, the American TV public, heard more sworn evidence than did the jury. The public, based on all the sworn evidence, thought Simpson guilty. The jury, hearing less of the sworn evidence, found him innocent.

The manner in which the trial was conducted was as controversial as was the verdict.

In the summer of 1996, multicultural conflicts continued as Islamic terrorists killed 19 United States military personnel in Khobar, Saudi Arabia. Additionally, they destroyed six apartment complexes.

In the summer of 1997, the NATO alliance extended invitations to once-Communist bloc countries, the Czech Republic, Hungary, and Poland, to join the alliance in two years.

In the 1997 fall, Iraq issued a proclamation stating it would shoot down UN surveillance aircraft. The planes were used to determine if Iraq was meeting the agreed-to surrender terms of the 1991 Iraqi/Kuwati War.

Early in 1998, President Bill Clinton, in a televised interview denied his sexual relationship with a White House intern, Monica Lewinsky. His continued denials and his resulting perjury before a grand jury led to his impeachment. The impeachment proceeding was initiated by the House of Representatives. The Senate determines if a person will be removed from office. The political party alignment in the legislature, rather than the issue, will generally determine the outcome. The president had the votes in the Senate to avoid removal, so his impeachment meant little politically.

Before his denial, Clinton's approval rating was 73% and at the end of his term, it was 66%.

Also early in 1998, Osama bin Laden, leader of the al-Qaeda terrorist cell, issued his declaration of war against Jews and Crusaders (Christians). This announcement encouraged world-wide terrorist attacks in the name of Islam against many people having only a passing interest in Muslims. This was the longest, on-going, wide-range multicultural conflict involving the United States since the 1860s and the wars with indigenous people.

In early summer of 1998, the United States Department of Justice and 20 states filed anti-trust charges against Microsoft. (AT&T had been broken up by the Justice Department for being too successful and it had, without crime, gained such a market advantage that it discouraged competition.) Microsoft and the Justice Department demonstrate that this particular unfair competition is no longer an issue in United States business. [*United States vs Microsoft* lawsuits and settlements.]

As multicultural conflicts continued in the summer of 1998, Osama bin Laden, through his al-Qaeda terrorists, attacked two United States embassies in Africa: Tanzania and Kenya. These attacks killed

24 and injured 4,500. The United States launched a cruise missile attack against al-Qaeda camps in Afghanistan and a chemical weapons plant in Sudan.

Late that summer, the United States Congress passed legislation stating that Saddam Hussein was the corrupting influence in Iraq and should be removed.

Early 1999, a new currency was introduced in Europe – the "Euro." This is to be a competitive tool to minimize United States influence and maximize the European.

In the spring of 2000, the United States census showed a population of 281 million, an increase of 13% since 1990. The South and West of the United States experienced the majority of the increase.

Also that spring, in the case of the United States vs. Microsoft, it was stated that Microsoft violated anti-trust laws by diminishing its rivals' capability to compete. [*United States vs Microsoft* lawsuits and settlements.]

During the presidential race in November 2000, George W. Bush and Al Gore were holding near-equal votes, but the dispute in Florida over "hanging chads" necessitated that the Supreme Court make a ruling. On December 12, the Supreme Court named Bush the winner. ("Hanging chads" is an expression based on the inability of the voter to completely clear his preferred candidate's ballot of the area in which the voting mechanism could register a vote.)

On September 11, 2001, Islamic terrorists hijacked four United States airliners and crashed one into the Pentagon in Arlington, VA, and two into the World Trade Center in New York City. The Trade Center fell. The fourth airliner crashed in Pennsylvania when passengers fought to terminate the plane's flight to its target. Including the Pentagon crash and airline passengers 2,977 Americans died. This was 600 more than died in the unprovoked Japanese attack on Pearl Harbor in 1941. The Pearl Harbor attack is what drew the United States into WWII.

All these September 11 attacks were by Osama bin Laden's al-Qaeda organization. So far, this was the most damaging multicultural attack on United States soil.

Because of the September 11 attack by al-Qaeda, which was supported by the Taliban government in Afghanistan, in October 2001, the United States military, with support of the United Kingdom, started the first attacks on al-Qaeda and the Taliban government in Afghanistan. The following month the Taliban government left the Afghanistan capital.

During the spring of 2002, the United States Department of State identified the seven nations which have state-sponsored terrorist programs: Iran, Iraq, Cuba, Libya, North Korea, Sudan, and Syria.

In the summer of 2002, Iraq, in violation of the terms of their 1991 Kuwaiti war surrender document, continued to thwart all efforts of UN weapons inspectors to determine if Iraq still had Scuds and a chemical weapons program.

This interference by Iraq had been continuing for several years. President Bush outlined the world problems being caused by Iraq and requested the UN to militarily remove Sadam Hussein. This did not go before the UN council because France assured the UN that they would veto it. This threat of veto made economic sense for France. Economics often supercedes principles when both are involved in the same decision.

The United States president also informed the UN that even without their support, the United States and others would attack Iraq. This was the "Coalition of the Willing."

In the fall of 2002, the United States Congress authorized the president to use military force as he thought necessary.

Also that fall, the UN passed Resolution 1441 which stated that Saddam Hussein and Iraq were to disarm or face serious consequences. This was mere UN show. Iraq had been so informed many times previously.

At the same time, NATO invited more ex-members of the now-defunct Soviet bloc to join NATO. These were Bulgaria, Estonia, Latvia, Lithuania, Romania, Slovakia, and Slovenia.

Early in 2003, the Space Shuttle Columbia exploded over Texas during reentry. All seven of the crew died. Some wing heat-shielding tiles had been damaged by ice falling from the fuel tank during lift-off. This damage had been observed in orbit and was a concern during the flight. There was nothing that could be done to correct the tile damage in orbit and this made the return more hazardous than usual.

The seven person crew: Commander Rick Husband, a previous Shuttle pilot; Pilot William McCool; Payload Commander Michael Anderson, in charge of mission science; and Payload Specialist Ilan Ramon, Israeli Air Force, the first Israeli astronaut. (The first Jew to be in space, Judith Resnik, an experienced engineer and pilot had died in the launch of a previous Shuttle in 1986.) Additionally, there were Mission Specialist Kalpana Chawla; Mission Specialist David Brown, responsible for scientific experiments; and Laurel Clark, working on biological experiments.

[The crew consisted of three white males; two females, one white and one of Indian descent; one black male; and one Israeli male. Such diversity is important to government agencies under the close scrutiny of Congress.]

On March 19, 2003, after additional mandates to Iraq from both the UN and the United States, which Iraq ignored or ridiculed, the War in Iraq began with the bombing of Iraqi forces headquarters and barracks in Baghdad. The United States coalition consisted of forces from the United States, United Kingdom, Australia, and Poland. Some of these were small – but still willing.

Three weeks later the coalition took control of Baghdad. Saddam Hussein had fled the capital.

Nine months later, in mid-December, Saddam Hussein was captured by United States 4th Infantry Division soldiers. He was hiding in a hole in a small town.

Early in 2004, the CIA stated that there were no weapons of mass destruction (WMD) in Iraq when the 2003 war began. Hussein would have been wise to not thwart UN weapons inspectors. Again, he demonstrated very poor judgment. He had previously had WMDs, as well as chemical weapons, and demonstrated them many times earlier. It is assumed that he sold the Scuds and launchers. The buyer could be a great threat to him and his family, if he should tell where the Scuds went. This threat was more serious than any that the vacillating UN could offer. Besides which, Iraq was relying on France's veto should the UN propose military action.

Also early in 2004, the Mars rover was continuing to analyze Martian surface conditions and materials and relay this data to Earth.

On July 4, 2004, the Freedom Tower was begun at the previous site of the World Trade Center in New York City.

In late 2004, President George W. Bush was re-elected.

In December 2004 - A 9.3 Richter scale earthquake on the bottom of the Indian Ocean set a tsunami in motion which killed 290,000 people from Sri Lanka to Indonesia.

In 2005, on August 29th, Hurricane Katrina made landfall on the United States Gulf of Mexico Coast. The city of New Orleans, much of which is below sea-level, was inundated with water from Lake Pontchartrain when the levees that protect the city broke. More than 1,300 people died from Louisiana to Alabama in one of the worst natural disasters in the United States.

In early 2006, the one billionth song was downloaded from the Internet. This process had put the few remaining physical and exclusive stores for such music out of business.

Late in 2006, the population of the United States reached 300 million. It took only 40 years to gain 100 million new people. It was in the mid-60s that the 200 millionth person had been added. The illegal immigration issues were being debated in an effort to determine if the United States was to have closed or open borders.

At the end of 2006, Sadam Hussein was found guilty of the murders of many Iraqis. He had been tried by a Special Iraqi Tribunal. He was hanged.

Early 2007, President George W. Bush announced a troop surge of 21,500 for the war in Iraq. This was requested by the new commander of Multi-National Forces – Iraq, Gen. David Petraeus. This was to slow down the violence that was thwarting the Iraqi government from reestablishing the nation's infrastructure.

By summer of 2007, with the new military surge in effect, there were positive signs in Iraq but they were not reported in the United States media. There had been a reduction of violent attacks against United States forces as well as against Iraqi civilians. However, the Iraqi government was still having problems with multicultural factions (religious sects) within its government.

Also in the summer, a plot to blow up JFK International Airport and sections of New York City was prevented when four men were arrested and charged with the development and planned execution of this plan. This was another multicultural plot. Those involved have subsequently received life sentences.

Late 2007, the Mitchell Report on the Steroids Scandal in baseball was published. It detailed 20 years of steroids abuse and 90 players were identified. The blame was placed on the players, their union, and the commissioner's office – thus making the drug abuse an endemic professional baseball procedure.

During the summer of 2008, it was announced that most of the goals of the Iraqi government had been met and it was stated that the deployment surge of 21,500 soldiers had made the difference.

In the fall of 2008, the United States Congress passed legislation to assist the distressed United States's banks. This economic problem, coupled with summer oil prices above $140 per barrel, deepened the world economic crises which had been in process all year. The bank assistance legislation was supported by President George W. Bush and both presidential candidates.

In November, 2008, Barack Hussein Obama, a Democratic Senator, handily won the election for president. He was the first African-American United States president. There were concerns over Obama's eligibility to be president because he could not produce his birth certificate showing that he was an American citizen. However, three years later, one was located and copies were presented for the public's observation.

In the spring of 2009, because of increased government spending which helped to put the nation in debt as much as ten trillion dollars over the next 10 years, a Conservative grass-roots "Tea Party" emerged with 750 protests across the nation. More than a half-million citizens were involved. The expanded debt under the plans of Obama was instrumental in the emergence of the Tea Party.

In the summer of 2009, an outbreak of the H1N1 virus, named "Swine Flu," was considered a pandemic by the World Health Organization. This was the first such designation since the Hong Kong Flu in 1967-1968. The H1N1 virus and the hybrids continue to threaten large areas. It had been the H1N1 virus which caused the pandemic at the end of World War I.

In the fall of 2009, the recession had continued to deepen as jobless claims climbed above 10%. This had occurred in spite of President Obama's efforts to supercharge the economy with an $831 billion stimulus (gift) package to American businesses and citizens. It had not worked.

At the end of 2009, President Obama announced a surge of 30,000 additional troops to Afghanistan. This was recommended by the military, but was still unpopular with the Liberal base of Obama's political party. The president had pledged to end both Middle Eastern wars. (The Afghan/Taliban war had been the United States response to the terrorist attacks on the United States on 9/11/2001.)

At Christmas of 2009, an al-Qaeda-trained Nigerian Muslim terrorist tried unsuccessfully to detonate a bomb on a United States airliner bound from the Netherlands to the United States. There were 289 passengers and crew on board. He confessed to the attempt and was sentenced to life in prison.

In March 2010, the socialized Health Care legislation was approved to extend benefits to most Americans – insured privately or not. This created a greater gulf between political parties and the public. This social medicine program takes the citizens' healthcare decisions from their hands and places it into those of the government. This was unpopular with the tax payers – but less so with those not working and so not paying the taxes which paid for the medical services.

The public disapproved of the bill because most of the public had private health insurance and they were satisfied with their health care. They were managing their own health needs. This new social health program is in addition to Medicaid and Medicare which are socialized health assistance programs from the administration of Lyndon Johnson.

Now, with forced government socialized health care, the entire American health care system was placed in limbo. This previous health care had been admired world-wide. Private insurance companies being large businesses were consequently upset when the way they had been doing business for generations was terminated – all people with private insurance had serious issues and these were not of their nor their insurance companies' making. This cost large sums of private money and thus impacted the stock market and all other investments relying on the financial bases of insurance companies.

Spring of 2010 - The United States Census of 2010 was conducted and it showed a 9.7% increase from the 2000 census with the United States having a total of 308,745,538 people. Again, there were debates relative to illegal entrants from Mexico. To enter a country illegally means that the country's laws have been violated. This defines a criminal act. This specifies that the perpetrator, the citizen of a foreign government, is a criminal. This is simple and straight-forward logic. The reasons for violating the law are irrelevant.

In April, a British Petroleum deep-water oil rig exploded in the Gulf of Mexico killing 11 workers. The explosion caused the largest oil spill in United States history and it seriously damaged the fishing and tourism industries of the United States Gulf States. British Petroleum promised to reimburse all individuals for their losses.

On October 3, 2010, the chancellor of Germany paid the last WWI reparation payment of $94,000,000 with interest. It took 96 years for the war debt to be paid and the terms of that war settled.

In the fall of 2010, as was expected by many, the Republican party won the majority of elections and took control of the House of Representatives with a gain of 63 seats. This demonstrated the largest gain of seats since 1948 and reflected the public's disagreement with President Obama's political agenda. Also instrumental in this change was the Tea Party movement to force the government to pay more attention to the national debt. This was one of the few Conservative movements in many years, and consequently, surprised both political parties.

In the spring of 2011, Congress finally passed the 2011 budget, which should have been approved by September 30, 2010. After six months of negotiations there was a $38 billion fiscal year cut in expenses. This was one of the first measures that showed the Tea Party's influence to try to get the federal deficit under control.

In the summer of 2011, Osama bin Laden, who masterminded the 9/11/2001 attacks on the World Trade Center, the Pentagon, and other locations, and the leader of the terrorist group, al-Qaeda, was killed after being hunted for 10 years. United States Navy Seals raided his specially designed and built compound in Pakistan. This was while the Pakistani government continued to assure the world that Osama bin Laden was not in Pakistan. His protected compound was 45 miles from a major Pakistani military base.

Also in the summer of 2011, NASA's Space Shuttle made its last landing at the Kennedy Space Center. This was the end of the NASA Shuttle Program. Congress did not suggest any long-term goals for NASA. NASA, being an agency of the legislature looks to that funding source for national aerospace priorities. It appeared that the NASA budget was sacrificed in the Obama Economic Stimulus Package. This had consumed much funding with little-to-no stimulus.

At the end of 2011, President Obama declared the Iraqi war to be over and ordered the combat troops to leave the country.

In the summer of 2012, Islamic terrorists attacked the American consulate in Libya and killed four Americans including Ambassador John Stevens. This was a year after Islamic extremists took over Lybia, killing their ruler, Muammar Gaddafi.

In the fall of 2012, the largest hurricane in recorded history, Sandy, had taken an unusual track up the East Coast and come ashore on the New Jersey coast near Atlantic City and the Long Island coasts of New York. This caused considerable damage to coastal towns and the general boroughs of Manhattan and Staten Island. The estimated cost was $65.6 billion. The hurricane was a Category 2 at its peak and had a diameter of 1,100 miles.

In the fall election of 2012, President Barack Obama won reelection. The legislature remained split.

In the spring of 2013, two Islamist brothers ignited two bombs near the finish line of the Boston Marathon. Three bystanders were killed and 264 were wounded in this cultural diversity attack. Of the wounded, 16 lost limbs; 3 lost both legs. The pair also killed a university policeman, shooting him six times. The city was shut down by civic authorities.

After the bombings, they highjacked a car from a Chinese National, who escaped and notified police. A shoot-out ensued, in which one police officer was critically wounded by a home-made hand grenade thrown by one of the terrorists.

One terrorist brother was apprehended by police, but the other brother drove the car toward them, running over his brother and dragging him, dead, a short distance. The driver later abandoned the vehicle and hid in the back of a boat parked at a residence. His position was confirmed by airborne thermal scanners.

The terrorist had no weapons when apprehended. He was sentenced to death but now lives in a maximum lock-down prison.

The brothers learned to make the bombs by viewing al-Qaeda webpages.

The brothers' family had come to the United States in 2002 seeking political asylum.

During the summer of 2013, Congress accused the IRS of targeting specific civic organizations for auditing and other federal investigations. This extra scrutiny started in 2010 with the gains of conservative groups in Congress. The IRS was managed by appointees of the Liberal president, Obama. The groups being investigated were exclusively groups such as the Tea Party, patriotic and religious organizations – all Conservative.

In the fall of 2013, the Affordable Care Act began to register citizens for the federal government (socialized medicine) health insurance program. There were many deviations and waivers in implementing the confusing rules and regulations of the program.

[At this point, there must be an aside by the author. This is near a cry of frustration. He started reading about this health care act so that he might better understand it and then present the gist of it in a concise manner for this book.

At first he was confused. Then as he read more, over the hours, he became amused. There is an expression in the area where he lives which is similar to "When you are...chin...-deep in alligators, it is hard to remember that all you were going to do was drain the swamp."

He continued his reading of the Affordable Care Act and found mutually exclusive terms. In time, he was becoming less amused. He has written complicated technical documents and he recognizes bureaucratic tripe when he sees it. He was directed to write such verbiage on occasion and he was very accomplished at doing this.

Therefore, he admits that he cannot reduce this Affordable Care Act to an understandable couple of paragraphs. He could write a book about it, but – "Do your own research. You will learn more that way." He apologizes but this is not his fault.]

On January 1, 2014, the beginning of total socialized medicine, known as Affordable Care Act, went into effect for millions of Americans. This was the largest social welfare program since 1935. The earlier act, Social Security, was begun during the Depression and was supposed to be temporary, but continues today. Like most Liberal changes, it is near impossible to "back up," thus making such changes dangerous. Liberals know this.

In the case of the Affordable Care Act, near 7.4 million citizens, given few choices, joined the system.

This complication necessitated that many individually-owned and local health clinics – clinics which had been providing for their patients for years (and working with the client's insurance company equally long), had to acquire a new tier of expensive paperwork management (highly-trained personnel) to cope with the varied and weekly-changing federal regulations. These clinics had to join consortiums to manage the government-mandated, virtual-document trail. This meant that the family doctors who once cared for their client's health, were now agents of a larger, faceless and distant paper-shuffling organization. Many doctors apologized to their life-long patients with, "I am just an employee, now."

In 2018, the expected cost of the program will be $700 billion. This will come from the taxes of the producing citizens.

Early 2014, Russia hosted the Winter Olympics and a few days after it closed, Russia annexed the Ukrainian territory of Crimea. There was widespread condemnation and limited sanctions by the United States. Russian expansionism had reappeared for the first time since the end of the Cold War in 1989.

Russia took note of the world's limited and shallow unhappiness over their actions. This was the same moderate level of concern as demonstrated with Hitler's "annexations" from 1935 to 1938. Russia, as Germany had done, just ignored the complaints.

In the summer of 2014, ISIS, an independent Islamist group, took over a large amount of territory in western Syria and northern Iraq. This conflict necessitated that Western Nations try to thwart another source of forced Islamic fundamentalism. On September 22, the United States and allies begin a bombing campaign to reduce their effectiveness. (Islamic fundamentalism requires strict obedience to a religious code interpreted by individuals, and as such represents a culturally diverse condition.)

Near this same time the first case of Ebola was certified to be in the United States. This was the result of travel from the countries of Liberia and West Africa. The virus in Africa has spread to 22,000 people; killing 9,000.

In the midterm elections in November, Republican lawmakers increased their majority in Congress. This removed the Legislature from the Obama administration's control for the final two years of his term.

In the spring of 2015, a black man died in police custody. This incident with others at the end of 2014 in Missouri, and more in 2015, led to the creation of the "Black Lives Matter" movement.

This was generated by the criticism of police brutality in poor minority and violent crime-ridden neighborhoods. The result was the citizens' list of appropriate responses for the police when the police are confronted with immediate, personal danger. This criticism included how the police could secure that public's good will.

There appeared to be no recommendation for any change in the attitude or behavior toward the police by the public in the poor minority and violent crime-ridden neighborhoods.

In the summer of 2015, full diplomatic relations were reestablished between the United States and Cuba for the first time in 54 years. The diplomatic relations had been terminated when Communist Cuba nationalized many United States-owned businesses.

Late 2015, Islamist-inspired terrorism in San Bernardino, California, killed 14. This had followed brutal attacks against citizens in Paris in November. These multicultural attacks and others are inspired by the rise of ISIS in Syria and Iraq, as well as in other countries around the world. (There are few places where harm and death are not being caused by multicultural/culturally diverse factions.)

In the spring of 2016, the most popular show on television ended its 15-year run. This was *American Idol* and it represented the desires of many Americans. Fame and celebrity status is the goal of most young Americans and this was demonstrated by the program having 31 million viewers in just 2006 alone. The TV program created celebrities of performers who were otherwise unknown. (The American Dream had changed since 1945.)

In the summer of 2016, ISIS, the radical Islamic terrorist group, made an attack in Orlando, FL, which killed 50 and wounded 53. Additional attacks occurred throughout the world, including complex attacks in Ankara, Istanbul, Brussels, and Nice. These multicultural attacks have demonstrated a variety of methods. (Again, cultures are generally defined by language and religion.)

In the fall of 2016, Donald Trump, a flamboyant billionaire businessman from New York, having no political nor military experience, won a surprising election over Democratic challenger Hilary Clinton. She was the former Secretary of State under Obama and First Lady during her husband, Bill Clinton's 8-year presidency. H. Clinton was representing the ongoing Democratic Obama liberal platform.

The results of the election shocked many and were received very poorly by the losers. They could not accept that their policy was currently unpopular with American voters. They looked for an excuse rather than adjust their policy to be more in line with what had been voted for.

At one time their loss was because of poor communication with the public; then it was because of confusing ballots in one small state area; then another loss was because of hanging chads in one area of a southern state; and this time the Russians did it – in some manner.

At the end of 2016, outgoing President Obama expelled 35 Russian diplomats from Washington because his own sources informed him that Russia was behind the loss of his party by "influencing the election in some manner." Details were not provided – if known. It was stated that no vote tallies were affected. Still, the possibility of an (imagined) influence could not, would not, be ignored as the cause for the loss.

Early in 2017, North Korea launched a ballistic missile over the Sea of Japan. This was perceived as a test of world resolve. North Korea continued its attempt to develop a deliverable nuclear weapon. North Korea stated that the United States territory of Guam was within their missiles' reach. This prompted more sanctions against North Korea. Their statement cost Guam millions in tourist dollars.

In the spring, a private aerospace firm, SpaceX, performed the first re-flight of an orbital-class rocket. It had landed vertically on a platform. SpaceX's goal is to reduce spaceflight costs and so initiate more cost-effective space tourism.

In the summer of 2017, the United States withdrew from the Paris Climate Agreement. More opposition had come forward to disagree with the premise that human-generated CO_2 was causing Global Warming. Climate change is accepted as it has always occurred. The reasons for it and the correction of those reasons have little current support other than one based entirely on politics and economics – not science.

The hurricane season of 2017 was very destructive in the Gulf of Mexico, Caribbean, and Atlantic coast areas. It began with Hurricane Harvey doing $125 billion in damage to the Houston area. Then Hurricane Irma, the strongest in Atlantic history, made land fall in Florida, and then only a little more than 10 days later, Hurricane Maria went ashore in Puerto Rico. These three hurricanes caused over $150 billion in damages.

At the end of 2017, as promised in his campaign, President Trump signed the largest tax cut and changes in the tax code since 1986. This was the Tax Cuts and Jobs Act which reduced rates and simplified the tax code.

In the winter of 2017/2018, a cold wave occurred with record low temperatures in the Midwestern and Eastern United States. On December 30, 2017, Omaha had a temperature of -15 degrees F. The previous record was set in 1884. Times Square in New York City had a temperature of 9 degrees F. with -4 degree F. wind chill.

Early in 2018, Turkey announced the beginning of a military offensive to capture a portion of northern Syria from Kurdish forces. This was another part of the ongoing multicultural Kurdish–Turkish conflict. Such ethnic cleansing can be dated in modern times since 1923.

Retail sale of marijuana began in California, the largest state to allow the sale of marijuana for fun.

Also in early 2018, there was a landslide in Southern California which killed at least 13 and injured 25. The main damage was in Montecito, California, which had been nearly burned out by the Thomas Fire at the end of 2017.

In early 2018, Senate Democrats blocked a bill that would have kept the government operating until mid-February. The government shutdown of 2018 had began.

About the same time, the SpaceX company successfully conducted the maiden flight of its most powerful rocket to date, the Falcon Heavy, at Cape Canaveral, Florida.

Trump approved the release of a controversial Republican memo accusing the FBI of abusing its powers during the inquiry into alleged Russian meddling of United States elections. The method of meddling was not defined. Special Counsel Robert Mueller announced that 13 Russians had been charged with interfering in the 2016 presidential election – in some manner.

Also early in 2018, in response to the Democratic shut down of the government, the Dow Jones share index had the biggest drop since the 2008 financial crisis. Thus, it can be demonstrated that Trump caused the Dow Jones drop – at the same time the Liberals shut down the government.

Trump announced the largest package of sanctions against North Korea. He had already established tariffs of 25% on steel and 10% on aluminum imports on other countries. This is less punitive than to balance trade deficits.

In mid-March, a shooting occurred at Marjory Stoneman Douglas High School in Parkland, Florida, resulting in 17 killed and 17 wounded. An expelled student, Nikolas Cruz, was the shooter. He was known to have behavioral problems and other issues.

In response to gun violence in the United States, and particularly because of the Parkland shooting, thousands of high school students organized protests – during school hours, rather than on weekends.

It was stated by the major health organizations that there was a massive opioid (fentanyl) epidemic in the United States and it was worse than first thought. In 2017, 47,000 abusers had died from opioid overdoses. This was 130 each day and 7,000 more deaths than occurring in auto accidents per year. The majority of the most dangerous pills are coming from Mexican drug cartels.

Islamic terrorists attacked in France and killed five people. In this multicultural attack, the perpetrator died, as well.

In the spring of 2018, 281 to 1,729 people died and more suffered injuries from a sarin chemical attack in the last rebel-held town near Damascus, Syria. This chemical was delivered by surface-to-surface rockets launched allegedly by the Bashar al-Assad regime. The United States, the United Kingdom, and France ordered the bombing of Syrian military bases in response to the sarin attack.

Also in the 2018 spring, a driver in Toronto drove a rented van through a crowd, killing 10 people and injuring 16. The driver, 25-year-old Alek Minassian was arrested. The same spring, Najafi Aghdam attacked YouTube headquarters in California and wounded three before killing herself. Both were multicultural attacks.

The state of Iowa approved the so-called "heartbeat" bill, which bans most abortions once a fetal heartbeat is detected.

The national unemployment rate reached 3.9 percent, the lowest rate since 2000.

The Trump administration announced an end to the special Temporary Protected Status program for 57,000 Hondurans.

The state of California became the world's fifth-largest economy, with the state's Gross Domestic Product surpassing that of the United Kingdom.

In late spring, the Senate Intelligence Committee released an unclassified version of its investigation into Russian "cyber attacks" in 2016. The conclusion was that Russian-affiliated hackers gained access to restricted elements of election infrastructure in a small number of states. This did not alter voter registration data nor affect vote totals. This also meant that they did not influence the outcome of the presidential election. ("Russian" in this report did not mean the Russian government.)

The National Centers for Environmental Information reported that April 2018 was the coldest month in the United States since 1997.

At the same time, the California Energy Commission introduced its 2019 Building Energy Efficiency Standards, requiring that all new homes be fitted with solar power after 2020. It is the first state in the United States to enact such a law. It is assumed that it applies to all homes – even those in known landslide- and wildfire-prone regions.

In the summer, 8 students and 2 teachers were killed and 10 others injured at Santa Fe High School in Texas. The shooter was a victim of bullying.

Also in the summer, a summit meeting was held between the United States and North Korea in Singapore. It was the first between a United States president and a North Korean leader.

During this time, the offices of a newspaper in Annapolis, Maryland, were attacked and five people were killed in the newsroom. The shooter, Jarrod Ramos, had a dispute with the newspaper. He had been consulting mental health professionals.

Summer wildfires in northern California had continued across large areas. The fires were declared the largest in the state's history. There were several deaths and hundreds of structures were destroyed.

Also in the summer, the 2018 Kivu Ebola outbreak started in the Congo. By November, it had become the second-deadliest, surpassing the 2013 West African Ebola virus epidemic.

Circumstances have led the Democratic National Committee to reverse its ban on accepting donations from the fossil fuel industry.

Highly publicized at the national level, the Iowan missing person case was resolved when an illegal immigrant led police to where he had left the body of Mollie Tibbetts.

A shooting occurred at a video game tournament in Jacksonville, Florida. David Katz, a professional player who had previously won $10,000 in another tournament, became angry at losing in Jacksonville. He left the facilities and returned with a hand gun. He killed 2 professional players who had defeated him in games. After firing at others, he committed suicide. Katz had wounded 10. He had been involuntarily committed to a mental institution on several occasions and was under doctors' care.

In late summer, Hurricane Florence became the first major hurricane of the 2018 season and made landfall in North Carolina, displacing more than a million people. A month later, Hurricane Michael came ashore at Mexico Beach, Florida. It was the most intense hurricane since Camille in 1969.

In the fall, Canada became the first industrial nation to legalize marijuana for fun.

Also that fall, 11 people were killed and 7 wounded during a shooting at the Pittsburgh, Pennsylvania, Tree of Life Synagogue. The shooter, Robert Boyers, a 46-year-old white, anti-Semitic extremist was arrested. This multicultural terrorist act was apparently far more offensive than previous similar acts and it received international attention in the media.

Also in the fall, 56-year-old Cesar Sayoc, Jr. was arrested in Plantation, Florida, in connection with mail bombing attempts. He had sent 16 "bombs" through the mail but none could detonate because he had not enclosed an ignition source. He had no group affiliations, but a long list of failed attempts at many things.

Near the same time, 800 United States soldiers were sent to the Mexico-United States border to reinforce it against the incoming hordes of Central Americans who will not go through normal, legal, and established channels for migration. This reinforcement effort was caused by the recurring illegal entry of many migrants sneaking across the southern United States border.

In early winter, 13 people including the shooter Ian David Long, were killed at the Borderline Bar and Grill in Thousand Oaks, California. The apparent reason was Post Traumatic Stress Disorder. He had been a machine gunner in Afghanistan.

During the same time, wildfires in southern and northern California killed 91 people with at least 1,000 missing. More than 250,000 residents had fled the fire. One fire in Butte County, California, was the deadliest and most destructive with 88 dead and 19,000 buildings destroyed.

In the winter, France experienced civil unrest in the form of social-media-driven people taking to the streets in yellow vests to protest their interpretations of unfair economic conditions. This movement reflects the growing application of modern crowd manipulation via the Internet. This is a populace movement with many issues and fanciful solutions.

At the end of the year, the United States government was shut down for 35 days by those in Congress who do not want to accept what the American people have stated they wanted the president to do.

Also at the end of the year, United States District Judge Reed O'Connor ruled that key elements of the (Obama) Affordable Care Act were unconstitutional. As usual, there is no suggestion of how this Liberal act can be corrected.

The government shutdown influenced the Dow Jones and it closed after its worst week since 2008. Political polarization outside the elective process is now controlling the nation's economy.

<u>Section III</u> – United States Society in 2018

Introduction

At some point in time, what "is" becomes what "was," and therefore, there is no present. In the time it takes to contemplate on the present, it has become the past. So there is only past and future – yet "future" is an abstract term and not at all assured for anyone – and the past is defined by history – that is the story of the past. This past, with consideration, is the only period in which there can be any faith, but there must be prudence in selecting the sources of recorded events – history. These are not always easy to recognize.

There was a time when a publication was available in elementary schools and it was called *Weekly Reader*. These had been edited to fit the education level of the grades to which they were delivered. They were handed out each Friday, hot off the press from a national organization. Students looked forward to receiving them. These were their "newspapers" and after sufficient time in class for the students to read them, the articles were then discussed. The idea was that the students, having read their *Weekly Reader* would then know what was going on in the world.

Though at this time, even with some students being only 10 years old (the author included), a few of the students understood that if was in print and had been sent to them in the mail, the news could have hardly been current.

The articles were not what Shakespeare called general, current talk, as "modern instances." They were major events presented in a language that the students could readily grasp.

Today it is assumed that everyone knows everything that is happening everywhere and almost immediately. This is an assumption that is patently incorrect.

It could be that some people are writing about "current (recently past) events", i.e., "contemporary history," but only in the manner in which they would have desired the events to have occurred. This could result in its being presented as history, but of exclusively good events, or it could be history of exclusively bad events – depending on the reporter's purpose and conviction. The reporters' recording of their version of history is called "creative history" or "revisionist history."

However, real or not, it is being printed and presented as the truth and it is being read. The reader is under the impression that "now he has been informed" – and he will vote accordingly.

There are those people who know they are being misled, yet they continue to read and listen to the media. Interestingly, they delude themselves by thinking that if they listen to enough untruths, they will know the truth.

The flaw in this conviction is too silly to discuss; and too silly for people to believe – and yet they do. There must be something else involved in these cases. Perhaps they want to hear only the untruths they like. There was one instance when the "news of the day" was proven to be a hoax. The response was, "Well, even if it is a hoax, I think it should be read!" This is less silly than dangerous!

In years past, this reporting was known as "yellow journalism." (This is discussed later.)

The media is now the most pervasive public opiate. In this light, there has been an American opioid epidemic for many years – certainly since the 1990s.

"History": What a detested word that is in the United States today! History is the record of what *was*. There are myths called "history" and they are to be considered as lore and not facts. These exist generally in primitive societies with exclusively oral communication (no written language).

A written record is required for there to be any qualification of the story of past times. As a written record, it can be studied, analyzed, and researched so that the validity of the record can be determined.

In a lot of exclusively oral societies there is an abundance of hope and faith, and this can quickly evolve into a religion; a religion that people will not only die for, but will kill for.

Thus, much of written history in today's press is modified to reinforce some social point or agenda. This can only be supported by imagination and "fact manipulation" – faith. "Faith" is that powerful word that is the foundation of most religions. Many of these religions are often just myths presented in some colorful and sincere manner.

Hoaxes do not disqualify history. Hoaxes demonstrate the need to <u>study</u> history.

History is what happened a minute ago.

Or maybe 100 years ago.

Someone may wonder in what way old history can have relevance today, and this is a good question, but dim people think that by just asking the question, then in some manner the question itself simply disqualifies the need for an answer. Or far worse, if precludes all need to even contemplate the question.

It is necessary to think about history to realize just how very much of history is relevant today. It really is likely that an understanding of history can assist a person in making wiser decisions.

Without understanding history, someone might be tempted to do something that seemed appealing at the time, but then he observes someone do it and it does not turn out well at all. Because of this observed result, he decides that there were a lot of hidden risks and these caused unintended, unpleasant consequences. So he decides to forego the current opportunity to repeat it.

In this case, the person will have just applied a constructive lesson from history!

Apparently, lessons from recent history are easier to apply than those of older history. In many cases it is assumed that recent history has more relevance than older history, as if human nature had changed.

History is a database of events just as a database in a computer is a database of numbers. These computer databases function as "look up tables" for the computer. Many computer operations may refer to these tables in nearly every computer function. People rely on such computer databases hourly, or constantly in some professions.

Consequently, historical databases should function for the citizen just as the numerical database functions in a computer. But for this to occur, some understanding of general history must make up the citizen's historical database.

Duke La Rochefaucauld wrote – "Many will complain of their memory, but few will complain of their judgment." He thought (correctly) that the former, "memory," was necessary for the latter, "judgment." He could have said the same thing about a lack of historical knowledge (experience) and bad judgment.

However, his comment's relevance can now be questioned. It was written a while back – in 1665, over 353 years ago. Perhaps it should just be ignored. Though it seems relevant, there are many people who would disregard it – it is just old stuff now.

So it is that few people will study history to answer the question of its relevance. It is too easy to rejoin the media's flocks – the ones with the dishonest shepherds. That shepherd will lead them to discover their voting preferences.

*****

To help explain the whys and the wherefores, the following will be a narrative based on the history of the near-current period. Then, those events will be used to explain how the United States got to be the society in which it presently finds itself.

Much of the information in this book has been a narration on a virtual time-line of history from 1945 to 2018. There was little editorializing or relating the associated parameters because to engage in discussions of the events would have been out of context with the flow of the history. To be best understood, history needs to be presented as a continuum.

Many of those mentioned historical events – those which seemed so fleeting at the time – have had significant, far-reaching results. The most important of these will be discussed in this section, and because of this, there will be some necessary repetition of earlier material to refresh the reader's memory.

A discussion of "who," "what," "when," and "where" is for the most part straight history; discussing "why" and "how" is historical essay and is much more speculative.

In understanding this *Section III*, there are two parallel points that need to be kept in mind; they both deal with context.

The first is that a person may commit an act that is legal and it may later become illegal. However, it would be agreed that he had not done something illegal because it is that legal condition at the time and place (context) that takes precedence over the act. As immoral/unethical as slavery was in Western society, at one time slavery was legal.

The reverse of this situation is abortion; though the questions of morality and ethics continue, it was once illegal, but now is legal.

There is a fine line in considering someone smoking marijuana at some place and time when it was illegal. That is a crime – that which is punishable by a stated procedure. One perpetrating a crime is a criminal; convicted or not.

A bare few seconds later, the same person doing the same thing at the same place would not be committing a crime – if in those few seconds the stated law was changed to permit it.

Many social changes are legislated and these always alter society suddenly – often at the stroke of midnight.

A noted pediatrician, Benjamin Spock, wrote that an infant should be put on its stomach to sleep. This recommendation may or may not be negligence. At the time he wrote these instructions for the new parent, this was the prescribed sleeping position so that should the infant regurgitate its food, this would not enter the lungs and asphyxiate the infant.

Now, however, with the current knowledge of Sudden Infant Death Syndrome, it is prescribed that the infant is placed on its back.

It is the context (time and place) of the condition that determines crime/neglect – or innocence.

And secondly – if someone has reliable information from a reliable source and repeats that information, it could hardly be called lying or deception. At the time, everyone would accept it to be the truth. However, knowledge gained well after the event may disqualify the previous information. In this case, had he lied? Or had everyone just been misinformed?

There is a reason for the inquiry, "What did you know and when did you know it?" This is usually asked to establish guilt, but it can also be used to confirm innocence.

Consequently, in any review of history, there must be diligence to keep context in mind.

Chapter 1 How the United States is Socially Today

It is difficult for anyone to qualify where they are in terms of social convention, but it can be done because it defines the current American living experience, and yet this is what makes it difficult – its familiarity.

It would be constructive to establish some standards to define what human relationships are supposed to be when compared to their purpose, and this is really about the basics.

– Standard of Living

During the eight years I was teaching adults, I would ask the students to offer suggestions as to what should be on a list to measure and qualify "Standard of Living." They were my students, though many were teachers themselves. As they called out some desired living criteria, I wrote each on the board. Then we would discuss each and start removing redundancies. A lot of mutually inclusive ones were removed as well. We would generally end up with a list similar to this:

1. Not going to bed hungry.
2. Not going to bed dirty.
3. Feeling safe.

The first criteria meant that citizens of the United States are to be sufficiently fed. There is still some hunger, but this is a small exception and not the norm. In truth, the citizen may well be over-fed.

The second criteria is straightforward as well, but there is a good by-product of this. Cleanliness may or may not be close to Godliness because there are a lot of people who are very close to their God(s) and these people are exceedingly dirty.

However, the by-product of cleanliness is better health. The citizens of the United States do not share in the illnesses and health conditions which afflict many in the world for no other reason than the United States citizens are clean – when they want to be.

The third may be easily accepted as well, but the citizens' current physical threats should be understood.

For this, statistics will give more valid information than the media; the media is agenda driven and politically based. This heavily influences what they report/promote and how they do it. Their publication is based on circulation – they kowtow to their subscribers because this will get the advertisements in the newspaper seen by more people and therefore increase the revenue.

Terrorists occupy a lot of media space and network time, but the citizen's personal threats from terrorists are minimal and this will likely remain so. After the United States has had enough legislation to reach the extent of the cultural diversity which infects so many other countries, then this may change.

So what is the greatest threat to the citizen's Standard of Living?

It is the United States Senate – just 100 individuals.

They can do what they want with anyone's and everyone's Standard of Living, and do this any time the mood strikes them. This even includes Americans' health care. Terrorists are not likely to influence this.

The risk of diseases can be ameliorated by healthier living habits.

The most prevalent physical risks are auto-related and this is very high. Though autos are becoming safer, the higher speed limits and the increase in distracted drivers will easily offset any vehicle safety improvements.

In 2016, there were 40,427 auto deaths and in 2017, 40,327. Serious injury statistics require a lot of research to gain any conclusion. It can be assumed that many in automobile accidents did not die, but were maimed – some for life.

The most prevalent cause of auto accidents (causing death or maiming) is chemically degraded driving, and second is likely caused by distracted driving (un-associated with chemicals; alcohol and marijuana, included). Most of the deaths and injuries that are caused by distractions could involve a cell phone in some manner, or in some cases, rowdy children could be contributing factors. Statistics of accidents caused by such distractions are difficult to attain, but logic demands that they be considered as contributing factors.

There are readers who would expect to see gun deaths listed as risks. Too often the gun death statistic is presented in the media as "total of gun deaths" as it relates to the media's desire for more gun laws, but 66% of the total reported gun deaths are from suicide – generally, male. In the absence of guns, this 66% of victims could find other means for suicide; such as pills and alcohol – which are preferred by females.

Also, there are a few thousand accidental gun deaths each year; however, these, like suicide, are not a deliberate physical threat to others.

So the real gun death threat is homicide – murder.

In 2016 there were 11,000 gun-related homicides. But this is a threat that does not apply equally to everyone. It varies geographically, and not everyone is necessarily at the same risk at the same place.

In the case of the individual's risk, it is true that Black Lives Matter. In 2015, 90% of all homicides were black against black. The concept of "Black Lives Matter" is by definition a racial issue and the burden for reducing this 90% rests with blacks. According to the Bureau of Justice statistics, blacks kill blacks in great numbers as indicated by the 90% black on black homicides.

When considering interracial violence (between blacks and whites) – between 2012 and 2015 there were 631,830 of these violent crimes, including homicide.

Blacks make up 13% of the United States population, yet committed over 85% of the violent crimes. This is 540,360 assaults on whites. Whites, with 61% of the population, committed 15%, or 91,470 assaults on blacks.

For each unarmed black male killed by a police officer, blacks have killed 18 police officers.

This implies that Black Lives Matter – but Black Lives Matter much more to whites than to blacks. Black-on-black killings may not be racial, but they certainly can be considered hate crimes.

Stray/random (accidental) bullets can easily kill and maim – in 2015 and 2016 combined, over 43 children were killed or maimed by drive-by shooters, but one nine-year-old was deliberately murdered because his father was a gang member and the killing of his son was gang retribution. All black on black.

It has been said by black Americans that white Americans can never understand the black experience. It could be suggested then that a parallel thought would be that the black American can never understand the white experience.

When it is considered that there are 340 million people in the United States, there can be a better idea as to an individual's physical risk of death from a fire arm.

While addressing Standard of Living, if is difficult to address the intellectual, philosophical, or spiritual condition of a person, and indeed, a nation. At one time in England it was required that the king must have his peace – not so surprisingly, it was called "The king's peace" – and it had best not be disturbed.

This concept was broadened, and by the time of England's colonization in America each man was to have his own peace. There may not be much discourse to define "peace" and the desire for peace varied. The greater the population density (people per square mile) the greater the possibility of having interaction with other people.

Having peace is difficult in an intrusive, self-occupied society. It is easy for such people to be rude. It could be expected that the more reserved the public, the more thoughtful they may be and the less interference there would be with others. Extreme examples are the hermit and the recluse. They would not likely interface with many people.

The antithesis of peace is noise, crowds, and general distractions to one's orderly preference and personal business.

In the United States today there is a large population which does not respect one's right to peace if it in any way inhibits their personal desire for anything. This is tantamount to the liberal idea that the individual's desire takes precedence over the desires everyone else; this is their idea of personal freedom.

There is a good technological solution for those who do not want the distraction of noise which sometime disturbs their peace. Fortunately, this distraction has become a little less so because of the greater use of hearing devices like ear buds and earphones. Before these were in use, young people would walk down a city street or village lane with a loud "boom box" playing on their shoulder.

One could say that personal music distractions are of a pleasant nature and it contributes to the hearer's sense of peace. It is possible that some walker could be so engrossed in his Pachelbel or Mozart that he would not hear an approaching vehicle such as a train – the train with an incredibly loud horn. This example is neither hypothetical nor singular.

Quiet personal reflection and introspection might be a thing of the past, yet it should be occurring during the most critical, early years of an individual's life. To one age group of the United States citizens, some peace and quiet would be enjoyable. To most other citizens, it appears that silence is a fearful condition and one that must be avoided, since they desire so little of it. As soon as they are conscious in the morning, the radio or TV is turned on. They call it "company."

Company used to be more personal.

Chapter 2 Family Myths

At one time, American parents taught their children quotes and adages from the Bible or from whichever religious doctrine they subscribed. These lessons were adjusted for the different ages of children. Some of these came from Benjamin Franklin's "Poor Richard's Almanack" (1732 - 1758), though the parents may not have known this because they were just repeating what they had been told as children themselves. This makes it basically their culture's lore – that is tribal knowledge or tradition. The quotes do not have to be true – just believed.

– Old-School Myths

Some of the more common proverbs and aphorisms being taught were:

- "An apple a day keeps the doctor away." This has been demonstrated to be untrue.
- "A stitch in time saves nine." Sometimes.
- "Wishing on a star." This can be disproved on any clear night.

○ "Beauty is only skin deep." Appears to be true. (But ugly is to the bone.)

○ "Cheaters never win." Certainly untrue; otherwise, they would not cheat.

○ "There is no perfect crime." This is an old thought.

○ "Crime does not pay." This is a very, very old thought.

○ "Let sleeping dogs lie." This has nothing to do with dogs but is instruction to leave well-enough alone. This is difficult for those people whose political philosophy requires change. Change is what defines them. They apparently believe that everything needs to be changed – and right now. Shakespeare had written: "How far your eyes can see I cannot tell, but striving to better, oft' we mar what is well." Many people have seen evidence of this.

○ "Birds of a feather flock together." This is true for birds and most creatures, and therefore appears to be a natural condition (seen in nature), yet for humans it is not to be. This "flocking" thought is very unpopular for humans – perhaps it is even subversive. This old statement is contrary to the thought that cultural diversity is good and the more diversity a society has, the better. There is a lot of historical evidence of this not being true.

○ "Opposites attract." But this does not mean that they will have a proper interface.

And the Golden Rule was near the top of most family lists:

○ "Do unto others as you would have them do unto you."

– New-School Myths

In modern day America there are many Modern Myths that sound nice, but cannot withstand any contemplation:

○ "Change is good." Unless changing something that is OK and then finding the change to be worse than the previous condition, and then learning that it cannot be changed back. A little foresight would have been useful; restraint appreciated even more.

○ "Americans have a right to know." There is no evidence of this in the Bill of Rights. This is a Modern Myth invented by the media to justify their printing anything at anytime anywhere. This means that they have neither responsibility nor accountability.

○ "If you can imagine it, you can do it." Parents tell their children some terrible untruths. It can emotionally maim them for life. Some children might work to gain fame on social media.

They had been told that there was nothing they could not achieve – then later, they wonder why they had not attained it.

Someone must have prevented it.

They will identify someone, or something to blame. It cannot be their fault. After all – there was nothing wrong with them! They must have been victimized! The near-constant thought that others are victimizing them becomes an immediate response to unpleasant circumstances.

Perhaps they will find someone to take to court – if they feel lucky.

○ "You are already a winner if you try." This cannot be demonstrated, so this belief will create very unreal expectations as the child becomes a young adult. Scoreless competition does not exist in the adult's life nor in the office nor on the playing field. (Nor in Nature.)

○ "We are all equal." This thought is in conflict with genetic science and all DNA studies. All individuals have both objective and subjective preferences encoded in them. Statistics gathered from identical twins raised in different environments demonstrate definite common, endemic, <u>subjective</u> preferences in each twin. It also disqualifies a lot of the nurture/nature beliefs.

From the time of the first cell division at about 30 hours in the womb, each individual will have been encoded by male parental genetic material. The cell already had the female's genetic material. People start becoming who they are when that first cell splits – the cell (egg) split because it had been fertilized. Humans are not equal after the cell split...that human did not exist before the split. Humans were never equal.

○ "You can be anything you want." This is more misinformation offered in the form of encouragement. The short kid from short parents should not be encouraged to consider playing professional basketball as a serious career choice. (Exceptions exist – that is why they are called exceptions. They are contrary to the rest of the world.)

○ "Pay the teachers more money and the public education system will improve." This does not work. It does not work again and again. The students did not need teachers being paid more. They did not need better teachers; the teachers needed better students. Students have a responsibility to the teacher. Bad students create bad teachers. (Unions are not guilds. A guild is established to maintain the quality of a product. A union is not established for this purpose.)

○ "There is only one race: the human race." This is nonsense and can be easily demonstrated to be so. But still a person is criticized for even addressing the issue. The United States Government keeps track of races – several of them. So there must be more than one.

Apparently, no one but governments are permitted to even recognize that there are different races. In the past when some governments did this, it turned out badly. Perhaps it should be an open subject for everyone to discuss. Even people on the street. Even scientists.

From the New York Times, December 24, 2018: "Women March activists are grappling with how they treat Jews – and whether they (Jews) should be counted as privileged white Americans or 'marginalized' minorities."

Apparently everyone is the same if it can only be determined in which of many narrow, multilayered categories they can be placed. There seems to be a lot of categories for such a world of similarities and general sameness and equality. The question appears to be a form of profiling and generalizing; both being Politically Incorrect.

The United States Government counts the number of members of several races in the United States. Therefore, the government is not accepting the all-one-race philosophy.

○ "If they are old enough to fight, they are old enough to vote." This is another Modern Myth based on ignorance and has far-reaching social/political effects. Or it might have been that some politicians found a way to increase the number of voters for their party. Altruism had nothing to do with it. Few young people are conservative. They are liberal without being aware of it; they want change.

It could be questioned as to what makes a good soldier. And then, what makes a good (informed) voter.

There may be different qualifications for being a good soldier and being a good voter. It is likely that being one disqualifies the other.

Unquestioning and following a leader is of paramount importance to being a good soldier, but when voting, that is not a good premise – it is a bad premise.

The good voter will consider the issues and then determine which socioeconomic philosophy (political party) could deliver the best responses to those issues. This would make a good voter, but a soldier weighing the pros and cons of an order could get that soldier – and many of his comrades – killed.

A good soldier does not evaluate the quality of what he is told to do; he <u>does</u> it.

A good voter should not vote for someone just because he is told to.

Elevating the young to adult importance gives small minds a lot of influence. The brain is not fully developed until age 25 and this defines functionality. The adult and teen use their brains in different ways. The inputs to the brain are supposed to be "life-long learning" (experience) and in an 18-year-old, that young life might be missing some important learning/experiences.

It could be said, "If they are old enough to vote for a senator, they are old enough to be a senator!" This sounds good, but now a person must be 30 years old to be a senator. This also seems to be some sort of ageist slight to our young American fighting men who can enlist when 18.

- "If they are old enough to elect the president, they are old enough to serve as president." This, too, sounds good – even if the voter is not 35 years old.

- "Man is causing global warming." Global warming has been explained many ways. One way to consider this likelihood is that this has happened before, but learning about this would require research and that would result in showing that the planet will respond to natural laws and that humans are just along for the ride – certainly, when it comes to human existence. The planet does not "need" humans.

However, the citizens of the United States are of a new generation. They believe that they are the paragons of the cosmos and control everything – certainly everything on the planet, and with this control comes responsibility. This thought makes humans the imagined perpetrators of all earthly phenomenon. Consequently, many are likely to find a lot of other people thinking that the sky is falling and feeling guilty that it is.

It should be considered that once when the sky was falling a piece of it hit Chicken Little on the head (it was an acorn) and Chicken Little informed Henny Penny as to the event. They went off to tell the king – perhaps to ask for a grant of more feed so they might spend their time studying why the sky was falling, how much time they have before it all falls, and what they could do to keep the sky up there where it belonged – but mostly, find out who was causing it to fall.

On the way to see the king, they told everyone they met until they had a whole crowd following along and concerned with the falling sky.

This analogy ended in a very understandable manner.

A sly fox came along and seeing a lot of gullible, good meals walking as a group, he talked them into going with him. Then the fox and his family had a feast.

The gist of this story is near 2,500 years old, and as folk tales are rated, it is a "20C." The moral is: "People should not get caught up in other people's hysteria and paranoia, or something bad might happen to them."

From 1823 until 1943, the clever fox took care of the ignorant rabble-rousers (barnyard activists). But then by 1943 and on, the idea of someone being eaten for the trouble they had caused seemed a little harsh and perhaps too gory for children.

In 1943, Disney presented another view so that after all the hysteria and civil disturbances, they all had a great meal together and lived happily ever after.

Thus the moral becomes: When people get involved in other people's issues and there is all the hysteria of large, noisy crowds, (rioting? looting?) – in the end, things work out fine. And they are all winners for just trying.

Chicken Little and Henny Penny did not know how to apply to the government for financial assistance to study "Animal's Influence in Causing Sky Instability."

After something about Sky Instability was in print, then the governments could establish offices and staff them to keep track of the impact of a falling sky. They could monitor the rate of money being spent on grants to study the sky's instability; catalog all the reports about it; and list the places where the barnyard researchers could go to read their reports to other forward-thinking, agreeable, and wise barnyard folks like themselves.

Then the nations could form large consortiums to intimidate other nations into agreeing with their premises and imagined solutions. During this time, each country would be demonstrating that they were not the ones causing the sky to break and fall but that someone else was...this would be the United States, most likely. The United States should be made to pay a bunch of money for their wrong-doings, or at least volunteer to damage their national production as recompense.

The activists would continue with this theme as long as it was satisfying for them – and funding was available.

Being good at public speaking, they might end up saying, "All we did was just point out that the climate was changing and it was getting warmer." This is a little weak – and a little late.

The liberal support for these issues still comes from those who have demonstrated before – they still oppose industry, capitalism, and free enterprise.

Chapter 3 Political Correctness

"Political Correctness" is not a new term. It has been in use since 1793 when it appeared in a United States Supreme Court judgment of a political lawsuit. It was also used in the 1880s. The first use of it in a more modern sense in the United States was in 1970, and it was used in the United Kingdom shortly thereafter.

The citizens of the United States should understand some meanings of the word so they can have a more literate interpretation of the concept.

This starts with the word "policy." This simply refers to a plan of action or a set of rules agreed on by a business, a government – most any group – listing what they will do in particular situations. This does not sound too interesting until someone is asked, "Do you want to know how you are expected to function so you can avoid conflicts?"

Most people would say, "Sure."

Now that the person has expressed an interest in "policy," he has become a "politician" by definition – an amateur – but a "politician" just the same.

A rather famous American politician in the 1950s and 1960s and one who was also a Statesman, said that he had been called a "professional politician" in a demeaning manner. He had replied, "Yes, I am a professional politician and I am a good one. Who would you want governing your nation's policies? An amateur or a professional?"

Everything associated with "policy" is "political" by the very nature of the subject.

What is interesting is that the policy being discussed is modified to declare that it is a "correct" policy relative to "correct" communication – written and spoken. This occurs in a nation which touts freedom of speech; but apparently, some people are more free than others and they have told the public which words and expressions are acceptable, and most other similar terms have become incorrect.

Another time when there was thorough Political Correctness was in 1930 Nazi Germany. They, too, had a very Politically Correct population and they had an enforcement system. Each citizen was to be proactive and they were to correct those citizens who transgressed.[5] If the transgressions continued, the inconsiderate person was to be reported so that they might receive more stern enlightenment.

At this time, those reporting the news in the German media were given permits, but only to those "whose opinions are politically

---

[5] "Proactive" is creating or controlling a situation by causing something to happen rather than responding to it after it has happened.

correct." [Actual quote – though this quote is in English rather than in German.]

More recently, the Political Correctness function can be dated from 1950 and the Soviet Bloc in Eastern Europe. In the eyes of the Socialists, this referred to the "correct" position on all political matters, defined then as "the party line." This included common speech among individuals.

At nearly the same time, Chairman Mao, the leader of the People's Republic of China and Chairman of the Communist Party of China, also had a pervasive Politically Correct communication system. Should a member of the public not abide by Chairman Mao's Politically Correct instruction, which defined Community Standards, they were sent away to be re-educated. No one wanted to be "re-educated" – but many were. They returned Politically Correct and sorry for the errors in their communication and offending Community Standards.

Chairman Mao also had the consideration for his people to put his sayings (all very Politically Correct examples) in a little red book. These were pocket-sized and each citizen was expected to have this book on his person...and be prepared to display the book. At certain times in public, they were to, en masse, hold the book well above their heads in a common display of their dedication to Political Correctness (and their desire to avoid re-education).

In the United States, it is fashionable to change words rather than concepts; consequently, Political Correctness is occasionally being called "Community Standards." This is just as arbitrary because it implies that someone else's judgment is determining what is to be said where and how. The community was not asked. But there are those people who claim to speak for the community. Mao did.

Things that are written and are inconsiderate of Community Standards will be "filtered" and the message will not appear on social media. It is explained in detail that this is not "censoring." The "filter" will protect the community in some manner by someone's subjective decisions.

Indeed, in some automated voice-to-text functions, a spoken "censor" may appear as "filter." Benjamin Franklin wrote/said,

"Whoever would overthrow the liberty of a nation must begin by subduing the freeness of speech."

*****

The purpose of modern Political Correctness/Community Standards is to avoid offense to any person. There are a few exceptions, however. It is permissible to offend Caucasians, members of the Christian faith, Southerners, and everyone so backward as to desire a traditional way of life. Not only is it permissible to offend those people – in the media it seems to be imperative.

If anything is traditional, then it is wrong by example of age. The tradition had originated before the current generation's time, so it could hardly have value. Tradition is thought to be insensitive, ignorant, and racist. The transgressors will require retraining by the proactive Politically Correct.

There may be no "re-education institutions" now, but many careers have come to an end (before retirement) when there was a comment made that was deemed Politically Incorrect – no matter how accurate the comment may have been nor when it was made. In this punishment, the idea of context is suspended and the past is judged by the current Politically Correct context of time and place. The previous time and place and convention are disregarded.

There are qualifiers for avoiding offense such as toward the marginalized (?) or to prevent others from insulting groups of people considered to be disadvantaged by some stated rating process – once it can be determined just what that rating/profiling system is.

Having a tenet that everyone is equal and then needing to create various categories to record their names to make sure that they are all treated fairly appears paradoxical, if not even politically incorrect. But this is the way Political Correctness is and the citizen is to accept it – not question it.

In public discourse, and occasionally in the media, "Political Correctness" is used in jest to imply that the expressed ideas lie somewhere between inane and excessive, though Political Correctness does empower the paranoid and the indignantly self-righteous.

Political Correctness is abbreviated "PC" so energy will not be wasted on so much effort, ink, and paper. "PC" has but two syllables whereas "Political Correctness" has seven. Consequently, the saving is significant. Also, by using "PC" the public might forget that it is a Liberal political effort forced on the public through intimidation – thus, trying to control everyone's freedom of speech. It can be imagined that in the future this will become "CS" – for "Community Standards" (six syllables).

The thinking is that if a list of offending words are not used, and new terms are created to describe the same thing as the old terms, then the new words will alter the definition of the condition. Thus will the offending conditions no longer exist. In such cases, apparently, blindness and deafness will be no more. However, "Rise, take up thy bed and walk" may have been documented as being successful but once.

The people who put this Political Correctness idea forward apparently never had anyone tell them to "play nice and don't say ugly things." They, being more self-aware, decided that a policy was needed to educate those not knowing this. Those people knowing it considered Political Correctness as a source of humor and Political Correctness was, in itself, the admission of poor upbringing.

Before Political Correctness became fashionable in the United States, when the offensive terms were used, they were meant to offend – and all using and hearing them knew it. It used to be called Free Speech, but this was before Political Correctness and its derivative, Community Standards. America is a more gentle nation now.

The Politically Correct want to be thought of as being modern. As if modern was good by their definition. In a liberal society all change is good. But it gives off the smell of righteous indignation – and when this is institutionalized, it is another form of brainwashing and elitism. It has been known as such through history and over the world. It empowers a caste system – something the Politically Correct profess does not exist.

Few things define the polarization of Americans as much as those touting Political Correctness and those who feel they do not need someone to tell them how to speak in the United States.

Again – "Whoever would overthrow the liberty of a nation must begin by subduing the freeness of speech."

Nothing in American history subdues the freeness of speech as does Political Correctness or prescribed Community Standards, or more correctly, the proactive citizens who are enforcing Political Correctness agendas by intimidation and all education policies.

Crude language and obscenities in public are not examples of freedom of speech. It is the imposition of those who lack a sense of decorum on those who do. But Liberalism states that the individual's desires/rights have precedence over the desires of the many. Yet, again, this freedom is denied to Caucasians, members of the Christian faith, Southerners, and Conservatives in general.

There are Conservatives who believe that "Political Correctness" and "Multiculturalism" is part of an overall Liberal conspiracy to undermine Judeo-Christian values. Or possibly just the Christian values.

There is a "life lesson" in this and it was demonstrated in a most unlikely manner.

A man was in his shop when his wife entered to ask him a question. At the same time their young son entered and went straight to his father's work bench. The son picked up a delicate jeweler's file and pushed the tip into a small hole; he immediately pulled it out and broke off the tip. The son had not been in the shop for more than 15 seconds.

They were all astounded!

The son blurted, "I didn't mean to do that!" (It certainly looked like he had.)

The father could only ask, "If you had meant to do that, what would you have done?"

There are things someone might do that have unintended consequences, yet it still looks exactly like that was their origninal intention.

So if there were a Liberal conspiracy to undermine Christian values, the Liberals should be doing exactly what they are doing. The reasons for their actions do deserve consideration; however, questioning Political Correctness is considered to be politically incorrect. This means that to the pro-actively Political Correct, this question would appear to be an attack and just another case of bigotry. (Bigotry is when someone believes something to be true but will not engage in serious discussions about the validity of the belief...as are the Politically Correct about some of their tenets.)

It has been observed that Political Correctness stymies conversation and general discourse; it can even inhibit the intellectual exchange of ideas and the expression of ideals. When done for any reason, this is not good. In its absolute truth of proactive application it does not just ignore bigotry; it does not even isolate bigotry. With Political Correctness, opinions are formed without discourse; thus, Political Correctness creates bigotry.

The Politically Correct's firm opinion comes without verbal dissent or debate. This is very bad for any society. A person could almost say that it is undemocratic.

Dictionaries used to be used to improve literary or oral communication. Semantics need to be put on a common level before any informative discourse can occur. Dictionaries defined the word, gave instruction on how to pronounce it, and then gave some history and source of the word; the etymology. That was all that was expected.

Now we know that dictionaries can do so much more.

With liberalization involved in everything and everywhere, the dictionary can be used as a tool to alter society by the dictionary's being rewritten to give social instruction – i.e., be Politically Correct. The speaker or writer will be told which words are politically incorrect with the warning that the word just defined is not to be used. The etymology will likely not be there because to explain the word's origin and history would be offensive to the Politically Correct. And if the word is not to be used, the origin does not matter. Not only is this history unnecessary, but giving the etymology could possibly disqualify the Politically Correct's interpretation of what they say the word "really" means.

In a popular, current dictionary, the singular "n-word" has 17 cases advising against using the word.

In the same dictionary, the "f-word" with its 5 entries and variations, has no suggestion of use. Meaning it can be used most anywhere without offense – or so the implication of the Politically Correct indicates and often demonstrates.

And anyone who expresses a preference for birds of his own feather will find himself in trouble with the Political Correctness/Community Standards proactive committee. At one time, this committee would have been called the Gestapo.

Chapter 4 Cultural Diversity
Introduction

A person can peruse history books for examples of multicultural countries, or for countries that have the cultural diversity for which the United States is striving. It should be remembered that culture involves the language, religion, social habits, cuisine, and the arts. In some cases in history, a large group of people considered themselves to be a common culture when all they shared were their language and religion, so it is assumed these are the primary identifiers of cultures.

It is difficult to anticipate the response of any one person to most any challenge, yet it is thought that the government can know what this would be for an entire nation. A legislated social change is difficult to correct if it does not work out as it was planned.

A nation does not need a country or borders to be determined a nation. Otherwise, there could be no indigenous American people's nations, as exist with Apache, Navaho, Cherokee, and 570 others. There are over 56 million United States acres dedicated to these 573 nations.

– Multiculturalism

Like Political Correctness, cultural diversity has become a mantra of liberal institutions, so this means schools and media. Like any good political program, these influence the children who are not to question what they are being told.

The Roman Catholic Church followed this principle a long time ago and it worked well. The expression, "Give us your child for the first seven years and we will give you the man" (or some variation of this) has been attributed to St. Ignatius Loyola, the creator of the Society of Jesus, in the early 1500s. They were known as Jesuits, and at the time within the church as "the Army of the Pope." They were to counter the increase of Protestantism.

It was assumed that the child could be so conditioned that he would perform in a prescribed manner as an adult. This is less clever than intuitive. In the United States today, the child can be in liberal government institutions from fetus to voting age.

(If desired, the reader can revisit the definitions of Liberal and Conservative on pages 216 – 218.)

Many people (the author included) have been taught in mandatory government employee classes that all cultures are the same and that we should value people the same – but no one should ever evaluate another. Having a room full of engineers told to "value without evaluation" is a little bizarre, but then much of the teachings about multiculturalism is. Yet to actually discuss this would be considered incorrect, and was not permitted in the classes.

The idea that all cultures are the same and we are all equal does not have much credence in many parts of the world where for centuries they have shared their real estate with other cultures.

Every hour somewhere on the globe one culture is trying to get rid of another culture. The idea that all people can learn to coexist requires that both sides have great fear about what will happen to them if they do not. This has actually been done a few places. It generally occurred because the feared one was a third culture which had far greater fire power and was willing to use it.

As stated in a popular, public encyclopedia, "Cultural diversity is the quality of diverse or different cultures, as opposed to monoculture, the global monoculture, or a homogenization of cultures, akin to cultural decay." This statement is incorrect. It is based more on philosophy and hope than on statistics. History demonstrates it to be untrue.

Monoculture is hardly decay and monocultural nations are not in decay because of the monoculture.

There are definitions of "civilization" which require that there be cultural diversity to even be considered a civilization. This, too, is simply philosophical hope and is inconsistent with the definition of the word "civilization." Yet, the definition can be changed if enough people wish to change it. [Remember Pluto.]

Public desire will take precedence over accuracy when public pressure is strong enough and the intimidation near-constant.

"Globalization is often said to have a negative effect on the world's cultural diversity." This, too, is from the popular, public encyclopedia. When there are definitions and statements that are negative about multidiversity, there are different comments.

In the same encyclopedia, in one case the comment was "some people do not believe this." An editorial addition in that sentence was "some people [weasel-words] do not believe this." The added "[weasel words]" is there to imply that the statement should be disregarded. (Weasel words are so named because a weasel can suck the insides from an egg and leave an empty shell, so weasel words remove the meaning of the statement.)

The bracketed interjection means that the writer should have listed every person who does not believe it, or at least give the number of people who do not believe it; and just saying "some people" was insufficient for the editor.

Then why was not "Globalization is often said to have a negative effect on the world's cultural diversity," edited to read "Globalization is often said [weasel-word] to have a negative effect on the world's cultural diversity."

The author should have stated how often it is said, and where it is said, and by whom. This omission of "[weasel word]" shows an agenda in the entire article and this should alert the reader to remember to apply the constant question of the Renaissance, "Does this really make sense?"

People must check their sources carefully, and when they do, they will see the political bias in many "true statements." The forum for the liberal view point is incredibly larger than that of the conservative. This is by the very nature of education, degrees, and the attitudes of the people desiring those degrees – and in their preferred professions.

If globalization of commerce is bad because it homogenizes disparate cultures, then this wide-ranging commerce could be stopped, but it is doubtful that some countries would want the lack of global commerce for long. Yet, the effort is there to stop it.

What is being done in places in Africa is that large populations are being deprived of electricity while living on top of extensive coal and oil deposits. The native families, possessing but a few goats and a mud hut, are being told to use only wind and solar energy. These power sources have been tried there by the government and found lacking. It costs money they do not have. The development of the coal and oil deposits would give them electrical power, jobs, and money.

But instead, they are destined to destroy their lungs and those of their children with the smoke from cooking over an open wood or dung fire inside their small mud huts.

Oil and coal reserves could revolutionize their economy, but these resources cannot be developed because "the environment must be protected." There is usually some reference to global warming involved.

"Cultural diversity can be seen as analogous to biodiversity" – also, from the public encyclopedia. This, too, sounds good. But it is nonsense. Biodiversity is a natural, evolutionary process. There is no desire there. It just is. It is natural – as in nature (when humans are not involved).

Cultural diversity is not natural. The fact that it exists a lot of places is the result of conflict – not peaceful, natural migration. Birds of a feather do flock together. That is natural. It is observed – repeatedly – everywhere.

Those who think monoculturalism is decay, and that without diversity there can be no civilization, will have to disqualify Japan's great success. They seem to be doing well, and the current Japan is not a very old society – but it is nearly a monocultural nation, and a large one. Basically, its governmental structure – even a major part of their then-national religion – made a huge and sudden change as recently as 1945. Their God told them that they would "have to endure the unendurable." They showed the world just how quickly a country with long traditions can excel in the modern world and particularly when not hampered by the confusion of multiculturalism.

All this can be said of South Korea, as well.

Strangely, it is proposed that a nation with multiple cultures is to do better than those with just one, and this is while saying that we are all the same and that no culture is better than another.

Apparently, they are not all the same or the United States would not need so many of them (besides for their art ... and food).

There are cultural purists who monitor the accents of cartoon characters. It seems that there is no accent for a villain that such purists will accept. The upper-class English accent of a villain lion was disliked, as were any other accents.[6]

The purist did not seem to mind the "American" accent of the hero, but wondered why the accents were different for others. A viewer might wonder what language and accent a lion would prefer to use. Or a hyena.

Some cultures do develop a persona. No one did this, but they themselves represent some sort of personality in common. It is part of their cultural identity...like music and food, but this seems to be a general attitude.

Some cultures appear to be easy going. Some are hard working and industrious. But we do need to recognize these differences. Some things about their cultural identity is religion-based and we do not agree with some of those things, so maybe some cultures are not as preferred as others.

Our culture frowns on human sacrifices, cannibalism, female infanticide, and the alteration of female genitalia. (However, male genitalia mutilation is acceptable – even preferred by some people.) These practices are quite old and have been well-integrated into some cultures. To truly value these cultures, Americans should reconsider how they value female infanticide. Not all cultures are equally valued even while American citizens are being told they are. A person growing up with Political Correctness might know these things but not admit them. Perhaps their freeness of speech is being inhibited.

There are terms even now for how to negotiate with someone to determine the lowest/highest selling price. There is a culture known for their really vigorous negotiating.

And it would be entertaining to discuss cultures to determine if there is one known for their organization, or lack of same – or the culture's work habits – or for their cleanliness. Perhaps there is a culture known for keeping their money in their pocket.

---

[6] When the author was a child, all villains had a German accent and appeared as the artists thought a German should appear. We were at war with Germany; consequently, Germans were believable villains.

The Politically Correct conclusion would have to be that they are all equal and valued the same. (Except for those engaged in human sacrifices, slavery, female infanticide, etc. ,etc.)

– Communication

With constant change, perfection cannot be attained and mediocrity is the best that can be expected. Yet even mediocrity cannot be experienced when there is bad communication – failure is more likely the result.

There is a simple question which escapes many people, but most people experience the results and do not like them.

It is known that the purpose of language is to communicate, so it is logical to consider what contributes to good communication. A principal purpose of communication is to eliminate confusion. Mixed accents and dialects contribute to complication and confusion and therefore degrade communication – the very purpose for which languages are developed.

For consideration, Person A and Person B are engaged in conversation:

#1. Person A is speaking his language A, and Person B is speaking his language B, and neither person understands the other's language.

#2 Person C speaking his language C, and Person A speaking language C. But Person A's accent is so heavy, Person C cannot understand Person A. Also, Person A may be nearly incapable of even making the sounds that are needed to communicate in language C.

The difference in #1 and #2 may be very little. Communication is being hampered.

One can see how politically incorrect such considerations are and a person must be insensitive for even broaching the general topic. Too few people today consider the relevance of what is being asked when that is what is important.

"Why even ask such a question?" is often the first and last thing, said. This is not an answer, but another question. Too often this question is intended to be a comment, but it is not. It is an implied comment, and this is only the old application of verbal intimidation.

If this subject is discussed at all, there will be a Politically Correct diatribe on the sins of insensitivity. (Apathy is now a mental disorder. Remember Pluto.)

For accurate oral communication to occur it should be clear in tone and be distinct – and must be understood.

This current era is called "The Information Age," but this could hardly be so with confusing oral communication. Being given information in a language or accent that the listener cannot understand is not fulfilling the purpose of oral communication.

Many people have terminated phone calls because they could not understand the person with whom they were trying to communicate. When people hear a language/accent they do not understand, and they just hang up, they are not being rude; they are just returning to their business which the caller had interrupted.

When multiple languages are discussed, it will be found that many people in the United States study Spanish for a second language. But in many schools, the second language is English since so many speak Spanish as a first (and only) language.

After English, Spanish is the most common language in the United States. More people speak Spanish in the United States than those who speak French, Chinese, Hawaiian, and all Indigenous People's languages combined.

In 2007, the United States had the second largest number of Spanish speaking people in the world; Mexico being first. The United States is ahead of Spain, Colombia, and Argentina. Only half of the United States Spanish speakers claim to speak English well.

English is not recognized as the official language in the United States. There was an active "English First" project to have English declared the official language, but it failed to get enough votes. When the "English First" project was presented, the Spanish speakers had already become that populous. (Conservatives are easy to pick off. They wait until the issue gets bad and then it will be too late to make any difference. Again, this is the "sitting target" syndrome.)

So in the United States culture, English cannot be included as one of the cultural identifiers. (It seems everyone has a culture so it could be assumed that the United States has a culture also – it is just not being discussed because it is so mixed and not all parts are accepted to be equally important. This statement might be unacceptable but it will not be debated.)

The Spanish language is formally identified at the state level in various states. In New Mexico more than 40% of the residents speak Spanish. This means that they "speak Spanish" – it does not mean they "can speak Spanish, but they speak English."

Communication would be more thorough when a group of 200 people were speaking a common language in a near-common accent. There would be little-to-no communication if the 200 people were each speaking a different language.

The extremely Politically Correct would sense a red flag being raised when such considerations of communication are contemplated. They are alert to these unpleasantries because they are sensitive people – meaning they are very sensitive about any challenges to their issues and agenda. Even the question would be considered offensive and thus preclude any discussion. ("Why would you even ask such a question?")

Being firm of opinion without discourse is considered bigotry many places. The location and reasons for this do not disqualify the term nor its application. When it occurs in Political Correctness, and it does often, it is still bigotry.

The people who think communication is best served by all people speaking a common language are being Politically Incorrect.

There could be a lot of satisfaction for the Politically Correct when they are on the phone seeking some important information on a serious issue and they contact some company who has outsourced their support services and it takes maybe two minutes to even determine what the agent's first language is. Once this is known, the person needing accurate information can then try to remember how the people being paid to provide the information pronounce English words.

The Politically Correct person's satisfaction will come from knowing they are on the phone all that time enjoying cultural diversity.

"Keen" from Hispanics means "Ken." This was worked out in high school many years ago, and from many weeks in Mexico. However, in high school they did not call themselves "Hispanics."

Multiculturalism is very, very old. Once it was a natural, evolutionary process. It was not created by legislated law.

There are engineers who experienced some of this language confusion in the control room of a large rocket engine test complex. Poor communication could destroy a multimillion-dollar rocket engine and test stand, but NASA was working to achieve congressionally mandated cultural diversity.

In Los Angeles, there are 140 cultures speaking 225 languages. When speaking of people, it is constructive that anthropological terms be used. Therefore, "culture" defines religion and language – among other things. But it is likely that their music is interesting and their cuisine is simply divine, but oral communication can be exasperating and inaccurate – and very, very time consuming. In business, this wasted time costs a company the same way as productive time helps the company prosper.

In hospital environments, miss-communication can be dangerous.

In London over 300 different languages are being spoken in schools. The United Kingdom can be considered the birthplace of the English language – a language which by its functionality has served the world well, and this common adoption was more by evolution in business than through legislation. Developing good communication in business is paramount.

Many people try to understand a new device's instruction manual – though supposedly written in English, it is difficult, if not impossible to understand some of them. This, too, is a natural product of the multicultural society in a global economy and therefore it should be valued.

The desire of many immigrants, legal and otherwise, is not to assimilate but to maintain a cultural separation while living in the United States.

When people forget the simple purpose of oral communication, they will believe anything.

Diversity puts an unnatural burden on the public with the philosophy that after a few generations we will have no problem communicating. This could be true, but businesses often function by fiscal year – 12 months – not generations.

If other countries are used as examples, it can be seen that when the alien culture does not assimilate, in a few generations there could be increased animosity, then later, armed conflict.

But maybe there will be super-fast I-Phone translators. It would be good if their batteries never needed charging. It is foolish to put any social system in place which requires yet another undefined technology to make it function seamlessly.

I-phones are answering essay questions with "yes" and "no" and this is happening so fast that the answer cannot be committed to human memory, and if it is not in human memory, there is no learning.

– Multicultural Conflict

Multiculturalism is the source of too many wars and too many terrorist acts. While this is not universal, just by observing history it can be considered a near-constant cultural condition.

The invited people to a country can hardly be told to "go back home." Therefore, this is another social change that can be legislated but not reversed if it turns out to be detrimental.

The attempt at multicultural reversal is generally done by warfare. From Croatia, Serbia, Albania, to the Levent deserts, to nearly every river valley in Africa, as well as the Palestinians and the Israelis. Even admitting that Israel existed caused a Nobel Peace Prize winner to be assassinated. There are some real cultural differences in the world.

Some of the attributes of multiculturalism can best be found where it has been in place a few years and, of course, the wonderful multiculturalism stability of Iraq is well known – as is that in India, Bangladesh, Pakistan, etc.

On three pages of a local newspaper, June 25, 2018, it was reported that:

– United States president is concerned about legislation to stop illegal aliens.

– The European Union is backing the idea of limiting African and Balkan migrants – their term for "illegal aliens."

– Mali's government says 16 people were killed in Fulani ethnic fighting. The death toll is now 32 civilians. It was reported that there was most likely more because many were already buried to hide the bodies.

– Egypt extended their state of emergency because of the killing of at least 44 people in the fighting between Islam and Coptic churchgoers.

– Nigeria reported 86 killed in clashes between those who herd and those who farm.

It could be that the many people in those varied places are not as aware of the importance of cultural diversity/multiculturalism as are the citizens of the United States.

Ethnic diversity/multiculturalism is a well-studied condition. There are United States citizens who should consider forgetting about unicorns, 24-hour rainbows, and wishing on a star. It would be more constructive that they do a literature search of "ethnic conflict" before supporting the legislation of laws which promise to create many more nations within the United States.

Diversity conflict continues worldwide, yet in spite of even the current evidence, the United States legislates that the United States will be a multicultural and culturally diverse nation. And this has been continuing for some time and it will only increase.

Diversity is not always good and there are many cultures who would prefer another culture to be extinct – and given enough fire power one of them would be. Again, there is no miss-communication between them. They have known each other through a few centuries of near-constant interfacing – and often fighting for long periods.

Chapter 5 Immigration: Legal and Otherwise

As mentioned earlier, the United States Government is the principal organization in the United States dealing in multiracial comparisons. It is doing this so that the government might adjust society to some model of "racial equality." This has been demonstrated to mean taking opportunity from one race and giving it to another.

(Much of the following is from United States Government sources.)

In 1988 the United States approved 1.4 million citizenship applications and most were from people who were in the United States illegally. More than 980,000 were from Mexico.

If Americans have "the right to know," then there should be a great effort to permit immigration to just those who speak English sufficiently well to function in most any job requiring oral discussions. This would be so Americans could exercise their right to know what the aliens are saying or trying to say.

To deny that many Americans hang up the phone when difficult-to-understand people call them is a statement too obvious to even discuss. And if this preference for understanding is considered, then accepting someone immigrating into a society using a different language would certainly decrease communication accuracy – and in a profit-oriented society, this would reduce the bottom-line by increasing product costs. In a charity-based society, the language would not matter much.

This disparate communication skill is assuming the United States' doctrine of equal pay for equal work is being enforced. This is another phrase that is absent of all logic. "Pay" is objective – it is a number. "Work," however, is not objective but subjective. If the boss says some employee is doing good work then the employee is; if however, the boss says that another employee is doing bad work, then that is true, as well. And both employees may have the same job title and be doing the same job.

The purpose of the work is to make the employer money. Employees who do this are valued. Those who cost the employer money are not valued.

So an efficient worker is valued over the less efficient – even when they have the same job title and are doing the same work – only one's work has more value to the employer than the other's.

Yet, the idea that because each has the same job title, then they must be doing the same work, and therefore have the same pay, is inconsistent with the very principles of commerce.

Still, "equal pay for equal work" is never to be interpreted that way. If the two workers have the same title, that is all that is to be considered; not their productivity. The fact that one employee might cost the company four times the amount of the other employee is to be irrelevant.

(The questions is – "Does this really make sense? Or is it just some cute-sounding political slogan?")

When the United States is compared with other countries with international migrants – legal or not – it can be seen that there are 244 million international migrants in the world. This was a 41% increase in 15 years. Thirty percent of the world's migrants live in just 20 countries. The largest number lives in the United States with nearly 47 million (19% of the world's total migrants). Second and third are Germany and Russia with 12 million each; Saudi Arabia has 10 million; and the United Kingdom, 9 million. Of these countries, the least in area is the United Kingdom.

India has had the largest number of people leaving – 16 million in 15 years – more than one million a year.

Mexico is second with 12 million citizens leaving.

Those leaving India can have many destinations; Mexico has but one.

By a 2012 Gallup survey, 640 million people would leave their country if they could. Of these, the most-preferred destination is the United States with 23% (147 million people) desiring to come. (Population of the United States in 2018 was 327 million.)

The second largest group, 7% (45 million people) would go to the United Kingdom. The next preferred country was Canada. The common language in these three countries is English; though 20% of the population in Canada speak French, many signs there are in both languages.

Therefore, 224 million people would go to an English-speaking country if they could and this is the same number of migrants that are currently living world-wide. It can be assumed that whatever their societies are, it is thought by them to be lacking. And these migrants will later bring their extended families to their countries of choice.

So 45 million immigrants would go to the United Kingdom. The United Kingdom has 66 million people but only 94,000 square miles; this is less than half the area of France. The United Kingdom has less area than the state of Michigan.

London, United Kingdom, is multiethnic and in government (public) schools in London, black and Asian children outnumber white British children nearly 3-to-1.

East Germany and the East/West wall was designed to prevent movement from the East to the West. The West demanded that this cease. It did. Now the West has found it necessary to govern the East-to-West movement. This is seen there as a "paper-work" wall.

Intelligent governments will find a way to protect their borders (and their culture) when it is necessary. A country which has an unprotected and uncontrolled border has no border other than a line on a map.

Some idealistic governments such as the United States have philosophy, rather than reality and history, to guide them.

Walls to keep in are considered to be a prison; walls to keep out are considered protection. Many nice homes in California have walls around them, and gated communities are common in the United States. These are to keep unknown people out. Apparently, walls are acceptable for homes but not nations.

Some countries have no physical borders and some just pretend they do.

There was a common game among children when some small area was marked off on the ground with a stick and then the child proclaimed, "This is mine and no one else can come in."

They always did.

A line on the ground is just that.

It is touted that lower-paid workers, immigrants (legal or not), can provide cheaper services for consumers. In some cases, either the labor cost for locals was excessive or the locals would not do the work, so there would be some jobs created because of cheaper labor. But this is not a "short-term exchange program." They come to stay.

There is the question of when the low-skilled people will bring their non-producing family, or how they will provide their families with basic human needs, such as health care.

One may wonder how much grass a lowly skilled immigrant can cut in Southern California to pay for just the basic health care of his family. And of course, at some point, he will need to declare his income (in cash) on his tax withholding statement.

It is difficult to determine what this cheaper labor will cost the tax payers. The illegal immigrant's "rights" are still being discussed at the legal level. However, when they get the right to vote, they will gain immediate clout to determine what rights they want. The tax payers' burden will likely exceed the alien's contributions to the tax base. Basic numbers indicate this.

Benjamin Franklin said, "When the people find that they can vote themselves money that will herald the end of the republic."

The democratic system is already flawed by having chronically unemployed citizens continually receiving benefits from the taxed citizens while many of these unemployed may have never contributed to that tax base.

A study linked the idea that as the illegal immigrant number increases, the public reduces their amount of volunteered charitable contributions. The researchers did not understand this, but a discussion with the public would have improved the researchers' comprehension. The time may come when the producers (tax payers) decide that their required tax burden is "charitable contribution" enough.

A historian at a Scot university said that the average life span of a democracy is 200 years. But it is likely that a long time after that democracy had ceased to exist, the citizens were still calling it a "democracy" – even it after had been a popular socialist state for four or five generations.

*****

According to national studies, such immigration into just the information technology industry reduced the wages of the United States computer scientists over 5%. This was presented as a good thing for the consumers.

This means that the local/indigenous citizens' starting salaries were reduced by $2,000 a year and the mid-level salaries were reduced by $6,000 a year.[7] The idea that lower-paid immigrants would force locals into better paying occupations seems rather tenuous. Anyone

---

7

By John Bound, et al, (May 19,2017) "Reservoir of foreign talent." Science Magazine.

who would suggest this idea as being constructive should consider that possibility in their own professions – should their profession be in the United States.

It was stated that research on illegal aliens is lacking, but it is still proposed by sociologists that illegal aliens have a positive effect on locals. This premise is being offered in lieu of research. Again it seems to be a Liberal philosophy – hope. The "studies show" what evidence does not support.

In such research there should be the basic question; are welfare and immigration related? Sociologists wonder if this is even worthy of research. It could be expected that the American tax payers would like to know – should the sociologists decide to address it. One would think that if the "positive" side of the issue were being measured, so would the "negative" side. Only then would there be a valid consideration of the value of illegal immigrants. This lack of information may be in the Politically Correct logic that cultures are to be valued, but certainly they are not to be evaluated; consequently, the negative impact is ordained to be nonexistent. Considering the positive vs. the negative would seem like an evaluation so, therefore, it is not to occur.

Just as it would be hard to find funding for research on the question, "Is Global Warming Caused By Humans?" and easier to get research funding on, "The Impact of Humans in Causing Global Warming," then perhaps "Determining the Positive Influences of Immigration" would be funded, but "Determining the Economic Impact of Immigration" would not.

The then-current intellectual community has generally established the criteria for awarding most research grants.

There was a study in 2016 which indicated that United States immigration between 1940 and 2010 increased the rate of high school completion. This seemed good but strange. The increase was only 0.3%. This was 3 more graduates out of each 1000 students over a 70-year period – this 70 years constitutes two generations. (Thirty years per generations is the common understanding.)

There could be many things besides immigration during this long period to cause 3 more graduates out of 1,000 students. There were no statistics offered for high school dropouts during the same period. Again this consideration of negatives would appear to be evaluating.

Because of set-asides and affirmative actions in the United States and the United Kingdom, it was found that elite colleges favored minority students over the locals. This is not how the government proves the similarities of cultures when some cultures are favored over others. The government will decide which is the favored culture while stating they are all the same.

Foreign students from South Korea or Japan might be favored by any school system desiring to improve its scholastic standings. These students would certainly make American teachers look better, even though these students are from monocultured countries. These students being put in a multiculturally diverse school may no longer perform at their customarily high standard.

*****

The statistics are entertaining in that one can see how a flaw in logic affects the future of the United States. The flaw is the insistence that a value can be placed on something which cannot be evaluated.

So the public is left with receiving information on all the positives of the world with no reporting of the negatives. This appears illogical.

What is not in dispute is that the illegal immigrants are in the United States <u>illegally</u>. They violated many laws to get here. Their reasons for doing so do not matter. They are violating the law. <u>Why</u> they are violating the law is irrelevant. Embezzlement is a crime and it does not matter how justified the embezzler may feel while doing it.

Perhaps there is more to the illegal immigration permission idea. If there is no agenda; it begs the question – "If there was a conspiracy, how would it be done?"

From the presented evidence, the only idea that is positive is that whichever political party can give the illegal aliens voting privileges then that party would prosper. And the political party which can provide tax payers' resources to these people will get these people's votes. This has been demonstrated to be successful in the past.

There is a heart-felt wish of illegal aliens that their children can be born in the United States. This and other medical care is at the United States tax payers' expense. The data on the amount of this expense is not easy to locate.

How the family of Mexican citizens – those who violated many United States laws to get here – is treated once they are here should be the Mexican citizen's consideration. It is rare when the illegal immigrants are referred to as "Mexican citizens," but that is what they are. They will remain Mexican citizens and most of their family will reside in Mexico for a while before they come to the United States as extended family.

Additionally, their children born in the United States can have dual citizenship – Mexico and the United States. This is being done a lot more often than first thought. The procedures for doing this are simple and instruction as to how children born in the United States can have dual citizenship is given step-by-step on the Internet.

The Mexican government does not overlook how many of their citizens are coming into the United States. And being here, they will still be Mexican citizens and their president will reside in Mexico. The influence of their voting in the United States will exceed any imagined Russian election involvement.

Could the president of Mexico influence United States elections?

How could he not?

*****

The idea that someone making more money one place than at another place, and that this has no impact on another person, implies that wealth is fluid and unlimited. It means that money has no objectivity nor does it have material substance. But it is not that way. If one person gains, someone else has less. Those who do not understand this must assume that the money in a wallet is self-perpetuating and replenishes itself each night while the owner sleeps.

After reading the glowing reports of how illegal immigration is constructive for everyone, one might wonder why any country would maintain any border. Or why any landowner would put up a fence around his property...or in California, walls around his property. And yet "trespassing laws" apply and are enforced many places. The pride of ownership might be involved in trespassing laws, but apparently not as it applies to the United States.

A 2014 study in the United Kingdom showed that immigration reduced house prices. The logic was that the indigenous/local people had, for whatever reason, decided to move to other places after immigrants took up residence in the local's neighborhood. The local people were selling in a neighborhood with houses that had depreciated in value for some reason. The seller sustained a loss of value. So it was true that immigrants did reduce home prices. And this was presented as a good thing and a recommendation for more immigration.

This is another way that immigration is shown in statistics to be good for the locals. Yet it can be shown that taking something way from person "A" and giving it to person "B" will greatly improve the life of person "B."

It is not logical to assume that he will leave his cultural mind-set at the Mexican border when he crosses over into the United States, even when it was the immigrant's own culture which created the previous environment he had determined to leave.

Something must be seriously wrong with Mexico and now their citizens, Mexicans, are coming north and things will be much better for the United States – according to sociologists' research.

Under the present conditions in the United States, the border cannot be controlled or it would have already been. An uncontrolled border is not a border but a mere international speed bump.

Chapter 6 Education
Introduction

Once there was a country where the people were enlightened, literate, fed, and clean.

Then, the unwashed masses arrived.

These masses did not come by invitation – quite the contrary. And they thought that their idea of government, though crude, was the best. The long-established society was disrupted and the Dark Ages had arrived in Europe. Almost all the people became illiterate, mostly pagan, and unruly. This continued for 500 years or so. (Sixteen generations!)

Then another culture arrived to change everything again. The people living there did not like this change either. Again, much of the language changed.

Much later the same thing happened at a different place in a different way. Instead of Angles, Saxons, Jutes, Frisians, Vikings, Normans, etc., who had arrived in Britain, these masses were home-grown hordes of "Johnnys."

And like the previous hordes, the Johnnys were not interested in literal education nor in convention – and certainly not in traditions. They were self-indulgent and absorbed with only their thinking. While stating that they were for freedom, they set about to enforce their idea of freedom on those who had for many generations before them enjoyed more freedom than that offered by all the Johnnys.

Many people can remember when they first heard of these Johnnys. The people had seen the bumper stickers warning of them. The bumper stickers asked, "Why can't Johnny read?"

Now Johnny and his clan have scattered and taken control of the land. They are grown, married, and have had many additional Johnnys and Joanies. They and their society have gone to work as journalists, publishers, editors, teachers, television writers, etc., – and they still cannot read. It shows in their poor writing.

This was acceptable in itself, but the worst part was that they were therefore ignorant of history.

History/tradition is disqualified by them as being "old fashioned" and as such, has no application in their perception of a better "modern" (Johnny-ed) world.

Their comments are too often without foundation or relevance, and it is not permitted to discuss their ideas, but they sound so good! Those who question them are disqualified by ridicule and intimidation rather than by rhetoric.

Then if the subsequent Johnnys are progressively more ignorant (and this would seem likely), then the ignorance is compounded because of their misinterpretation of information, and still worse is that they believe misinformation. (Some Johnnys might be right by chance, but chance is not a good thing to rely on.)

Many of their parents practiced the sensual: "If it feels good, do it!" Or, "I ain't a'hurtin' nobody!" ('At the moment,' being implied.)

The more astute could refer to these people as being "Yahoos."[8]

In this time and place, a different age began. It was not one of darkness, but certainly not one of light. It was only dim. Someday those years of the 1960s will be referred to as the beginning of "The United States' Dim Ages. This was when there were a limited number of good options for serious, time-critical social problems, but the populous was unknowing and functionally illiterate.[9] (And it was not socially acceptable to discuss this; it might cause them to feel bad.) Their general education scores were not good, but they did not care; they thought really well of themselves.

– Making the Grade

Who would have a better understanding of scoring systems than would school teachers?

[Again the author can speak from experience.]

Early on I was not confused by the way the teachers did the scoring. I knew my numbers. I knew what an "A" was numerically and I knew how to derive the averages of various combinations of grades. I knew that if I answered 10 out of 10 true/false questions correctly (though rarely occurring,) I would expect 100% on my sheet. If I answered 7 of the 10 correctly, which was much more likely, then I would have a 70% for the test and this was passing – barely. (Sixty-nine was an "F" – as in "Failing.')

I wondered, 'How difficult could this be? It was simple math.' That was the only kind of math I knew.

Yet, one day I heard the teacher say something about "grading on a curve."

8

Yahoos were the creation of Jonathon Swift in 1726 and were described as being crude, brutish, filthy, and obscenely coarse, near-humans.

9

A person who cannot associate various terms within one article and relate the parameters.

Now, I was scared! I knew what a curve was! I had had many curve balls thrown my direction. The ball appeared to take one path but would suddenly veer to another path...and I did not hit the ball very often.

And with the curved grading, I had lost control of my own sense of accomplishment – as small as that might have been at the time. I would do the best I could and receive a score that was un-associated with simple math.

It appeared that I was being given extra credit, but not everyone was getting this "little bit extra." The cute, smart girl that I knew really well and who was always in the "A" class had to do more than I did on the same test that I had in my "B" class. So the grade given was not the numerical score – it was adjusted in some manner...some changing, curving manner.

I did not know it, but at that point, the American education system had gone to Hell...but it was a much more kind system. No longer was it objective but it had became less firm and much more "adjustable" for circumstances. The same accomplishments of a dumb kid counted for more than those of a smart kid. I saw this. I experienced this. I understood when it was happening. But I was just too cowardly to depend on it. It might switch back when I was not looking and my "D" (which was OK with me) become an "F." (HORRORS!)

– World Education

The importance of education varies among countries and states. The deficiencies in education do not depend on money spent on each child. This has been demonstrated over and over in the United States. The deficiencies are occurring when the basics are being overwhelmed by new and varying teaching techniques with each promising improved education...but not delivering. The result is that another generation of Johnnys get short-changed in school.

The United States spends more per student than any country, yet overall, education in the United States is only #14 best in the world.[10] However, this covered all tiers of education from the lowest to the highest. This may provide an overall score, but it does not address the basic one: Johnny's reading ability and his functioning with math.

In the world the United States is #40 in math, #24 in science, and #24 in reading.

United States law requires school attendance from 5 to 8 years old to nearly 18. The general ratio of attendance in the three principal types of schools is that 87% of the students are in public schools, 10% are in private schools, and 3% are being home schooled.

United States student loans are now nearly $1.5 trillion. This is staggering when the effectiveness of education is considered and the likelihood that the graduate students, when practicing in the fields in which they have been educated, will not have enough income to even pay back the student loans.

So the United States will try something else. In Liberal political philosophy the United States will not go back to what was working before. Doing that might appear to be some traditional method – interpreted to mean "inadequate" – no matter what the evidence is to the contrary.

It is difficult to excel in any discipline if basic math and English skills are lacking. And in English, this includes reading and proper speech. The term "proper speech" is often considered to be judgmental and therefore it is discouraged. "Proper" as used in this case means "for which speech was intended – effective communication."

When mouth noises are made and there is no communication, then maybe some people are not speaking a common language, or perhaps it is a common language but poorly spoken.

It should be considered what Johnny knows and not what Johnny's technology knows. Not all Johnnys can afford to walk

---

10

According to a refereed, independent United Kingdom publishing and education company's survey.

around with a $363 iPhone (up 10% over last year) with a yearly service cost averaging $960.

Interestingly, Finland had been #1on the list of best in the world education, but it is now displaced by three Asian countries: South Korea, Japan, and Singapore (as well as Hong Kong – though Hong Kong is not a country but a defined economic region in China). The top two countries are very monocultural.

The relationship of education and economic growth seems related, but one does not guarantee the other. Money spent on education does not automatically produce better education so this better education must relate to something else.

While it appears intuitively obvious that those students who excel in the lower grades will continue to do well in higher academia, as well that the underperforming students in the lower grades are likely to not do well in higher education, there is still no one-to-one correlation. (Again, there are exceptions, but the fact that exceptions exist validates the condition considered to be the norm.)

Among European nations, Finland is ranked first with the United Kingdom second; on a global scale Finland is fifth and the United Kingdom is sixth.

Of interest is that Poland is tenth on a global scale. Poland was a Communist Bloc state from 1947 until their Solidarity Revolution in 1989 when they started reestablishing their own independent country. Poland has separate schools for national minorities. "Separate is not equal" has no meaning to them. This separate school concept would have to improve communication in all the schools. To serve the individual needs of their students, there would have to be differences in the schools. This means that while they are not the same (and they should not be), education is offered equally to each group.

Poland had a major educational reform in 1999 when the amount of time in certain classes was changed so there was a gain of nearly a full year to be dedicated to core subjects – reading, grammar, and math. These simple changes affected their rankings in world education.

Additionally, the Polish teaching positions were elevated in civil ranking so that violent crimes against them warranted stronger penalties. The school principals could assign aggressive students to community service and the student's parents could be fined. A teacher not reporting violent acts in school could face a prison sentence.

Poland's educational system now has advanced past Denmark, Germany, Russia, the United States, Switzerland, and France, plus others. Such a change was profound and required courage on the part of the government and teaching organizations. The citizenry had to see the need for such a change.

The top 40 countries in education are:

1. South Korea
2. Japan
3. Singapore
4, Hong Kong
5. Finland
6. The United Kingdom
7. Canada
8. The Netherlands
9. Ireland
10. Poland
11. Denmark
12. Germany
13. Russia
14. The United States
15. Australia
16. New Zealand
17. Israel
18. Belgium
19. The Czech Republic
20. Switzerland
21. Norway
22. Hungary
23. France
24. Sweden
25. Italy
26. Austria
27. Slovenia
28. Portugal

29. Spain
30. Bulgaria
31. Romania
32. Chile
33. Greece
34. Turkey
35. Thailand
36. Colombia
37. Argentina
38. Brazil
39. Mexico
40. Indonesia

The best way to improve a nation's scholastic rating would be to flood the nation with bright, educated students with a desire to learn and having a discipline to sacrifice the moment for a better tomorrow – this is called "foresight."

The reverse of this would be the best way to reduce the effectiveness of an education system. This would be when a school was flooded with students with poor preparatory schooling and students who would rather not even be there. Then, not only are these students counted in the negative, they are reducing the level of education of those who are in the classrooms to learn.

Few nations would do this deliberately, but many nations have been forced into this situation by world politics.

Yet, some nations have volunteered for this educational setback. The idea is that the underachievers will prosper by emulating the students who are setting a good example. This is hard to accept no matter how many times it is written. When demonstrated, the outcome was poor. The underachievers created distractions and this interfered with the attention of the inspired students. It also sapped the teacher's time and energy.

The United States education system (#14) will continue to be engulfed with the young from the #39 nation on the list. It would not be too extreme to expect the United States to go further down in the rankings – or perhaps sociologists can develop a grading system based on a curve and the United States could suddenly leap to #1.

If given this grading task, it would be wise to develop a curve based on how good the students feel about themselves when leaving school.

Some of the better performing schools in the world might produce tired students with nagging questions about self-worth, but having a burning desire to excel. The American parent would likely think, 'Well, that certainly was not any fun for them! They are young. They are supposed to be enjoying their youth!'

Therefore, a better grading system might ignore knowledge and deal with sensitive issues like feelings. The students can get their education later.

Japan is the 10th most populated country in the world with 127 million people, of which 98.5% are ethnically Japanese. This is as close to being ethnically pure as can be determined for a developed nation.

South Korea has 50 million people, of which 96% are ethnically Korean. This, too, would be considered ethnically pure.

Both Japan and South Korea are highly educated, high-output industrial countries, but no one has been telling them that they need more cultures. They seem to like what they have and it is working well for them.

In world education, out of the top 40 nations, South Korea is ranked #1 and Japan is ranked #2. Perhaps a part of these high ratings is the singular culture and the ease of communication.

The United States has 327 million people and is the third most populous country; it is listed as one of the 17 most megadiverse countries, and it is adding one person every 13 seconds.

Immigration (legal and otherwise) in the United States increased from 20 million people in 1990 to 40 million in 2010. There is no reason to assume that this number will do anything but increase – and not linearly.

From 2000 to 2010 the United States Hispanic population increased by 43% while non-Hispanics in the United States increased less than 5%. The increase in population in the United States is "Hispanic from Mexico," or worded differently, they are Mexican citizens coming uninvited to live in the United States. It is only assumed that their political alliance will shift from Mexico to the

United States. Or they may bring their Mexican culture to the United States – this would be the culture that created the social system that they felt compelled to leave.

In education, Mexico is #39 out of the 40 listed countries. They do, however, out-rank Indonesia. It can be assumed that there are studies to show how the American education system will benefit from the addition of illegal aliens from the 39th country in education.

*****

In the United States, high school students are graduating that are unable to use a look-up table or balance a checkbook, and the entrance standards in some two-year colleges are quite low. But the responsibility of the teacher is to teach. The responsibility of the student is to learn. This takes effort by both parties; students and teachers.

The teachers are not getting enough students who want to learn, or those who do want to learn are being held back by other students – either by their lack of desire to learn (which saps the time and effort of the teacher) or by those students who are actively distracting everyone.

The idea of teachers inspiring students to want to learn is possibly in opposition with a family, or, indeed, a complete society, which has digressed to the point that there is no stigma for failure. In such a society it is believed that it is always someone else's fault for their failures.

Chapter 7 The Media

Introduction

At the current time it appears the population prefers a fun hoax to any truth. It is thought that a statement is fact even if it is reported out of context by a person who heard it from another person who was not present at the time of the event, nor were they authorized to address the subject, nor were they even associated with any party in question – but it is still accepted as fact when the source of the information cannot be identified nor can the "facts" be confirmed because "they" spoke only under the condition of anonymity.

This explains the media of today – and from whence the public gets its "facts."

– Influence

If someone were reading of the social state of any country, it would be logical to think they would be interested in the greatest social influence in that country. The most influence in the United States still lies with the media (printed material, electronic, and TV). The media is the vehicle to be ridden to stardom and celebrity status! This certainly includes the political institutions.

The media influences American opinion and considering that Americans vote their opinions, then it is intuitively obvious the media affects the way Americans vote. The media is a greater influence on American elections than any Russian internet manipulators who may be guilty of doing something or other.

The media now has no responsibility to anyone for anything while claiming without fact that they are performing a public service. They repeatedly post "facts" as being "from a source not wishing to be identified nor were they a party to the event, nor were they authorized to speak to the press, etc...", but the media liked it.

So by printing these stories, the stories become the News and the Truth – because the citizens of the United States have a right to know – thus is the media's slant on reality.

The citizens post comments on social media and do not check their sources – nor does the media check theirs.

Each citizen should pay attention when they read a newspaper report of any event of which they have personal knowledge. Then they should consider if there were any glaring errors in that report.

The only time the author has found accuracy in media reporting was when it was submitted by him under his byline. However, on one occasion he was "quoted" as having said that a particular bridge was "8 miles long." This was in a local newspaper and every person in the town knew it could not be "8 miles." He had stated it being "eight-tenths of a mile long." The reporter was sitting within 10 feet of him taking notes.

Maybe the reporter was supporting the "other side" of the town hall meeting issue and his making it "8 miles long" was a good way to disqualify the point the author was making. Or perhaps the reporter was functionally illiterate.

For all other general articles of which the citizen knows little, he should assume that every article may have the same type of errors that were evident in the article with which the citizen was familiar.

These errors may be due to neglect, ignorance of craft, or it could be to deliberately deceive the public. To assume that the media reports the truth is too unbelievable to even consider.

The American public can see through some degree of non-truths and event vacuums...sometimes...when they want to.

As far back as the mid-1700s, it was understood that personal assumptions based on partial truths did not improve anyone's accuracy of contemplation. The good Doctor Johnson wrote in 1759, "Between falsehood and useless truth, there is little difference. Gold which cannot be spent will make no man rich, so it is that knowledge which cannot be applied will make no man wise."

Reading several sources of lies will never reveal the truth, and reading equally biased but opposing views will not make the citizen more informed. They will just read until they find something they like and then assume that to be the truth – no matter how outlandish. This means that many people will select the source of their misinformation – and vote accordingly.

At one time there were newspapers which had editors who demanded that the reporters reveal their sources. "Did you check your source?" was the common question from the editor's desk to the cub reporter. But they were reporting important events and they wanted to report them first. The best way to report first is to have the copy ready for press as the event is taking place. In the case of TV, this means before it happens, but they give it their best guess as to what is likely to happen next.

Some newspapers are little more than a political party's constant campaign forum. And if politics are involved, the campaigning is non-stop. These newspapers are easy to produce when no one holds the newspapers accountable for what they print. The newspapers disqualify their own sources, yet still print the story. And the public believes it because the media knows there are those who want to believe it. Desire supersedes truth.

All this authority and power/influence were given to the media by the public. The public did not challenge the media. The public simply acquiesced. Rarely will some group rise up and call for boycotts of products advertised by an untruthful media.

A letter to the editor might make the writer feel better, but calling for a boycott on an international social media forum might be more important – providing that the letter is not removed from the social media when opposing activists complain.

A Washington newspaper is one of the Liberal's forums, and then poorly operated local papers pick up the Washington newspaper's syndicated stories. Many of the local editors seem to approve the articles without even reading them. Perhaps the article is the length that the editor needed to complete a newsprint column. Practicality and accuracy are not friends. The media believes in H. H. Munro's – "A little inaccuracy saves tons of explanation."

A Washington newspaper article on December 5, 2018, had the lead-line – "Campaign Arm for House GOP Admits Hacking." ("GOP" is accurately translated into "Republican Party/ Conservative.")

Considering the current claims of "damaging hacking by Russians" (against the Liberals) this admission by the Conservative GOP Campaign Arm's hacking is very damaging for the GOP – as the bold lead-line was meant to convey.

Reading the whole article, however, the reader learns that the admission was <u>not</u> that the GOP was <u>doing</u> the hacking, but rather that the GOP had <u>received</u> the hacking. The paper did not have an accurate lead-line. This would have been "GOP Victim of Cyber-Attack."

When one considers the newspaper's political bias, he can understand why that newspaper printed the article that way. This style of reporting is not new. It is called in the business "yellow journalism" and it comes from a few years back. Yellow journalism defines the media which invests in little research or reporting of the facts, but functions by sensationalism and fabrication while giving no sources.

William Randoph Hearst, the publishing mogul of the New York Journal, and Joseph Pulitzer, the owner of the New York World, started representing powerful people who wanted Spain to sell Cuba to the United States. These people had plans for Cuba. Spain did not want to sell Cuba.

The newspapers continued to tell of the hardships that were being forced on the Cuban people by the distant, uncaring, tyrannical Spanish government. Because of the reporting, the citizens of the United States felt sorry for the Cubans.

Then there was another seasonal revolution in Cuba, but it was, as most were, stalemated with sporadic battles-of-opportunity by one side or the other. The New York newspapers kept publishing articles about the atrocities perpetrated by the government against agrarian Cuban citizens. The newspapers continued to propose that the United States should intercede in the revolutionaries' cause and then govern Cuba as an American territory. This was the desire of powerful businessmen in the United States.

Small, local skirmishes in Cuba would be magnified in the newspapers to read as major battles.

Hearst paid famous artist Frederic Remington to go to Cuba and by his planned, dramatic illustrations show the brutality of the war in Cuba. Remington went down and became bored with nothing to do in a rather peaceful Cuba, and in January 1897 he wired Hearst, "Everything is quiet. There is no trouble. There will be no war. I wish to return."

It was reported that Hearst wired back, "Please remain. You furnish pictures. I will furnish war."

A little later, when the United States battleship Maine exploded in the Havana harbor, Hearst ran the headline, "The War Ship Maine was Split in Two by an Enemy's Infernal Machine. There were 260 American deaths." Exciting illustrations accompanied the article.

A lot of people in Congress and most newspaper readers demanded that the United States declare war on Spain. This resulted in the United States being in a short war with Spain and Spain having no claim on Cuba.

Additionally, Guam and Puerto Rico would become United States territories, and for $20 million to Spain, the Philippines would have no alliances with Spain but with only the United States. The people in the Philippines thought they could do as well being self-governed. This was not permitted by Spain or the United States.

Thus the Hearst/Pulitzer type of newspaper reporting gained the name of "Yellow Journalism." It continues today because it works so well on a gullible public.

The press does not report the truth about historical events but rather recreates them.[11]

Another example of this was the reporting in May 1970 that "some students at Kent State University, Kent, Ohio, had a peaceful protest against the bombing of Cambodia by United State forces. They clashed with Ohio National Guardsmen on the campus. The result was that four students were killed by National Guard bullets."

Someone might wonder, 'Why was the National Guard even there? There were lots of demonstrations in the past that never justified mobilizing the National Guard.'

The National Guard back then did not have the attention it has today. Then, they were referred to as "weekend warriors" because they were committed to one weekend drill a month. (Today, they are an active complement to the United States Army and may serve with them on extended tours around the world.)

The following information is from newspapers being published at the time of the events.

On Friday, May 1st, "students, bikers, and out-of-town youths" clashed with local police. That evening the peaceful protestors threw rocks and bottles at the police officers and they lit several bonfires. [Fires excite; public fires excite the most. The Nazis knew this; as did the Ku Klux Klan.]

Bars were closed early because of the excessive drinking by the peaceful mob. Then because of the bar closings, students and others began to break windows and loot stores – and not just for liquor. The entire Kent police department, plus other police from nearby towns

---

11

In 1976, an investigation team determined that the Maine explosion was caused by an internal ship fire that set off the ammunition stores of the ship's powder magazine. This was an accident. There were no outside influences. At this point the truth makes little difference.

tried to quell the rioting. The next day, Saturday, the crowds had increased and the mayor declared a state of emergency and requested the governor to send the Ohio National Guard to protect property. The National Guard began to arrive that evening. When they arrived, they found the ROTC (Reserve Officer Training Corps) building at the university in flames.

When firefighters arrived on campus, students and non-students, at times as many as 2,000, jeered them and the fire hoses were sliced with knives. This occurred while the firefighters were trying to get water to the fire in an effort to extinguish it and limit the spread of flames to adjacent buildings. The National Guard was now trying to protect both the firefighters and themselves by using tear gas to disperse the crowd which was growing more bold and moving against the National Guard. The fire continued.

May 3rd, Sunday, there were 1,000 National Guardsmen on the campus. The governor accused the protesters of being unpatriotic as they continued to damage campus property.

The National Guard was outnumbered and were ordered to fix bayonets on their weapons for their own safety. All requests for the crowd to disperse and let the firefighters do their work were ignored.

On May 4th, Monday, some classes started and many students went to class. Protestors started rioting again and the university officials tried to ban the assembly of students for demonstrations.

The crowds grew and the National Guard again tried to use tear gas, but a change in wind dispersed the gas too rapidly. The crowds were throwing the tear gas canisters back at the National Guard and then the mob started throwing rocks. The crowd was shouting slogans such as "Pigs off campus!" Many rioters were non-students but activists just the same.

The crowds were approaching the National Guard. Seventy-seven Guardsmen were ordered to advance on the mob and 29 of the Guardsmen were separated from their group and found themselves being backed into a "vee" in high, chain-link fences. The Guardsmen were well-outnumbered and feared for their lives. They finally opened fire. The firing lasted 13 seconds – 67 shots were fired.

When the firing stopped, nine students were wounded and four were dead. For only 13 casualties from that size mob and when 67 shots were fired by a group of 29 guardsmen, it is apparent that some guardsmen were showing a lot of restraint. Two of the four dead were not part of the mob, but were dead elsewhere on the campus. These two were an average of 345 feet away. (Over a football field's length.)

These two could hardly have been targeted by the National Guard and this indicates that some Guardsmen were firing randomly over the mob's heads in an effort to get the rioters to back away from them.

It was understood by many people that after the rioting, looting, arson, and then the mob attacking young people like themselves (but these attacked young people were armed), then the natural result might be death.

Images show young Guardsmen, some younger than the rioters, looking confused – or scared.

Any unarmed person who challenges someone who is armed is showing very poor judgment. If the aggressive person has his judgment impaired by chemicals (alcohol included) then perhaps this was the reason for his dangerous behavior yet it was hardly an excuse.

Two of the four casualties were dead because of a riot that they were not a part of and it was the rioters who caused the shootings. The rioting could have stopped at any time and there would have been no shooting and much less property damaged or destroyed. Had the rioting stopped when the police had first arrived, there would have been no National Guard called out.

Each individual in a mob is responsible for the mob's action and the results. Anonymity in a mob/crowd does not justify criminal behavior but it often encourages it just the same.

Yet, in history, the "Kent State Killings" was labeled by the media as "excessive police response" with the National Guard being "the perpetrators."

According to the media, the rioting, looting, arsonist activists were apparently blameless.

Yellow Journalism.

The most recent source of media humor for many was the continued reporting of BP's (British Petroleum's) unfair treatment of

Gulf of Mexico small fishing businesses. The fishing industry was damaged by the BP drilling rig explosion and subsequent oil flowing into the Gulf. It was reported that BP had not been reimbursing the businesses for their claimed losses.

BP said that they would cover all losses, and to determine that loss, official tax withholding statements would be accepted by BP as proof of income before and after the oil spill. This not only seemed reasonable, but it was a clever way of determining loss.

However, in many, many cases these records were not provided, so the seafood company losses could not be determined. Those people not providing the tax withholding statements, which they certainly should have had, went to the media with a lot of the common complaints of the big-man-taking-advantage-of-the-little-man stories. Many small businesses operate on a cash basis so the in 1665 – needed paperwork might not be that accessible.

There are many reasons why these people did not receive compensation, and failure to provide the requested documents is but one. If the media is involved, the truth is difficult to determine.

Also, like global warming, anything about the horrors of big oil people destroying the planet makes good Liberal press, even when the candid images shown on the front page of the newspaper were impossibilities. The image as presented could not exist in nature, so perhaps it was a staged photo with a hoax for a story. Additionally, the TV news exposés were ludicrous to people who have eaten much shrimp – yet, the media's complaints and charges continued. All fresh shrimp have a dark "vein" down their backs; it is their natural digestive track. It is not crude oil.

The stories were upsetting in areas where the readers and viewers knew little about the seafood industry and their products, or when readers are possibly functionally illiterate.

Yellow Journalism.

The media is obvious, yet their deception works on enough people.

A recent newspaper headline read, "Black Mississippians Twice as Likely To Be Denied A Home Loan."

This behavior hardly seems fair and it is easy to imagine a lot of unhappy black people when they read that. The article was filled with one fact after another and the accuracy was easily accepted. The statistics were from a federally publicized database. However, the selection of the reported data was interesting.

As the various parameters of numerical data were read, the reader could consider each comparison of data and the text of the article. It was learned what the annual income was for Mississippians when compared to that of someone living in New York. This was interesting, but it was hardly relevant to the headline and one could wonder why it was there. Such literary distraction in the media is expected, still, the article had salient information.

Also well down in the long article it was learned that black Mississippians had an average income of $48,000 and the white Mississippian had an average income of $72,000.

This, in itself has nothing to do with loan approval because the amount of the requested loan was not listed. More important to the loan approval process might be the current debt and fiscal responsibility of the applicant in paying back previous financial obligations.

Additionally, the amount of the requested loan would make a difference in who is accepted and who is not, as would be the offered down payment on the item. If these were known, they were not in the article, but they are important points to consider when determining who is and who is not a good financial risk.

But the article was not about numerical accuracy or even about the understanding of the issue. All the mass of database information was just there, and to someone who is borderline, functionally illiterate it looked impressive and they would assume it supported the headline. The entire article was a little laborious to wade through, so it is likely that all the general reader saw was the headline. And the media is aware of this.

For someone who is literate and can associate various terms within one article and relate those parameters, then there were a lot of questions in the <u>reason</u> for the headline and the <u>purpose</u> of the headline. But maybe the reasons were not in the article but only in the implication. The headline was believable, but questions exist as to why it was true and if there was any discrimination in the loan approval process based on race? In the article, it appeared the approval process was based on financial conditions.

With all else being equal, one might expect there would be a difference in loan approval rates for people wanting to buy the same home when one makes less than 2/3rds per year than that of the other applicant. But with no mention of debt, even this is inconclusive.

There are a lot of times when the functionally illiterate would get the wrong impression by just reading headlines, banners, and parade signs in the media.

Yellow journalism.

– Social Media

Anyone reading the details of recent history will see that the height of many young people's (and too many other's) ambition is to become famous. An excessive number of people yearn to be celebrities. How they become celebrities seems to be of little importance.

Someone could wonder how this came about – this desire for fame. It was not built into those people living at the start of this social history.

Some people create their fame by committing horrific acts against their fellow man. It could be then proposed that was a successful life. His name would be everywhere on the physical and electronic media – sometimes for days – maybe months. Fifteen minutes of fame is not long enough for a lot of people. However, the day could come when 15 minutes of anonymity would be enjoyed.

Now, however, it seems that the citizen can be that celebrity. They can produce YouTube videos of anything they want, providing some pro-activist does not disapprove of it. The citizen can self-publish and have his books for sale on the Internet; however, in many cases graffiti on the side of a box car would likely be read by more people.

On social media there are the solicitations for "thumbs up" and "subscribe to me."

"American Idol," etc., has been replaced at the grassroots level by Facebook's constant pictures while few people turn down any "friend" request. The number of friends is more important than the actual friends.

And there is always the "do you like me?"

"I like you."

"Will you be my friend?"

But then there is the crushing humiliation when someone "unfriends" another. All this permits older adults to relive their similar, third-grade schoolyard angst.

Social Media is about "likes," power, and dominance. This is so popular that the business is now worth over $97 billion. Their stock continues to be recommended as "buy" for investors. The desire for recognition is making a lot of money for people, and that might be one of its greatest contributions. But to some families it can never offset the tragedy caused them by media bullies, or their being exposed to public reprisals for virtual slights.

Facebook et al. are like the many beauty pageants for every age of creature that exists. It is the market for the advertisements as seen with each opening by grandma to see how the grandkids are doing – provided that the kids have not "unfriended" her – and she can tolerate their cute vulgarities. Grandchildren are using language in front of Grandma that they would not want their Grandma using – and the grandchildren see no hypocrisy in this. They would prefer unfriending granny rather than their being imposed upon to clean up their vocabulary.

Some folks can excel by performance, and their names become household words; others have to pay for any degree of popularity.

Facebook is just one of many public forums. Malcontents use Facebook as a weapon and instead of drawing blood, they draw tears of disappointment. Perhaps malcontents have a right to entertainment the same as everyone else.

Faux socializing is still faux.

Virtual (socializing) means "implied."

However, if there is one thing the citizens were in 2018, it was self-centered and becoming more so. Consequently, righteous indignation now has no bounds and the citizen will complain to everyone about any and everything. With the media it is, "Americans have a right to know;" with the public it is, "Americans have a desire to hear something about it" – "it" being what was eaten at lunch.

Never in the history of the planet have more people been taking more images of themselves and sharing them with everyone else on the planet. Yes, it is easier now, but this latent desire to share their image with everyone known...as well as those unknown... is relatively new.

There was a recent time (in living memory) when people were too shy to want their photographs taken. Having one's photograph taken was considered to be vainglorious and it demonstrated a level of conceit to which one should not confess, much less demonstrate. Taking photos of others without their permission was offensive and the photographers were so informed.

Today, there seem to be no shy people – nor modest ones. The proliferation of cameras, still and video, allows those who want to share their image to do so – instantly – constantly. Thus, there is the home-grown, self-fostered celebrity status. "Hits" and "thumbs up" define the popularity index.

The implication is: 'I admired you, so now it is your turn to admire me.' In this, those on social media in 2018 have become a huge, mutual admiration society.

With all the cameras it has become just too easy. However, there should be the axiom – "Opportunity does not obligation create."

Americans are told by a computer when to click or tap a screen so one computer can communicate with another computer, and in that manner, someone they have never met nor would recognize on the street, will receive a computerized "Happy Birthday."

This will take place when the sender does not even know the birth date of their parents or grandparents. But it just takes a tap on a screen and a warm, heart-felt congratulatory message appears somewhere to add importance to someone's day. Such a "congratulation" is accepted in the same sense of affection as it was tendered.

It might be thought that the sender had received an email from a computer to do so, 'But still <u>he had to do the tapping!</u> That certainly indicates interest – maybe even affection!'

Celebrity status has no bounds nor are any means too petty.

Instead of the computer telling another computer to tell someone to send the message, it seems more efficient in this information age that the computer would skip the middle man and just send the "Happy Birthday" message itself.

*****

There is a strange condition of the mother who would bribe everyone in a school system to get her daughter on the high school cheer leader team, and then the young lady does bumps and grinds in public that got 1950-strippers jailed for performing in out-of-the-way, private lounges.

These non-adult cheer leaders are doing this in front of their teachers, the school body, and parents. And for the finale, she jumps high in the air, does a split – to expose her crotch to the faces of a stand full of citizens. If someone took a high-definition image at that moment and posted it on the World Wide Web, the mother would be bursting with fierce indignation and a defense that would seem more of an attack.

This is showing a strange sense of prioritizing.

The girl is seen by many more people than just those in the stands.

This is fame on social media.

(And Mom could have secretly planted the photographer in the stands.)

Section IV – The New Generations and Their Social Influences

Introduction

When considering where a society is on any timescale, first it should be determined if there were any seminal events (sudden or otherwise) that changed the society from what it was to what it is. Sometimes there are few significant influences over long periods. During those times society was stable and changes were slow (evolutionary), and what changes there were occurred in a seamless fashion. The people who were satisfied were happy and content to remain so; this defines the acceptable status quo.

Those who were unhappy still had a known set of circumstances by which they could make the changes that they thought could create the condition they desired. This could be a major revolution with a lot of bloodshed – or perhaps just learning a new craft/trade from the library or technical school. This might increase their chances for better employment with increased income. There is always a way.

During the period addressed by this study there was one particular, profound change in United States society and this influence continues today. And strangely, though it happened unintentionally, it can still be traced back to a single date: July 14, 1946.

If this change was good, no one can take credit for it because it was so unexpected.

If this change was bad, no one can be faulted because the extent of the change could not have been anticipated. But when the public had started this change, they had taken the first, irreversible steps to the society which exists in the United States in 2018 – and beyond.

No one was guilty of neglect or of any nefarious plotting, nor was there any subterfuge or deceit. Indeed, all intentions were not only inoffensive, they were also admirable!

And now, in hindsight, it can be determined that the responses were quite reasonable for the time. It all started with a simple, innocent little book.

July 14, 1946, a noted pediatrician published a comprehensive handbook: "The Common Sense Book of Baby and Child Care." This unassuming little book was to help young, modern parents raise their children. At the time, it would have been difficult to find any harm in this.

The author was Dr. Benjamin Spock.[12]

The many, many new parents of the just-married group at the end of World War II were not living near their parents and grandparents because of the national mobility that the prosperous age was causing. Consequently, when these newly-married couples were starting their families, their own family members (those who could share their experienced child-care instruction) were not readily available to the new parents. The experienced parents would have explained a traditional manner of raising a child.

With the publication of the child-raising book and the following, dedicated application of Dr. Spock's recommendations, there was a revolutionary change in infant and child care. This effort produced a different child, and this in-turn, a different adult – the adult who would then become a parent and influence his children.

Consequently, the book could be considered a breaking point between "traditional child rearing" and "systematic child rearing." And this, in general, created a new attitude. Therefore, in short order there was the New Child and the New Adult. And all this was from a pocket book.

In 1943, a contemporary popular writer, Ayn Rand, had her book "The Fountain Head," published, and then in 1957, "Atlas Shrugged" was published. Both books expounded on her philosophy, "Objectivism." These and her subsequent books were widely read – particularly among the intelligentsia. "The Fountainhead" became a high-budget movie.

---

[12] Dr. Spock was first mentioned on page 73, but then with just general comments. To have provided detail of him at that time would have been out of context. In this Section IV, *The New Generations and Social Influences*, there is a more thorough accounting of his significant history and influence.

Yet, Dr. Spock's unpretentious, nonintellectual, and literal pocket book about baby care has affected the United States far more so than has any part of the new philosophy of Objectivism.

Dr. Spock's book and its influence brought about a greater social change in the United States than even the end of WWII. All social changes are experiments – and most cannot be reversed. Many parents started raising their children by Spock's book and this represented the beginning of a social change. Though it was profound, it went unnoticed at the time.

Some social changes are abrupt and sometimes the changes are by armed revolution. Or just as abruptly, they might be accomplished by social engineers when a new order of society goes into effect with a law being enforced (or repealed) at the stroke of midnight. This might be by public/political persuasion or, seemingly, by social whim.

Dr. Spock's influence continues and our current society of 2018 is its unintended legacy.

Chapter 1 The Accidental Revolutionary

Benjamin Spock was born in Connecticut in May 1903. His father had been educated at Yale University and became a lawyer for a large railroad company. Benjamin Spock appears to have had a privileged childhood and attended the best schools. He did well in them, graduating with honors. He attended Yale and, while enrolled there, he won an Olympic gold medal in Paris for the Eight-Man Rowing Event.

Additionally, his academic/medical achievements were significant and he graduated first in his class from Columbia University's prestigious College for Physicians and Surgeons.

In 1927 Spock married his first wife, also from Connecticut. She helped him with his research and writing.

In 1946, Spock published "The Common Sense Book of Baby and Child Care." This was a little different set of ideas and instructions from what was traditional for the time and what had been published before. His book was a tremendous success. The first year, it sold 750,000 copies and by 1952 it had sold over 4 million.

When the United States became more involved in the Vietnam War, Spock, and many others, became vocally opposed to it and he joined in anti-war demonstrations.

He was involved in the politics of "The New Left." In 1967 he was encouraged to run as the vice-presidential candidate in the United States presidential race, and in 1972 he entered the presidential race as the presidential candidate for the socialist People's Party. In 1976, he was their vice-president candidate.

His wife was also active in Liberal causes and she was the mother of two sons. The Spocks were divorced in 1976 and that year he married a woman 40 years his junior. When first married, she was not as politically active as he, but she later joined him in Liberal issues and civil demonstrations.

They were arrested in demonstrations, and following one arrest, she sued officials of the Washington, D.C., government for sexual discrimination. With the support of the ACLU, she won her case against the mayor and police department for subjecting her to a more thorough search than they performed on others.

Spock was successful in business and public affairs and, as a professional, he always looked the part by dressing well. He generally wore Brooks Brothers suits and did not switch to something less expensive (denim) until he was 75 years old.

He did dress informally aboard his yachts where he and his wife lived for nearly 20 years. For quite a few years, they lived on their yacht in the British Virgin Islands. He was physically active most of his life. However, when Spock became seriously ill, he moved ashore.

His wife maintained an ongoing managerial function in his writing business.

Benjamin Spock died in 1998.

There is good reason to believe that Dr. Benjamin Spock has been the most influential man in American society since Adoph Hitler. For this to be explained in detail would require another book; however, the rationale can be presented simply. Comparing a known individual like Spock with an enigma like Hitler inspires serious considerations rather than mere media babble. In the serious thoughts lie the significance of the comparison.

Hitler caused WWII and this caused the biggest social effect on the planet from 1933 until 1991 when once again Germany was one country. That is a significant period of time with a great impact on humanity. During this wartime period, by Hitler's orders, six million Jews and near one million Romani (Gypsies) were sent to death camps. This has to be one of those pivotal points on most any historical time line. Hitler's brutality and infamy does not mean that he was not influential. Even examples to be avoided serve the public with all the accompanying warnings.

Some people thought Dr. Spock rated this level of societal influence. As an example, in 1999, *Life* magazine named Dr. Spock among the 100 most important people of the 20th century. To qualify Dr. Spock's social influence by the judgment of the *Time/Life* publishing empire, the other people that the publisher recognized can be considered.

Life's parent publication, *Time* magazine, had named Adolph Hitler the most important person in 1938 for his industrialization of Germany. Hitler's image appeared as such on the magazine's cover that year. The "most important person of the year" was an on-going feature of the magazine.

In 1939, by *Time/Life*'s judgment the most important person was Soviet Premiere Joseph Stalin. In the 1930s, Stalin had industrialized the medieval agrarian population of Russia. In 1947, shortly after WWII ended, *Time* again recognized Stalin. This time because he was the pivotal figure in the downfall of Berlin and the defeat of Germany. Additionally, he was then controlling most all of Eastern Europe.

In 1957, *Time* magazine recognized Soviet Premiere Nikita Khrushchev as the most important person. In just 10 years, he had nearly single-handedly destroyed the concept of Stalinism that had so damaged the Soviet Union.

And in 1979 *Time/Life* publications put an image of Ayatollah Khomeini on the cover as the most important. He was the revolutionary leader in Iran who over-threw the Persian monarchy to establish the Fundamentalist Islamic State, the Republic of Iran – with himself as the supreme political and religious leader for life.

Therefore, it can often be demonstrated that the most important influences in people's lives are people who had a great negative societal history. Social influences can come about for a variety of reasons and in many forms.

All these leaders who were recognized by *Time/Life* and referenced here caused considerable hardship for many millions of people, yet they were recognized by one of the most popular publishers in the world. Their cover portraits were prominently displayed on newsstands in most all countries.

All these people had instituted change.

Benjamin Spock had no negative agenda in his ground-breaking social change. It was just a trustworthy little book, "The Common Sense Book of Baby and Child Care." This was a book that appeared to come at the best time for many young families.

Chapter 2 The Book

"The Common Sense Book of Baby and Child Care" is one of the best-selling books in history. It sold 500,000 copies in the first six months, and in the first five years sold 4 million copies. It has now sold over 50 million copies in more than 40 languages.

In his book, Dr. Spock involved axioms and many disciplines – pediatric medicine, philosophy, and infant psychology. However, psychology is abstruse. This work still hinges on Dr. Sigmund Freud's seminal work of the 1890s. When this medical field is applied in the intellectual community of adults, it is very difficult to do so predictably because it is near metaphysical. To compare hidden agendas in the adult mind with those persuasions in an infant's mind is very risky, but the effort took place nonetheless.

After Dr. Spock's telling parents that they knew more than they thought, he told them what to think. Additionally, he told them, basically, what the infant was thinking. It looked so good on those 638 pages. (The author re-read "The Common Sense Book of Baby and Child Care" in preparation for this book.)

Dr. Spock used a lot more philosophy than medicine. His philosophy was contrary to tradition and this tradition went back in Western Society to perhaps – maybe to the first humans.

The many, many new American parents in the just-married group at the end of World War II did not have the benefit of their parents' and grandparents' counsel in child care. But with Dr. Spock's book and the dedicated application of the Spock child-raising ideas, there was a revolutionary change in infant and child care. And this produced a revolutionary child.

This could be considered the break between "traditional child rearing" and "modern child rearing." His new approach produced a new sort of child and that child grew to have children, and therefore Dr. Spock's influence continues generation after generation.

Even if the first generation of Spock-children did not read his book to raise their own children, they would have been imprinted by their parents' training in "proper" parent/child relationships. The impact continues today in nearly every American home and this has been a more long-lasting social change in the United States than had been the end of WWII.

All social changes should be considered experiments – and few of these can be reversed. It has been 72 years since the publication of Dr. Spock's book. At some point it will have to be called "the traditional method of raising children."

These modern parents were being taught by "The Common Sense Book of Baby and Child Care" that the child was a member of the family and should, therefore, be integrated into the functioning family unit. This philosophy sounded so good and seemed to make sense. This is why it was applied in so many young families.

According to the book, the child should be involved in the family and not treated as an outsider. This inclusion would foster a greater sense of belonging. Apparently, the child was to be treated not as just a child but as a miraculous child; one who could easily be integrated into adult society. This appealed to parents and child alike.

Many liberal parents were raising children by "The Common Sense Book of Baby and Child Care."

Conservative parents would have had a lot of issues with Dr. Spock's teaching. They would see it as a significant break from the way they understood children were to be raised – meaning – the way they were raised. Theirs was the traditional way. And they, being conservative, were more likely to desire an acceptable status quo rather than try some new idea to change a very old tradition.

A person generally does not need a book to explain what tradition and the status quo is. Such books as "The Common Sense Book of Baby and Child Care" are meant to change from tradition – and it did.

In a developed, industrialized, modern nation, "Common Sense" usually meant "traditional," but not in the case of this book. The book was well-marketed. Dr. Spock became very popular.

Though this change was not so noticed in the beginning, neither is an acorn falling from an oak tree, yet time shows a significant change. And it took time for the impact of Spock-child ideas to mature. The fact that the change took time to recognize does not make it any less revolutionary. The change was abrupt – but the results, the impact, took a few years to notice – maybe seven or so.

For social instruction, it is less important now for new parents to read his book because these parents were imprinted with behavior to which they themselves were exposed when younger. They had been childhood friends with some who may have been "Spock-raised" and so they saw the way their child-friends were treated in their homes and in-turn how that child treated his parents. This is the "avalanche effect in raising children" – the children from a "Spock couple" will in turn influence their children accordingly. <u>This is not conjecture if social statistics are believed</u>.

It has been written that any parents who show affection to their children and encourage them to be themselves have Dr. Spock to thank. However, those who were raised in the 1930s and before 1946 can only wonder how their parents knew to do this before "The Common Sense Book of Baby and Child Care."

[Again, here, the author can speak from experience.]

We were not encouraged to be ourselves – we already were ourselves. But we knew we had a lot of maturing to do. We were encouraged to be the person we would like to be. There are many children who, when they did become the person they wanted to be, had become adults whom their parents would not want living next door. This defines wholesome parenting – not cloning.

Mostly we were encouraged to be self-sufficient and a credit to society. This defined the "adult." In society the desire was to blend, not upset – nor "activate."

With the consistent application of the child-rearing principles in Dr. Spock's book, homes had become debating arenas where the child had the same authority as the parents, but the children were louder and more persistent. This created a home-life of contention and competition...and worse, the child came to feel that he was always entitled to accommodation. And he expected it right then. Children have never been known for their patience.

This new child, when deprived, feels that he is a victim and his parents should be punished in some manner for victimizing him. He would think of some way to get even. However, being but a child, his judgment might be suspect and his response inappropriate.

As society was changing, many people started asking what had happened. Spock's book kept being mentioned. What he had written in the book seemed innocent enough, but the book's success was greater than anyone could have imagined. There were many, many parents applying his book in every detail in raising their children. These parents were content in the knowledge that they were raising modern, healthy children.

Yet, in a 1968 New York Times interview, Dr. Spock admitted that his book contributed to an increase of permissive parenting in the United States. He said that the parents were afraid to impose on the child in any way. In a following book edition he did say that parents should set standards of behavior and ask for respect. (Not "require" nor "demand," but "ask.")

However, there were already a lot of his earlier books in print and application. By Spock's not addressing the overall message, it meant that these children, as adults, would continue to create narcissistic children.

The success of his book encouraged other notables to agree with him and then the creation of another entitled generation continued.

Chapter 3 The Results
Introduction

There have been passing comments offered by the author on his life and to some extent that of his wife's, but these were not to imply that there were no books to advise the young family in child care. Even then young, new parents were on the move and not living next door to relatives. But this was not because of industrial growth – quite the contrary – it was because of industrial stagnation – the Depression. This scattering of families was because of the absence of jobs in a nation of organized scarcity.

Yet, apparently, even without books, children were being born and raised and society was progressing by the same advances and setbacks as that which had occurred before and after such modern child-raising books were available.

Considering the expectations of American parents of 1935, or of even 1835, there were many similarities. The same could be said of Western European parents of 1735 and earlier.

Back then the child was given what tasks he could perform as soon as he was old enough to walk without the immediate prospect of falling. Many people lived on farms and there was always something needing done there and children going about their chores freed the adults for tasks which only they could perform.

A child's small size and nimbleness permitted him to get into small spaces and gather eggs more efficiently than could an adult. This was not "make-work" – this task was necessary and it contributed to the welfare of the family. Children knew they were expected to "help out."

In the cities, the same considerations applied to the child worker. In the textile mills there was a lot of lint in the air which would collect in various places and ball up. Should one of these balls float into a loom, many yards of valuable cloth could be compromised. It was a good job for a child to scoot around under machines and stairs and around doorways and gather this lint before it could damage the production of fabric. This was a never-ending and necessary task.

The only distinction was that the lad did a child's work for a child's wage until he was 16, then he was expected to do an adult's job for an adult's wage. And once he was earning the adult's wage, he could enter the company of adults; this would include visits to the local drinking halls.

Some young men could be assigned to a tradesman in a village, or to the church, and so elevate himself in society. In all this, there was no consideration for "play time." The child was a financial burden and needed to contribute to his upkeep as well as he could. Children understood this. This had been built into (their) traditional child rearing.

It had been in the late 1500s of Elizabethan England that there were Poor Relief Acts. These regulations made each parish responsible for the poor children in their area. This was church charity and an old idea and practice.

In the 1600s, adults started seeing children as separate beings and they, being innocent, deserved an adequate level of nurturing.

The English philosopher John Locke was significant in changing the thinking in parental responsibility. In 1690, he stated that a child's mind was blank at birth and it was the duty of the parents to set in the child's mind the proper ideas of convention. His belief was that the child could be led into getting an education and then the child would willingly enter a higher plane of study and understanding.

The increase of capitalism and the rise of the middle class encouraged the acceptance of child rights. But these rights were very basic, in that the poor child had a right to sustenance and an acceptance in society, and there was to be a communal concern for the child's soul.

Jean-Jacques Rousseau (1712 - 1778) enlarged on Locke's ideas of children's rights with the idea that childhood was for fun and games. He proposed that the hardships of being an adult in an adult world was so harsh that children should not have to face this until the short childhood days were over (around 12 years old). He made the point that once these days were lost they were gone forever. (This is not true today, but back then "retirement" meant "death.")

While Rousseau's ideas are worthy of consideration, his life and parenting history are examples to be avoided. Philosophers are often this way. What they write or say has precedence over what they did. Rousseau's political essays defining Liberalism, Conservatism, and Socialism are valid even today.

In the late 1700s, the general idea being presented in art was that the child was innocent and had an angelic countenance. This idea became popular. While at the same time (1744) children's books became more easily read so that they might continue to inspire and entertain the young mind. These led to the general belief that children should learn to read and write and draw and enjoy a more pure intellectual existence.

This idealistic view of childhood continued during the Romantic period (1800 - 1850) with the exception of the Calvinist's view that the child had an animal's mind with all its inhuman responses. According to Calvinists, this was the child (or adult) without discipline. The Calvinists believed that both needed a lot of disciplining. (A lot of disciplining!)

In 1960, it was argued by French historian Philippe Ariès that "childhood" was a concept created by modern society. He found, and it can be readily determined by many social histories, that before the 1600s children were mini-adults physically, and child-rearing activities were appropriate for the circumstances, this is for the context – time and place. This states it was appropriate in both family and village life.

This is not as it is today where all families look at TV.

[From the author's personal experiences.]

Both my and my wife's family knew from experiences that when we were poor or low, low middle-class, we did not have any government person making a big issue of telling us that we had fallen through the safety net of poverty, or some such, nor were we told that we deserved more than we had. We just did not have much and that was because of circumstances, but we believed that better days were coming. I remember no talk that would even hint at victimization.

When my wife was very young, she was picking cotton with her mother and sisters when they learned that her father had gotten a job in the oil fields. She immediately dropped her cotton sack and walked out of the field. Indeed, better days were coming!

We were not watching TV and seeing how rich people lived all the time we were being poor. There was no TV then, and the radios required the listener's imagination. To the poor, radio "life" was healthy and inspiring; TV life for the poor is discouraging, depressing, and debilitating.

– The New Child

Dr. Spock taught parents to accommodate the feelings of the child and consider his preferences. Before then the children had learned self-denial/restraint and to respect/obey authority. The first level of authority in the child's life were his two parents (two). If the child had asked the parents who the top level of authority was in the parents' lives, they would have likely said "God." This was, in their belief, that He was a "Heavenly Father" and the only true judge.

In a structured society everyone experienced various levels of authority to which they would have to ascribe or they might suffer the consequences for their contrary behavior. This worked for children – this worked for adults. But this changed for children in the modern era.

Now, self-indulgence took the place of self-control and self-denial. However, "self" still remained paramount.

To determine who was running the household, it would often depend on who had the most energy since supposedly they were all equal in the family unit.

No one was identified as the family leader. It was democracy in action – a loud and sometimes hurtful democracy with no accepted authority. In one sense, it could be a mob mentality.

Generally, the most dynamic and persistent person has the most influence. This certainly describes a child and not his working parents. This would naturally teach the child to defy unpleasant decisions and demand that his desires be satisfied, and they generally were satisfied in this environment. Gratification became the norm. Even Dr. Spock acknowledged this later.

Authority was dismissed by the very definition of the word "self," and "self" was the decision criteria.

[The author, growing up before "The Common Sense Book of Baby and Child Care" can address the expectations of the child before 1946.]

As children, we were prepared for the rigors of adulthood. The boys played rough-and-tumble games and were taught to "be men." The girls played with dolls and were taught to "be good mothers."

Besides "men do not cry," we boys were taught to grit our teeth, clench our fists, and learn to bear what we could not change. We knew that life was not fair. Life just was. We were to cope. We were not special. We were just kids and sometimes there was bad luck. This was no one's fault. The word "victimization" was not used then because it was not yet a social precept.

The parents were the child's role models. The parents knew this and took this responsibility seriously. After becoming parents, they altered their own behavior accordingly.

We were taught to respect authority – we had better – especially when the authority was armed. Some authority was armed with a gun; some with a paddle. Both deserved consideration and we respected them.

There would be a lot of times when we would want something, but we did not get it without some effort. The effort might be earning better grades in school or presenting a more cheerful attitude when asked to perform a chore around the house.

In these life-lessons we would gain self-respect and self-confidence and in general, social acceptance. We were supposed to have pride in ourselves, and we were right to desire that others respect us. If someone hit us, we hit them back. This would teach them to leave us alone. This actually worked really well. I know from experience – and not just mine, but I observed playground behavior around me. Standing up for ourselves did not always work, but it worked a lot better than our other choice – run tell the teacher. The teacher would hear about it later anyway from students. She understood about bullies and had experience with them. The school had a way of taming them – this was a long time ago.

We knew that telling a teacher was putting our responsibility off on someone else. We did this when we accepted that we could not take care of ourselves. But we were trying hard to learn to take care of our business because transferring our responsibility to others was the least preferred response.

We had figured out in our own minds basically what a Roman had said a long time ago – "To fight with a little guy is bullying; to fight with a big guy is stupid; to fight with someone our size could be a real bad fight."[13] Best would be not to fight anyone and try to be nice to everybody. We found things went better when we did this.

However – during the first generation of the new children being raised by "The Common Sense Book of Baby and Child Care," there were parents starting to speak up about the new child-training principles. Some said that Dr. Spock's approach would foster a sense of self-indulgence instead of self-control. It was understood that children certainly needed to be taught routines and learn self-control because their natural responses were generally not socially acceptable.

By making children active members of the family, the children justifiably assumed that they could speak up and they did. They started arguing with adults without anticipating punishment, and in general they developed a child/parent relationship where the leadership role of the parent was sometimes difficult to determine.

Parents were telling their child that they were his "best friends." This is quite a demotion from that of being his "parents."

There were parents who thought that "Mother," "please," and other words that indicated any semblance of rank would instill in the child a sense of subservience within the family unit. Many parents were having their child use first names for them, but this never became that popular because it was awkward in society.

In every discussion, the child had the advantage. They could be more persistent. They could be louder, and they could be petulant and use any personal device to get what they wanted.

Such levels of self-indulgence were difficult for the adults to attain because they had responsibilities. The child had no responsibility, but still expected to be satisfied. The children could tell the parents exactly what they wanted. They had seen it on TV.

They could define the item by general identity and then by the manufacturer, the model number and the price – and the source.

13

Seneca (4 BC - 65 AD) A basic social thought, presented here in kid-English.

TV had already done the "market research" for the child. The parents just had to go get the item from wherever they were sent. The parent was TV's "delivery system." In this situation, parents had become the first Amazon Prime, but a free one for the child customer.

In time, the child was learning to manipulate the parents, and in a short period, he assumed that it would always be that way. By experience, he expected satisfaction. There was no self-sacrifice and he only had to make sure that the parents understood exactly what was desired. Such gratification only required some loud and persistent "communication."

Near-instant gratification came to be seen as a right of childhood. And many of their playmates were learning the same lesson. Such reinforcement of an assumed right makes its expectation more firm.

Previous, traditional child-rearing had a very stern overtone because it was a product of a hardworking environment. Fathers did not want their sons to grow up to be sissies, but to be tough – therefore, childhood was a non-combative boot camp where the child was prepared for a rough, hard, and sometimes unfair adulthood.

Spock thought children needed affection and nurturing of the more emotional kind. The hardships of young adulthood would come soon enough.

However, in prescribing a more sensitive fostering, he did not allow for the natural tyrannical desire in children. They want what they want when they want it and to have it refused will cause retaliation.

The child was becoming the entitled member of the family. If he were refused, the child, as expected, would resent it and rebel at the rejection of his expressed desires. He had not been taught that he demanded too many things, instead, he naturally wondered why his parents hated him. He may ask in a loud voice from a faux wounded soul, "Why do you hate me!!!"

This is always painful for the parent to hear. Every time. And it will generally have the effect desired by the child. The child learns by example.

Something had gone wrong.

The child had been coddled and loved and often experienced acts of affection, but now he has decided that his parents must hate him and that the parents are victimizing him. This new parent understood how to get back in the good graces of their child – with more accommodation of the child's desires (not needs). This would restore the harmony in the family – for a while. The child can desire many things from watching TV.

In due course, Dr. Spock's influence had children who had learned to sass their parents, and this demonstrated the lack of respect the child had for his benefactors. If children did not respect their parents, they were not likely to respect the next level of authority – school officials.

By the 1960s it was not unusual that after a family visit to family friends, some adult would ask, "Did you hear the mouth on that kid?! If I had spoken to my parents like that, I would have gotten an immediate smack across the mouth."

And in a lot of families, the child would have. The child would not become a tyrant because of this, but rather he would definitely learn that there are times when he should keep his thoughts and feelings to himself. Shakespeare wrote, "Mind your speech lest ye mar your fortune." This is good advice for all children – as well as for their parents.

Teens, having more mobility than younger children, started to show less moral restraint. "If it feels good, do it." That did not come from some child's imagination. It was a natural response to how they were being raised.

The teen crime rate and truancy started to increase as SAT scores started to decrease. Young people became more interested in their short-term pleasures than having any concern for their own long-term best interests.

The young had no reason to respect the authority of the school teacher nor that of the school administrators — or any other authority with whom they disagreed. If the young did not understand the reasons for the authority's comments (and in the youth's lack of life-lessons they would misunderstand many things), then they had no interest in obeying a regulation for which they could not understand the reason. THAT to them was tyranny and they learned this from lenient parents, not strict ones. They should have learned about such "tyranny" at home and how to work with it or cope with it.

The parents made sure that the school administrators respected their child's uniqueness. Education suffered from this. This created poor students. Poor students created poor teachers. This resulted in poor education for everyone. The teachers were being blamed for faults caused by poor parenting.

The modern solution is to get the child out of the home and into an educational institution as soon as possible. Thus, there was Kindergarten for children 5 years old, though some parents held their child back until he was 6. Kindergarten prepared them to enter the first grade of Elementary School. Kindergarten is still not required in all states.

Then later it was necessary that there be a Head Start program to prepare the child for Kindergarten. This is for the child who is 3 and 4.

Yet, later, it became desirable to have an Early Head Start to prepare the child for Head Start. Early Head Start is for infants and toddlers under 3 – <u>and</u> for pregnant women!

If the future mom is in Early Head Start then the full life-range is covered. A person who was in an education facility from fetus to 18 years old should have a superb education! But it might be a rather expensive one for the taxpayers, because after 18, the student can then be in another school as an undergraduate or postgraduate.

Undergraduates can borrow $12,500 a year up to $57,500 total and postgraduates can borrow $20,500 a year up to $138,500. The undergraduate loans will be "forgiven" in 20 years; the postgraduate in 25 years.

Someone else had put up the money for the loans to start with – the producers paying taxes. Adding the burden of "forgiven" student loans to the real cost of education in the United States is certainly a lot of money. It is only assumed that the taxpayers will see a return on their investment.

Money does not promise better education, nor does the increase of schools, nor does the time spent in schools.

– The New Adult

The only influence that the New Adult could tolerate was one which gave him something, and Liberal/Socialist governments do give.

Conservative governments generally just offer opportunity and expect effort in return. When choosing how the New Adult should vote, it was obvious – "Why vote for a Conservative? What did they ever give me?"

The New Adult wanted to be fair, but by their understanding of "fair." This means, take from the rich and give to the poor. In doing this, there would be fewer rich people and fewer poor people. This shows a misunderstanding of basic production and civic responsibility.

Robin Hood is a folktale. Liberal governments are real – and expensive.

Socialist leanings are consistent with a society which does not practice personal responsibility – they want someone else to make the hard decisions for them – and then do the hard work. They have been taught to receive, but being required to contribute something in return seems rather demanding. They could indignantly but correctly think, 'That is not a gift. That is a swap!' This, they did not need. Particularly if it involved restraint, self-control, or self-denial.

Any authority that expected something from them was disliked and should be replaced. Many took to the streets. Dr. Spock was there with them defying authority – and they all thought themselves noble while doing so. Dr. Spock's political convictions put him in the camp of legions of young people who were often perceived as living dangerous, free-and-easy lives. And the majority of them were much influenced by him.

Because they were part of a mob, they thought that they gained individual importance, and at the same time, they thought they could divorce themselves from the behavior of the mob. Mob behavior does not work that way. The sense of personal responsibility goes down in a mob. This comes from the idea of anonymity. Responsibility and anonymity are thought to be mutually exclusive. This could be the reason a robber wears a mask.

The individual will still need to make his own decisions – the first of which is whether or not to join the mob.

The free-love and self-indulgence of the era was easy to understand in the age of "If it feels good, do it." The Sexual Revolution was spinning up – as were Sexually Transmitted Diseases. This became so endemic in the new generations that it was talked about so much it was unpleasant to hear. This took away some of the fun.

Discussing Sexually Transmitted Diseases sounded like there was to be some responsibility and control involved. It would be more pleasant to drop those offending words and just use the initials. "STD" sounded ever so much nicer – as in "Standard." The adult was learning to reshape concepts by renaming them and even inventing words. This procedure is very familiar today.

The Sexual Revolution that started in the 1960s is over and the citizen lost. Before the sexual revolution there were about five identified Sexually Transmitted Diseases – now there are over 50. There are a lot of ways to have sex, so there are a lot of variations in the chemical mixes and hybrids possible from a multitude of individuals coming from many continents and cultures.

It is very unlikely that in the few years of a little pocket book's influence, which saw its first products on the streets in the early 1960s, that human nature had changed.

People can change their appearance in a few minutes. They can change their personality in a few weeks. They can change their character only by extreme events which are generally well outside the likelihood of statistics, but to change their very nature would take some serious influences for a long time. There are a few million years of preparation to this point, but something had changed. And it had changed in a very short period.

The public's simple response to opportunity has changed. Sometimes they should say "yes" but sometimes, it should be "no."

Yet there is the thought still of 'if it feel good, do it.' If someone said "no" to this, they might think it to be some form of self-abuse, or so the entitled could think.

Parents are responsible for teaching the child self-control. This is difficult to do with the entitled child.

In a dynamic social situation, whether business or school, self-control is expected. Biting the tongue to keep from speaking and keeping thoughts inside is an exercise in self-control.

Leaving other people's property alone is an exercise of self-control if one is tempted to make that property his own.

In the last 60 years, the nation has experienced a moral collapse. The lack of self-control and the increase of indulgence, along with the sense of entitlement, will have a negative influence on most any stable, traditional society.

Since 1960, the rate of violent crimes has more than tripled. Every day there are news reports of heinous crimes unheard of in America two generations ago. Children murder their playmates, their teachers, and their parents. Teenage mothers abandon their newborn babies in trash cans, and every year students commit carnage on their classmates. The American culture has sunk so low that children are no longer safe with their teachers in school or at church – scores of men and women are arrested every year for preying on the children under their care.

There will always be a weapon. As the self-absorbed become smarter, the gun will be deemed old fashioned. It will become as outdated as the spear or stone club. A strange powder tossed in a school ventilation system will not work as fast as a gun, but it will do more long-term harm.

Dr. Spock had his legions of imitators because it is easy to jump on a successful and lucrative bandwagon. They knowingly smiled and nodded at his endemic wisdom, but not everybody agreed with his philosophy in raising children.

A nationally recognized and respected motivational speaker and author, Dr. Norman Vincent Peale, decided that Dr. Spock's philosophical advice was the root of the national problem. He alleged that "the United States was paying the price of two generations that followed the Dr. Spock baby plan of instant gratification."

Also, in the 1968 New York Times interview, Dr. Spock stated he "would be proud if the idealism and militancy of youth today were caused by my book."

And many thought it had.

It has been suggested that there was a hidden agenda in the publication of his book.

Dr. Spock was a very, very smart man – but not that smart. The results were unintended, but he liked the results just the same and he was happy if he had unknowingly caused them. This does not indicate a long-range plot. His comments reflect that he is just taking advantage of circumstances...as many people do.

He did later reverse himself on male circumcision – he decided it was unnecessary and circumcision really did not reduce cervical cancer. Now, more is known about medicine and this includes female cancer.

Some of Spock's recommended procedures were wrong because he did not have knowledge of Sudden Infant Death Syndrome, and that babies should not be put on their stomachs for the night as he recommended. However, when the book was published, this information was current in pediatric teaching. Surely, he cannot be faulted for this.

Some of his pediatric advice continued to cause questions. He wrote that parents and nutrition experts should place children over the age of two on a vegan diet. His co-author, another pediatrician, publically said that Spock's statements were extreme and that few parents would be able to properly plan the diets for the young. The co-author said that the results would be young people suffering from nutritional deficiencies.

Again, there was no suggestion that the child should be treated sternly and taught that he was not an adult but was a child, and children do not determine how a household is to function. Yet, supposedly, the young person was to be a vegan by the mere acceptance of his advice.

[The author again writes from experience –]

The people that my generation had grown up with were doing sufficiently well, but after Dr. Spock's book, it was learned that we were all raised incorrectly – indeed, dangerously! We all seemed to have been raised violently by negligent and abusive parents.

My wife being "made of sugar and spice and everything nice" was a more fit parent than I was, but then, she should have been. We had a few hundred thousand years of genetic history in us. Men and women's genetic makeups are not the same because of this. There are a lot of subjective preferences built into each's gene pool.

The issue became that it was Dr. Spock's coddling that appealed to the young parents, but the problem with a lot of philosophies is that humans (animals) respond to challenge and response; they are not as logical and mechanical as one might prefer - they do not react the same each time to the same stimuli – even when that same stimuli occurs only 15 minutes apart.

The parents always had more legal authority and responsibility; however, apparently, they could not exercise it without exposing the child to damaging tyrannical lessons. All the new parental instruction did not create a quiet household of known social positions and boundaries in the family. Instead it created a near-constant atmosphere of confrontation and competition. The home became a coliseum for a war of wills. The natural, child-competition with parents became the new rules of engagement on the home battlefield.

"Because I said so" had been the ultimate conclusion between parent and child differences for a very long time, and this had worked, but now this was considered to be unacceptable in modern child rearing. Such demonstrations of power over the child might lessen the child's self-esteem. He might think that he was not the parents' equal just because he was of a smaller form. So there was less peace until the parents acquiesced to the child early and often.

Besides "parents" might have become "parent." If "parent," the parent is working and other people are providing the social education the child requires. These people would be professionals and many with modern liberal educations – just as Dr. Spock's books advised.

And again, "Liberal" means change and "Conservative" means tradition. Dr. Spock broke with tradition and replaced it with a change – a Liberal philosophy.

The new parents had been taught that the child was a member of the family and if he was to learn responsibility he should be involved in many of the family dynamics. Also in populist thinking, punishment only made children victims of adult oppression and such punishment would foster a child desiring to employ physical violence himself. It was being stated that any hands-on punishment would make the child a bully and teach the child brutality.

Again this logic sounds good, but elevating the child to adult importance created a small mind with a lot of influence. The brain of a child is missing a lot of "life-long learning" – experience.

Gone were the previous days of children being children and outside the business of adults. Gone were the days when they were to be seen and not heard.

The new Liberal way has not worked out too well. There is more youth violence today and the social media is the weapon of choice. Before Dr. Spock, the bully might get a smack in the mouth by the victim's older brother – but not now. There is no hitting. At least not physical, but on social media some child can be destroyed socially and spiritually.

At some point, the focus of the bullying, the victim, might resort to the simple expediency of suicide. This is extreme in itself and might also reflect the disillusioned new child in the real, sometimes brutal world. The bullying target might not have been prepared for a harsh world. He might have been coddled and told many untruths.

*****

It became obvious that there was a lack of descriptive terms for the generations of children raised by the Spock book and then for these children as adults. This condition was noticed in the early 60s when the first Spock children were becoming adults and could then function independently of parents.

These generations were grouped by age because it was assumed they had similar psyches and therefore had similar responses to marketing. These names of the generations are the results of consumer sampling and media identity. They are generally humourous and exaggerated in writing and reporting.

The cute and whimsical names of generations are:

Traditionalist or Silent Generation – Born before 1945
Baby Boomers or Me Generation – Born 1946 - 1964
Generation X – Born 1965 - 1976
Millennials or Gen Y – Born 1977 - 1995
Gen Z, iGen, or Centennials – Born 1996 - ?

These names are for the most part products of marketing research and if "Z" is the last letter of the alphabet, then it might be assumed there will be no generation after "Z." There probably will be, but since they are not heavy consumers yet, no market research or generation name is necessary.

– Infantile Entitlement Syndrome (IES)

After considerable reading, research, and thought, it was determined that there should be a term to define the new social condition being discussed. This term would apply to those who matured after the new child development program, "The Common Sense Book of Baby and Child Care" came into being in the mid-1940s. This was a definite break from traditional child development.

Freudian classifications are used for infant phases. Other researchers use terms like narcissism, grandiosity, and indulgence. There is a narcissism phase in Freudian infant psychology. It is explained that as the infants grow, they are to lose much of this narcissism and become less self-centered and a more responsible child, and then adult. But this is only possible if parents apply correct procedures in their rearing and this requires responsible parents with a desire to produce a socially compliant child and adult.[14]

The author determined that what describes the product of Dr. Spock's social restructuring is "Infantile Entitlement" (IE). This term is consistent with other's research, as well as how the child was imprinted when much of Dr. Spock's philosophy was put into practice. And as a philosophy, his was very, very good, and that was its appeal – and that was also its unrecognized danger. Some philosophies might be good, but rarely when executed by mere man.

In time, these children experiencing Infantile Entitlement (IE) became adults and they wondered why things were not happening in the way they expected and/or had been taught. Now as adults they became parents, and whether they bought the Dr. Spock book or not, they would use their parents as role models. This, however, does not mean that they respected them. The parents were just there in the

---

14

James L. Fosshage & Sandra G. Hershberg (2014) *Specialness, Grandiosity, Omnipotence, Entitlement, and Indulgence: Changing Theories of Narcissism, Attitudes, and Culture, Psychoanalytic Inquiry, 34:5, 381-382, DOI: 10.1080/07351690.2013.846046*

background. It is difficult for them not to relate their lives to those of their children. The more satisfied the adult is with his own upbringing, the more likely this is to occur.

IE is not a binary function; it is not "on" / "off." It is not a digital function but is analog – there are levels in IE. There could be a trace of it in an adult because of his association with friends who were at a lower degree of IE – meaning their parents were applying less of the philosophy than another set of parents. And children do key off other children. This is the source of – "Why can't I have one?! John has one – and so does Martha!"

Hence, there will be a second generation with IE inclinations. The extent of the IE influences will vary by the natural variability of human responses, so IE is not a fixed condition but rather an influence. Some adults would have been more influenced than others; consequently, IE can be considered as a "syndrome" and there would be a variation of the syndrome, or a spectrum of influence. So concluding that someone was influenced by, or having IE, they may be at the low end of the IE Syndrome (IES) spectrum rather than at the high end, which would have been a greater influence.

However, their parents being raised by the Dr. Spock book will be somewhere on the IES spectrum themselves.

So the influence of IES can be passed on and can logically be considered as if IES were a communicable disease or genetic trait rather than just a social condition. Many conditions today are called diseases, so IE can be considered a syndrome that one might inherit socially – as if it were mores, or expected behavior.

In the case of someone on the IES spectrum, the natural thought process could be that there is no reason that one spouse should tolerate indignities from a mate who thinks that he is more entitled than his spouse. It was easier living at home. They knew they were special there. So they go back home – with or without their children.

Dr. Spock's book correctly taught that children needed affection and nurturing of the more emotional kind. But tough lessons and preparation for the setbacks and hardships of the adult life were missing, and some of these hardships became real soon enough. Because the young adult was unprepared, these problems and setbacks seemed worse than if they had had older, traditional training.

This compounding of the IES can be understood to be passed on with each new generation. The possibility of a return to a more stern but constructive child-raising process would not be at all likely.

Traditional child-rearing is now considered barbaric at most any level – indeed, it can easily be criminal and result in a chargeable offense. Social services have removed children from homes for less. Surrendering children to the institution of government has never been easier – after all, there is Early Head Start available.

Consequently, by 1963 the first generation of IES children was 23 years old and many were unhappy. Things were not as wonderful as what they had experienced at home. Yet, drugs can make things seem better. In 1976 there was the first generation of Spock babies producing their own babies in their own image, and in 2018 there would have been the third generation already 12 years old.

The IES by any name is well into the social psyche and many of these people are generating new laws to eliminate a lot of tradition.

This IES will continue and we see evidence of it daily.

They do not know that in their sense of entitlement (which they acquired unconsciously when they were very, very young) they can have no appreciation for the moment because they have no understanding of history. History is not likely to be important to someone who is entitled, special, and in general, uniquely grand.

They might likely be with only one parent present and they may see the other only on holidays and birthdays. This, then, is more of a temporary diversion than a constant influence. In this case, the child will be experiencing only one level of influence with the predominant parent. This may be good or bad, but it does reduce the range of influences to which the child could be exposed should there be two full-time parents. However, with only one parent, the child is more likely to spend his most formative years in institutions organized and operated by adults similar to the child's parent. And the parent that the child sees only on special occasions will likely be bringing gifts and acquiescing to the child's desires.

Those suffering from narcissism or some level of IES are not likely to think they could be wrong about something as important as child-rearing.

However, should these people show bad judgment and hard times befall them because of their actions, they will likely not blame themselves, nor in other cases, accept that it was just uncontrolled circumstances. They will think that someone else must have caused it ... so someone else should fix it. Or, indeed, there may be a plot – or even a conspiracy. They can become paranoid rather than accept personal responsibility. Accepting responsibility was not in the regimen of youth in the last few generations. Feeling victimized was.

It has been proposed by trustworthy professionals (after the product of Dr. Spock's books had been observed) that Dr. Spock's philosophy led to the child's expectation of instant gratification and generations of people unfamiliar with a final "No."

The IES people were being treated as adults when very young, so when they became larger, their emotional level at maturity could be suspect.

There were not enough popular wars to motivate them and the young person wanted to fight only in his choice of wars and in only his way. Again, this is an IES authority issue and we know when parents started teaching their children that they, the children, were just small adults in the family and should be involved in family decisions.

There are certainly non-IES children/adults, but they are in the growing-smaller minority. Some of them may be found in the military. There is no draft. Mixing the two types of young soldiers (draftees and volunteers) may not make a good military today. Only in a volunteer army will there be found young people dedicated to an idea greater than themselves. Putting something before themselves may be a key idea, but perhaps one completely lacking in the person high on the IES spectrum.

It was proposed by Ayn Rand in the Objectivism philosophy that those people performing charitable work were doing it for selfish reasons because doing it made them feel better about themselves. Also, it would be preferred that someone else bear all the expenses.

There is on-going, real evidence of IES and it is being forced on everyone. It affects daily writing, the press, performing arts, education, and politics. It affects the public's speech and the very word choices that they can and cannot use.

It is called – "Political Correctness."

This is founded on the principle that we are all the same and we are all wonderful and no one is to make anyone feel less entitled. The government has "sensitivity" classes for its workers. (There are no "de-sensitivity classes" for the overly sensitive.) Rather than address the singular problem, the government addresses the general group. To address the singular person could be construed to be discrimination; the higher on the IES spectrum the person is, the more likely this would occur.

Instead, the producing people will need to accommodate a singular problem. This is very inefficient but it is safer in a Politically Correct environment. It is basically a Liberal tenet that the individual has precedence over the group. This is what individual freedom means in a liberal society.

A society with varying traces of IES is not likely to be one that compromises.

Sometimes society sees changes in the government with which it simply disagrees. The solution is to change the elected officials. However, one political side was not raised to understand "No." When they lose an election, to them, that is the unacceptable "No." They have been taught that "No" is just a momentary response. They want to change it to a "Yes." There are things that a political party can do to achieve this end.

Consequently, since they have a difficult time accepting a "No," they will look to see who did it to them rather than accept that the things they wanted, the nation did not want at that time. So they will blame hypothetical communication problems, a questionable census, or maybe a confusing ballot, or hanging chads, or recently, rather than accept a "No" to their desires, they blamed a foreign government's computer meddling – in some form. Some "cause" will be found rather than accept the "No." There will be near-constant whining, finger pointing at shadows, and, with smoke and mirrors, load the media with insinuation. Even if it does not gain the desired end, they will feel much better about themselves for having done it.

It is no surprise that people with IES will do this. It is their social system. Like children, they cannot stop complaining and blaming. It cannot be their fault.

By this point the reader is aware of the IE child and adult. And the reader can recognize the IES (Infantile Entitlement Syndrome) at some spectrum/influence level in United States' daily functions and this includes their government and how it operates/functions.

If those possessing some degree of IES do not get what they want, they can just schedule a bigger march, and if looting occurs then it is not their fault. If they had been given what they wanted, there would have been no march, so the looting is someone else's fault.

This is the IES child's thinking and now the children are grown IES adults. The march is their "group pout." Rioting is their "temper tantrum." The fault must be that of big business, the rich people, environment-destroying industries, or even the rich nations– it must be something or someone's fault that caused their peaceful marchers to turn to looting.

The parallel between throwing a toy in rage and smashing a store display window is easily compared.

Section V – Government Policy and Economics

Introduction

Independently of the size of the government, whether it be one of a huge nation or of a small-town civic organization, there must be an understanding by the members about how that organization will function. This specified method could exist on a single sheet of paper and be as little as a boiler-plate constitution with minimal bylaws copied from some old, dog-eared paperback at the library; but regardless of source or size, there will be a management document dutifully approved by the membership. This document will define the manner by which the organization's members will conduct business. This is that government's policy; simple or complex.

This government can take many forms because what might serve one community may not serve another. One government might function most efficiently with an elected board of directors conducting almost all business and having just occasional contact with the membership. The business will be conducted by the board (as defined by the organization's constitution) while the membership is left to enjoy the group's activities.

Yet, some organization, based on the temperament of the membership, might require detailed documentation and exacting leadership using a firm hand to keep the heated discussions from escalating to the physical.

Regardless, there can be an adopted policy which will best serve that particular group of people and their interests.

In smaller organizations, the activity of the group is more important than prescribing the detail of how business will be conducted, yet even in small towns, cliques may form and then the most dominant personalities create factions. These factions may support issues with far more vigor than the organization's small budget and limited meeting time can justify – or even allow.

These factions at the state and federal level are called "political parties." Political parties are groups of people sharing a common socioeconomic philosophy and promotion of the same. These philosophies are varied in many degrees, but primarily they define how the party thinks a society is to be organized, and how other's wealth should be dedicated to their interpretation of what is best for the citizens. In extreme cases, the philosophy nearly becomes a religion, and then, too often, the core beliefs of the individual party may supersede all other interests or business, great or small. As the leadership of the parties becomes more intense, they may not recognize when they had started dealing with excessive energy on even minor issues. Personal indignation and pride can further solidify party opinion until it is too dense and weighty to function efficiently.

Since political parties are based on socioeconomic philosophy, it behooves the voter to understand what these philosophies are.

Most comments involving politics should be qualified, so in this case, almost every following statement in this section is related to federal politics, but still some parts will apply to state politics. Since this varies from state-to-state, the reader will be required to determine which applies to his state.

Chapter 1 The Citizen's Political Decisions

Political party operations at the federal and state level are complicated, but <u>personal</u> political decisions are <u>very</u> simple. More voters should be aware of this. There are only a few things that the voter in the United States needs to know to be able to vote as an informed citizen – even if that citizen is a member of a legislature. All the confusing detail in group politics just represents smoke for the players to dodge in and out of – and they are very adept at knowing which cloud of confusion to use when.

On most any voting issue there is little to decide if the voter knows that the basis of a political party is the adoption of the philosophy which defines the party's methods and aims for governing the citizenry.

Fortunately for the voter in the United States, there are generally just two viable choices in political philosophies: Conservatism and Liberalism.

The political party names are not that important – what they practice is and this is the main thing the citizen needs to understand. (The details of these are provided later in this section.)

One person may be an economic Conservative yet be a social Liberal, but this is dealing with philosophy and specific applications. At the current time in the United States, the political polarization is extreme because it is thought by political party members that their preferred philosophy must be applied 100% of the time and to every issue – no matter how ill-fitting that application may be.

In the citizen's political party selection process, the citizen should not vote based on the personality of that individual who will be voting in the Legislature. It takes a lot of party support and party money to get elected and the party spending the money would need to know that the legislative voter will vote the way the party wants when it is important. He can display his integrity and indignation on the minor things – things that do not matter – but never on the important things that the party is supporting.

What is most important are the concerns of the businesses and lobbyists who contribute the most money to that political party. These organizations putting up the money have a right to expect that their interests will be served in the Legislature. If it is not, they will find some other place to invest their money (to buy political support).

And all politics is about money.

Only.

Even the smallest social issue can have a price tag.

Chapter 2 Conservatism Defined and Described

Conservatism is a socioeconomic philosophy suggesting a more traditional (for them) social construction. This desire is based on the respect for traditional institutions which have been demonstrated to function for the public's general well-being. These represent stability and perpetuate the generally acceptable status quo.

They believe that what a person earns is the property of that person – this is wealth of any sort – and property rights are very important because they inspire industry; both institutionally and at the personal level.

The Conservative believes that the government should only do for the citizen what the citizen cannot do for himself. Human fragility is recognized, but also recognized are the life choices which might have led to that fragility.

Conservatives want to conserve/preserve stability. They resist revolutionary changes that will always disrupt the citizen's peaceful and preferred status quo. Change is to be evolutionary and it must be done in a seamless manner. If it is a great change, it should be put into effect in steps.

However, Conservatism in the extreme becomes stagnant and forces a rigidity on the population that will not change easily, even when the need of change becomes obvious.

In the United States, Conservatism generally means the Republican Party, also known as the GOP, for "Grand Old Party." In illustrations, the party is sometimes portrayed by an elephant. This is from a cartoon by Thomas Nash in 1874.

The states which usually support this party are considered to be "Red." (Not associated with Communism.)

Chapter 3 Liberalism Defined and Described

Liberalism is a socioeconomic philosophy that is based on the belief that a government is to administer to the citizen. It is the citizen's responsibility to determine what each's preferences are. This, they define as "personal freedom." In its minor form, it encourages civil disobedience, however, personal freedom is still considered supreme. This, to the extreme, will produce anarchy. In practice, it is difficult to balance anarchy and constitutional government, but the effort is made nonetheless.

In the practice of personal freedom, each individual will have precedence over the other. The effort to reach this impossible end is what represents the philosophical aim of Liberalism.

Liberalism seeks to replace the norms because nothing is without flaw and there is nothing in society that cannot be improved and this can be done immediately. Liberalism promises change.

The individual has precedence over the whole, but the government will administer to the population as it deems appropriate at that moment. This is expensive but all citizens contribute to the treasury (government's bank) as the government defines their (the government's and citizen's) needs.

The long-term effort of Liberalism will create and expand the socialist state since the government is responsible for all aspects of the citizens' lives. The citizen will have few options or opportunities since the government will have all the information and opportunity to make the decisions for the citizen.

However, historically, Liberalism has been the foundation for revolutionaries.

In the United States, Liberalism generally means the Democratic Party. The states which usually support this party are considered to be "Blue." The party is sometimes portrayed by a donkey – also from an 1874 cartoon by Thomas Nash.

Chapter 4 Comparing Conservatism and Liberalism

Fortunately, all the American voter is left with is a simple choice and this <u>does not require any media inputs</u> to make a decision. The political parties are <u>not</u> going to change their socioeconomic philosophies. Whomever is elected will do in office what the party who put up the money to get him elected wants done. It does not matter who that person is.

The voters should take the system as it is and not as they would like it to be. They should vote for the socioeconomic philosophy (Conservative or Liberal) that he thinks best serves the nation – not what best serves himself.

They should not waste a vote "to send a message." The parties cannot be swayed to change their philosophies. Use a messaging system to send a message; vote to install a philosophy.

*****

In comparing the Conservatives and Liberals, Conservatives are generally not so sure of their personal convictions and, therefore, they rely on precedence and tradition (general convention) as much as possible. If things are going good, they would rather not change anything unless there is a fallback position in case the change does not produce the results they expected. The Conservative is relying on a stable status quo.

The Conservative will offer options and opportunity. Citizens may or may not involve themselves as they desire.

Over time this lack of change shifts the stability into stagnation. In the distant past, Liberal influences on the Conservative moderated this tendency toward stagnation. Often the best of both philosophies, Conservative and Liberal were applied.

Liberals appear very sure of their convictions, and rather than provide options for the citizen, they will enact laws to make sure everyone has the courage of their (Liberal) convictions. The error in this logic lies in the inability to reverse a bad decision. Rather than go back to a previous condition, they continue with the changes until there is no stability nor anticipation of a comfortable social condition.

In practice, there is a good proposition for Liberal politics, particularly as it naturally evolves into a socialist state. The Liberal party gives favors to the public and the public in turn votes for more favors. This is a win-win situation for Liberals.

However, many of the recipients may not be contributing to the source of the favors, the treasury. There are other people making the contributions and their contributions are not voluntary but are required by law.

When it is thought that this Liberal largesse is damaging the long-term health of the national economy, the Conservatives might want to reduce the damage by removing some of the favors.

This will result in even more votes for the Liberals. Therefore, this is win-win-win for Liberal politics.

However, long in the past, conservative influences moderated the liberal socialist tendency, and the best of both Liberalism and Conservatism were enjoyed by the citizen.

Change identifies the Liberal.

Yet, when Conservatives want to change to something new, then at that point they are liberal in their actions; but when they want to change back, or return, to a previous condition, that too, is change, but recovery is not liberal. Re-acquiring something that was lost is hardly a gain; it is to reestablish an earlier status quo – this is Conservative.

Chapter 5 Recognizing Political Reality

The voter needs to understand that successful politicians at the level of the Federal Legislature are but professionals who have no shame and they have a very narrow and exclusive concept of honor. They do, however, have a very acute sense of denial, thus precluding any doubt or guilt of previous actions. Too much honor would interfere in their assigned responsibilities to their party.

This does not mean that they cannot function as very dedicated and adept legislators. They serve their party with conviction and consistency. However, this loyalty is not to the nation but to their party.

This is understood by the party and the legislator, but rarely by the voter. Once the voter accepts this, he would not place any sense of ethics or morality on a federal candidate, thus making the voter's decisions even easier. It does not matter what the candidate says. They want to get elected. They have an expensive staff to advise them on what to say and where to say it. And this speech/conviction can reverse in only 50 miles on the campaign trail.

There are major axioms in federal politics and these are nonpartisan. The politician must live by the knowledge that –

1. Only my party can properly guide the nation. The other party will destroy the nation. There can be no surrender. There can be no compromise. We must appear consistent and firm for our voters.
2. I must do anything it takes to get elected.
   This requires lots of money. I must do what it takes to get the money.
3. If I am elected, I must get re-elected. The re-election process starts the day after the election.
   This requires lots of money. I must do what it takes to get the money.
4. When in the Legislature, I must do what my party wants. The upside of this is that it does not require any effort on my part to understand any act or budget. Others will tell me what to say and how to vote.

There is no number five.

*****

The United States Legislature can make very strict rules and be very verbal about corporate executives when the executive leaves a company. This, the Legislature calls a "Golden Parachute." The worst thing about highly-paid corporate CEOs is that they inspire federal legislators, and this causes the elected officials to be even more ambitious.

These corporate executives are personally responsible for business profits which are greater than many countries' total income. One bad decision can cost the company/investors a lot of money.

One can wonder how much someone should be paid who is ultimately responsible for a company like Apple.

Apple is worth $945 <u>billion</u> – and its net income in 2016 was $53 <u>billion</u>. Apple will likely be the first <u>trillion dollar company</u> on the planet – making iPhones. Other companies are very close behind it.

No legislator is personally responsible for that amount of money.

Any team of managers who do nothing but permit the company to continue in this manner is doing good. There are no decisions that they can make that are guaranteed to show the same increase in profits. Unless it was expected, any reduction in <u>rate</u> of gain is considered "under performing." Serious questions would be asked if their next annual gain was "only" $52.9 billion. This would constitute a "loss."

In the federal government, there are 435 representatives in the Legislature. They serve a term of but two years. The representative will make $174,000 a year for each of his two years in office. However, they will each get <u>239</u> days off each year – this is <u>34 weeks</u>! Therefore, they are "working" for only 18 weeks. And they are getting $174,000 for these 18 weeks. This is tantamount to getting nearly $10,000 each week. Of course, they must also campaign during their time off, and all meetings with the public are actually campaign opportunities. Besides, there are a lot of fund-raisers they need to attend.

Then after serving three terms (necessary to have the required five years of legislative service), which is really serving only 108 weeks (equivalent to 2 years), they could retire, and receive $17,000 a year for life – plus other benefits. This is the minimum; the actual amount depends on how many terms were served. Additionally, there are many retirement benefits; some too complicated to unravel.

To most Americans, this in itself defines a "Golden Parachute" and one not requiring an actual retirement! So they must be in Washington for the 140-day average session; or rather they should be. The rest of the time they can consult and go about the business that they enjoy – politicking, e.g., promoting self.

There are 226 retired representatives – whose names start with "A, B, or C." There are many more retired representatives whose names start with the other 23 letters.

All this pay and these benefits, they regulate themselves. CEOs do not control their salary nor benefits. They sign contracts defining income options. They can take it or leave it.

The legislators can manipulate the law and its interpretation to gain increased income. They also set their own salaries with almost the same considerations as many corporate boards when the boards are creating signing packages for hiring the next CEO.

*****

It is believed by many that the United States can only survive and prosper if there is a Liberal government. They believe that <u>anything</u> that will attain that end is justified, and it does not matter how much it might hurt the Unites States in the short term, it is thought to be worth it in the end.

The nation's governing document has not changed that much, but the politicians (and the citizens) have.

There are some things that are new in 2018.

Political polarization is the most vocal and venomous as it has been in maybe 150 years. The lack of cooperation by legislators at the federal level inhibits progress because constructive change can never come by a wholly conservative nor a wholly liberal political philosophy. Without cooperation, the nation is locked into back and forth see-sawing of extremism and even more polarization. In this condition, there can be change, but not necessarily constructive change.

The extent of civic polarization comes from the media, but an indiscriminate public compounds the media's biased reporting.

In the study of distrustful cultures (other than the current United States political parties), the idea of one trusting the other can spell the doom of one. This is no minor consideration!

This means that every suggestion by one is justifiably considered suspect by the other.

There is no evidence that this circle of distrust and cynicism can be interrupted and certainly not over the short term. But over the long term – as in a century – a new attitude can emerge. Some nations do not have that long to change a legislative attitude and still be able to maintain their position in a global economy.

The more culturally diverse the nation is, the more likely there will be no consensus.

*****

There used to be liberal Conservatives who were more liberal than some conservative Liberals and often it would depend on the issue as to how some of these "independently minded" politicians voted. This was a long time ago when the elective offices did not cost as much money to obtain as they do today. Now the smart political parties know how to govern their own parties; however, not all political parties are smart.

In the 1950s such consideration of issues created the idea of statesmanship, or how persuasively a person could make his points but still be flexible enough to concede some points to the other side. Ultimatums were rare because they locked out any idea of agreement or negotiation.

Politics is no longer a statesman's business. Politicians used to say, "Get your people to talk to my people and let's see what we can work out." This meant "Let's get our staffs together and let them hash it out until we have a better view of where we really differ. Then we can see what we need to do to break any sort of deadlock."

This is a very old concept and now it is a long-forgotten process known as "compromise." It was based on, "I will yield some of my position and you yield some of yours; otherwise, the government will be shut down, and we all have far too much pride in America to permit this. We must remember that the United States government always comes first and the people depend on us. We can do this."

In this old way, what was produced might not be entirely what either party wanted, but it was the best that could be done and it was for the United States' citizens. The result was a moderate approach with a little of each's ideas incorporated into the final act.

The intent was always to resolve the conflict. Now the aim is to perpetuate or even increase the conflict for another four years and in this way the voters can see which party is causing all the trouble – it is thought. Each party has its own media support, but new laws can preclude any follow-up negotiations.

With the passage of time "compromise" changed to become a negative term. It was decided that "compromise" was for the weak and indecisive. Now it is thought that "a compromising person" has no firm convictions.

This term "compromise" is like the term "a discriminating person." The discriminating person was someone with high standards, principles, and good taste, and one who would not accept just anything. They would hold out for their ideals. This was a real luxury that only the individual who was responsible for just himself could enjoy.

Now, of course, no one is to discriminate – or he might be accused of "discriminating," a very bad act. And then it became true that in the United States, the citizen became less discriminating in nearly all things. They would settle for the lowest price and that was the only criteria. (Enter Walmart.)

*****

The purpose in politics is get elected. Second, stay elected. There is no third, campaigning and quest for money never ends.

In 2012 the average cost to run for the United States Senate was $10.5 million – that is for just one of 100 seats. A Senator's salary is $174,000 per year (plus benefits).

In the 2016 presidential and congressional election, $6.5 billion was spent – the presidential election alone consumed $2.4 billion of that.

It could be imagined that some honest fellow might decide that he wanted to work for his nation directly and run for the United States Senate. There will be $10.5 million spent to get him elected to a $0.17

million job. And this is ignoring the huge expenses of his running in the primaries, and run-off elections should they occur.

Much of this money goes to the media through the agents (lobbyists) of the political party.

These elections are the most expensive and extensive public communication efforts there are, and in the United States, it occurs at least every two years; each four years there is a presidential election and each two years there is a Congressional election. It is estimated that the election in 2020 will cost $5.2 billion.

Therefore, it cannot seriously be proposed by any political party that the voters were uninformed; perhaps misinformed, but not uninformed.

Yet often the losers will claim that there was either poor communication on their part or some type of illegal manipulation of the election process. This thinking is preferred rather than just admit that the public <u>was</u> informed and at that particular time, the losers' party <u>was not</u> the preferred one.

The manipulation claims may come in many imaginative ways.

In the last presidential election, the loser was well-known in American politics and raised more than $700 million for the campaign. The winner was a non-politician who raised a little over one-half as much ($400 million).

The party that is in power generally has the advantage, but the downside is that the public will know how they had been doing their jobs while in office. With the current United States political system, there can be a split Legislature and one side can blame the other for any unhappiness the citizens experience. It would be difficult to unravel the blame game even if the media was telling the United States citizens the truth.

Public Assistance (welfare/charity) in the beginning was intended to be a short-term solution. It was not to define a lifestyle for multiple generations, but who then would have thought that a possibility. This is the way of Liberal politics.

Social Security was supposed to be a short-term correction, and now people depend on it. Liberal governments enable dependency on the government. It promises it it creates it. Dependency maintains Liberal/Socialist governments.

Even after a 2009 Liberal government gave away $831 billion on a spending initiative to "jump start" the economy, unemployment went above 10%. The money given away by the Liberal government had come from the taxes of producing Americans who would have rather kept a little more of their income than have a law remove it from them to give to others.

Giving money to nonproductive people discourages effort. Most people work to get money. They would stop working if their employer stopped paying them. They would stay home if the employer would give them the same money anyway. [Actually, in this example, the producers would use their new free time to find other work to increase their income.]

Party affiliation is considered more important than Americanism – and Nationalism is thought to be bad by definition. Patriotism has no value in politics either, nor in sports.

A party relishes the losses of the other party – even when the loss is the United States' loss. At the best, this condition can rapidly approach sedition; at the worst, revolution.

The Liberals once published a White Paper that indicated that they had lost the election because they had forgotten what they were to be. They had forgotten that if they lost, they were, by definition, to be "the opposition party" and meant to oppose all legislation put forward by the other party. The implication is that if the party put into authority by the voting of the citizens found a cure for cancer, it should be opposed on principle.

Many lack the ability to accept that at any given moment their party's ideas may be unappealing to many United States citizens, and this is the focus of the problem. It has its origin in the beginning of this history (1946) and the following perpetuation of Infantile Entitlement Syndrome.

The Conservative president in 2018 will continue to have opposition from the Liberal media who claim that the president was elected by some Russian's manipulation of public favor in the election, but this does not make sense. In logic, this is the opposite of reality.

The Liberal presidential candidate, when Secretary of State, had official communication channels which were secure, but they were also recorded and archived. So she was using other email channels.

Perhaps the Secretary did not want traceability of all her correspondence. It would seem that if the person running for the presidency was using insecure communication channels, then the Russians would have wanted that person to be president – and not that bombastic, non-politician opposing her.

Businesses have to get big loans for the long term for them to expand. And they must have some confidence in the financial environment before they commit to multimillion-dollar contracts. A political party based on change (Liberal) takes away their expectations of what any market might be doing in the next few years. So they delay increasing their business and try to protect their market. This creates a fiscal condition where it would be prudent to have little expansion – while the economies of other countries continue to expand. No expansion means, among other things, no increased employment.

However, if the government (president and legislature) is business-friendly and wants to support the status quo (Conservative) then the business leaders have some idea of how they should plan. Businesses grow, profits are made, the unemployed are hired, and more people are working and paying taxes. This is all providing that the Legislature is doing its job and not locking down the nation's business.

It is an unpopular thought, but the truth is that the rich do not need the poor. The reverse is the truth. The poor need the rich because the rich will be the source of their employment – the poor do not need another poor person. The poor do prefer a very liberal government, however. And the more liberal, the better.

One wealthy Conservative was buying failing drugstores and modernizing them. He said that the best thing he could do for unemployed people was put them to work. This would give workers and their families both income and personal pride. He was criticized by the Liberal media for saying this. From reading the article it appeared that putting people to work was some sort of exploitation. It is never suggested, but the worker can easily exploit his employer by underperforming.

The same wealthy Conservative was also criticized for not having a large corporate-funded program for public welfare. Providing employment seemed to be bad to the Liberals, while just giving the money away was constructive.

*****

American Liberal activism is a model of revolution and it is a common political tool. They control campuses where the next generations are being educated. Liberal's activism is a perfect design to influence many people many places.

American Conservative activism is an anomaly. It is that rare.

The Conservatives will organize but on very few occasions. The most obvious conservative movement resulted in the creation of the Confederate States of America. This was to preserve their Southern way of life – a life much different from that in the North.

This Southern War for Independence, which was very similar to the American War for Independence, was not successful for many reasons.

The most recent Conservative public activity was the Tea Party. And like most Conservative activism it was short-lived. They had a point to make. They made it. It was not to be an on-going source of marches with issues being manufactured and members touting ridiculous slogans.

The Tea Party resisted all excessive government spending; Conservative and Liberal. When Conservatives are in office, the people who elected them seem to hibernate; Liberals never stop campaigning. Liberals do not accept that the nation has selected a new idea with a new president. He is the president of the United States, but he is not "their" president, so they remain on the offensive with campaigning attacks – such is their sense of righteous indignation.

Indignation is a strange phenomenon and it seems that only the human has it. It requires contemplation and this is something the rest of the animal kingdom lacks.

One can wonder why the Liberals are the ones who are activists and who are spurred to action by social wrongs, real or imagined. The Conservative is rarely indignant when the Liberal wants to change his status quo.

The times that the Conservative has even been vocal is countermanded by the media as being unwholesome or backward ("the

Conservatives are opposing change!!!"), whereas the indignation of the Liberal is considered positive and progressive.

And the Conservative citizens permit the media to do this.

Indignation requires that a sense of blame be placed on someone by the indignant. Blaming others exonerates the indignant of any blame. This is a good tool for the hypocrite. The first one to get indignant is positive and there is no defense because defense is thought to be the tool of the guilty.

Today, if accused, the accused are found guilty in the public forum – the media. No report or study can exonerate them. All positive results can be reported as being but "typical political posturing." The Liberal activist is rarely accused of this in the media.

Much can be learned from reading on the subject of indignation.[15] Indignation can serve when an individual wants to reveal circumstances which protect his ego and are flattering to him. This is biased because such an individual will want to take credit for the good outcomes of his indignation while avoiding the blame for the bad.

When the indignant band together, then the cohort is self-perpetuating in that their empathy is increased. This can easily "ramp-up" their sense of indignation and this results in more extreme behavior. They "drive" each other.

Hence their propensity for summoning crowds and marches.

The Conservatives are rarely anything but stationary targets.

*****

Everything is about votes. Those in office want to stay there – where they can best serve the nation. If one group routinely helps the poor, and the poor vote, then the more poor there are, then the more votes they would get for helping them. This is not buying votes, but is rather rewarding voters for their votes.

This defines the Socialist Government. "Socialist Democracy" is a real term and has been used often in other countries. It can apply to the United States, as well.

15

C.H. Miller, et al – "Indignation, defensive attribution, and implicit theories of moral character" *Dissertation Abstracts International: Section B; The Sciences of Engineering.*

It is often said, "The Conservatives never gave me anything."

"Gave" is the operative word.

The only thing the Conservatives offer is opportunity. This used to be the only thing requested by the down and out. This used to inspire. "Just give me a chance." "Just give me a job."

Times change.

The other way, Liberalism, functions by debilitation and lack of opportunity. The Liberal offers change, but ensures that the unproductive will be content to remain so because they have been told that their condition is not their fault. They are told that they have been victimized...in some manner. Therefore, they become a large population having no stigma for failure. Nor guilt.

Many remember when President Kennedy said, "Ask not what your country can do for you, but what you can do for your country." It, like many Liberals' statements sounds so very good. It just needs to look and sound good because if it is said and people believe it, then it does not have to be done. They already believe it. Their memory will not last long enough to recall that it was just a short term gesture.

And if someone brings it up later?

Then they do what all propagandists do – when they cannot deliver pie in the sky, they quickly redefine "pie" or "sky."

Redefining terms is a common political ploy. Today, "homeless" does not just mean someone without basic protection from the weather and having no address where he abides. It now means any family living with another family out of necessity. It could be debated that both families sharing the home are "homeless." And the homeless can include students living in a hotel.

Changing the definition of homeless to include these people can now show how some political party has increased the number of "homeless," or at least how some Government social office should have an increase in their budget and staffing.

This is not new. A political party wanted to prove they could reduce inflation. They did. They removed the price increase of autos from the formula for computing inflation. Inflation went down when auto inflation was removed. The next year, they reduced it again....by removing the increase in housing cost from the formula.

There is always a way.

Section VI – Reflection

Introduction

People who do not think that things are bad, when others are saying that they are all on a train bound for Hell, most likely think this way because people have been saying this for years. Or possibly, they are young (inexperienced) and have no understanding of how things were in the past – their history. Or possibly the past has been presented in very bad terms in their schools – making today seem great. This would certainly foster a sense of well being – providing current events are ignored.

The experienced adult's doubting is based on the assumption that either (a) there is no movement or (b) there is no Hell.

It is rarely proposed that things are getting better, but only that (a) or (b) is the case.

There is no reason to believe things are static. And if things are changing, logically then the direction is established also.

The considerations then become:

"How far away is Hell?"

"How big is Hell?"

"How fast is the train moving?"

"How long is it before the train gets to downtown Hell?"

It is assumed that the train passengers will recognize it and not like it.

There is the mantra that the only thing that is constant is change. Yet, with constant change there is no prediction of tomorrow – no anticipation of a stable life. A stable, traditional life was what the many just-marrieds were desiring when they started their families at the end of WWII, yet back in 1946 they were unknowingly sowing the seeds that eliminated the tradition they were seeking. Then those children became adults and produced the citizens of today.

Constant change destroys confidence because that which was enjoyed today will be changed tomorrow, and this makes the world unpredictable. Perfect change is chaos, but few people have desired chaos as a living condition.

Now it is accepted that what was learned today will be irrelevant tomorrow. This is true in the home, on the streets, and in the work place – indeed, even in the churches. The churches are the institutions which should be the most stable, but they are not.

If the statements from the churches are correct, God has changed His mind many times in just recent years. So apparently, even God is not stable. Liberal changes reach even to Heaven. But it has been said that Christianity was not tried and found lacking, but rather it was tried and found difficult.

When constant change is accepted as the status quo, there is no tradition nor dependability and everyone has become liberal – this means living with change and in limbo while thinking that is the way citizens are to live. There is precedence for this.

Chapter 1 The Food Chain And Upward Mobility

At one time humans were not very significant and they probably knew it. They did not think that they were the most wonderful things in existence. However, the other animals knew of the human's importance. The other animals, at least the carnivores, knew that humans were not very smart, and better yet, they were not at all fast, and they had no claws nor slashing teeth. Mostly they were easily caught and soft, but there were some parts which were satisfyingly crunchable. In general, humans were rather satisfying meals.

But humans were also wonderfully resilient.

First, in very small family tribes (seven or eight) they managed to acquire fire (500,000 BC). Fire was not being made by them but rather it was captured from nature and nurtured.

Then to make up for having no claws nor long teeth, they got some personal defense with sharp stones tied to sticks (300,000 BC).

In time, their fire-making became dependable and more meat (protein for more brain power) could be consumed. The date of the first fire-making groups is difficult to determine since remnants of prehistoric campfire sites do not indicate if the previous fire was started from a nurtured, natural fire or from a fire generated by those people using that campsite.

Their scavenging at other animal's kill sites still continued, but in time this was left behind in their upward mobility quest.

The one thing that humans wanted foremost was comfort. They wanted to be fed and be free from threats. Without expressing it, they kept this in mind and each new comfort, no matter how minor or tenuous, was built upon.

Then with larger tribes (50 or so) something new happened and humans developed a different way of looking at things (50,000 BC). They seemed to have received, recognized, or developed an inner *spirit* – they wanted art with body paint and baubles. And they gained music. At first it was rudimentary, but different igneous rocks when struck against others had a pleasant sound and with predictable repetition, rhythm was enjoyed. Skins over hollow gourds sounded good when struck with hand or stick.

And in some manner they developed a sense of awe – they discovered religion and constructed artifacts in an attempt to make sense of it and perhaps apply it for their own purposes.

They became more contemplative and could think in the abstract and this is demonstrated by their grave goods and burial rituals. Their language became much more complex since the mind then required a greater dimension for communication. Abstract thinking propelled the language from cursory grunts and squeals to a more articulate intellectual faculty.

This alone helped humans, *homo sapiens* (Cro-magnon in this case) accelerate on the long evolutionary and scientific trail to become humans in the current millennium.

Still desiring comfort, humans now zip across the landscape or fly through the sky in environment-controlled vehicles. They can retire to a safe home with control of their environment.

All of this was upward mobility for human comfort.

This development and desire, from wherever it had first come, continues today unabated. Only now, comfort comes in the form of iPhones, computers, and computer-controlled environments for vehicles and homes.

It can be imagined (with good reason) that when that first human actually started a fire in some cold, dark cave lying deep in a dangerous wilderness, the event was marked by some nearby, startled individual yelling the equivalent of, "NO! NO! Get rid of it! It will get loose and kill us all!"

The person who had made the fire was liberal. He wanted change.

The short-sighted, yelling person was conservative and did not want any more changes.

One desired a different tomorrow; the other wanted to maintain a familiar status quo that worked. To the conservative person, tomorrow should be a repeat of a survivable today.

Now after some 502,018 years of using fire, the Liberal still wants change; the Conservative still wants to leave the status quo alone.

Today, that Liberal who started that first fire would immediately make a law that all caves were thereafter to have someone make fire or there would be some penalty for the offending cave dwellers for not having such a person. Using this current analogy, the law would also require that all nurtured fires be extinguished and only the created fires be used – otherwise, there would be serious penalties.

The conservative person is a success because he has what he wants and he would like to keep it. But this cannot happen if Liberals keep changing everything.

Conservatism is a temporary condition. It starts at the time the individual is content with his place in the scheme of things and he wants to enjoy it for as long as he can. He accepts change providing it is not disrupting his way of life and it is only an opportunity which he can utilize or ignore. However, law is not that way. It rules.

If the conservative person is fortunate, he can enjoy his preference for the rest of his life. However, chances are that he cannot do this because that which makes humans human will interfere with his comfort/satisfaction.

Change to a conservative person is bad enough but it is tolerable. What galls is replacement. He is having things taken away from him and other things are being forced on him. These replacements are often things he did not need nor did he want. And in a lot of cases the new things are not as good as the older things that had been replaced.

Conservative people can mount an armed attack on the liberal people. This has worked a few places for a while, but this is no way to govern people.

Many people will want change. First, to improve unpleasant circumstances for themselves, but then they will force those changes on others ... to "bring them up to speed"..."get them on the same page"..."to update and modernize them. They will thank us later." Self-righteousness is a powerful stimulant.

Without an active military to prevent major social changes, Conservatism will be pushed aside by Liberalism.

Some Liberals may become conservative when successful and comfortable, but there will be many younger Liberals who will prevent this. Besides, the once-Liberal-now-being-conservative will not know he had become conservative. He will just say that he is a Liberal while withdrawing from politics. Nothing marks a Conservative more accurately than this.

The conservative person will drag his feet at all changes that upset what he has and has worked for. Even in this there is some profit for society. If more people dragged their feet, the train to Hell might be slowed some and not get there as soon.

This means, "Until after I am dead."

Chapter 2 Moderation and Acceptance

There have most likely been conservative activists, but this would mean a conservative person on attack to oppose change. Only rarely do Conservatives even recognize a pending change, and when they do, it is almost always too late to reject. They are happy and contented and wonder why anyone would want to change anything.

In some cases these changes will be extreme, such as in the South and with racial integration. They did not want to change, and they thought for good reasons, but a change was necessary at some point and they understood this.

But when?

Later.

This generally meant "After I am dead."

Someone should not be faulted for wanting a status quo and stability – particularly when those people desiring it are so inert. They are not proposing a change. They are just there – sitting ducks.

The Conservative Southerners thought that integration of the schools would lead to generally poor education and to intermarriages. The blacks had their schools and the whites had theirs. It was thought that they were equal in that each served their communities.

Again, a new, cute term came to entertain the media – "Separate is not equal."

That statement is not at all true in many examples. A dollar in one pocket is separate from the dollar in another pocket, yet they are equal. But equal is not always fair. The donkey and elephant are both beasts of burden, but it would be unfair to expect the donkey to carry a load equal to that of the elephant.

However, the buzzword and catch phrase in the media supersedes thought.[16]

Most people would agree that poor education would be bad, but the Southern Conservatives were not sure about what would be bad about intermarriages.

The Southern Conservative did not want any change and this indicates the problem with Conservatives. Nature had established the races, and proximity had rendered the concern about intermarriages to a mooted point. It was proposed that if color/races were ignored then everything would be better. The government would not permit this. Races had to be tracked to make sure things were fair.

Surely one race is as good as another. The public can think about this – but they must never discuss it because now everyone is an activist, or at least proactive.

Therefore, Conservatives are just the targets – stationary ones. They are at home. They come out to vote and then go back inside.

The most firm Conservatives are the opposites of activists. They are either hermits or recluses. They would prefer to be left alone.

16

A noted Supreme Court Judge, Justice O. W. Homes, Jr. wrote: "A good catchword can obscure analysis for fifty years."

Again, it is easy to victimize such an obliging target.

Many people heard the governor of Alabama telling how integration would damage American education, but we really do not know if it did or it did not. It is one of <u>those</u> subjects! It is easy to compare the American education system with all the rest of the world's, but it is hard to do it by American geographical areas and by year.

This governor said the same about change and homosexuals teaching school. At the time, many people thought that maybe those people just wanted to be school teachers and they should have that opportunity. Good school teachers are always in demand. But the governor said that they would evangelize and start pushing their life-style on other people.

This was considered to be the ramblings of a typical, bigoted Southern politician.

This was "teacher discrimination" and it was eliminated quite a while back so it is easy to see how they have gotten what they wanted. They had said that they just wanted to be accepted and have the same job opportunities as others and to just quietly blend into society.

Not surprising to many people, now that they are well-integrated into society they are making all sorts of political statements and marching to alter society to be a different way – the way that they want it – just as the bigoted Southern politician had said and feared they would do.

First, people desire equality. Once that is attained, they want and strive for superiority to make up for the times they were not treated equally. This is less about equality than about envy...they want to become those they had resented. This is not at all about equality – it is about vengeance and retribution. History demonstrates this...over and over.

Those who do not know their history...

– The 24-hour Status Quo

In change, something good can be realized, but one cannot depend on it lasting because tomorrow it will be left behind for another change. It is not just the computers that are being forced to change for the sake of change (updated). The individual is being updated as well, and this can be done on a 24-hour media cycle.

And with marketing, it is not just change. Those who resist the change cannot just keep doing what they have been doing – because "change" is not just the creation of options and opportunity. Now it means "replacement" – often forced by various individuals/markets.

In a digital world it is "this or that." It is not "both." It can be neither, but not both.

When a society has their sense of stability removed (and against their will) and it is replaced by something different, it is "theft of comfort" or the "creation of discomfort." It changes their status quo and disturbs their peace.

This will make many Conservatives feel threatened and at the same time disenfranchised. Their standard of living is being altered and not to their liking, and it is being done by changing the law. Individuals could respond to this with antisocial behavior. But it will be individually. The whole of Conservatism cannot be activated. Contentment defines them.

It is accepted that complete Conservatism (no changes to tradition) will bring stagnation and soon there will be a backward society incapable of recognizing new opportunities.

One may wonder which is better – Conservatism or Liberalism. The answer is neither – for 100% of the time.

Since it is hard for social changes to reverse, then almost as bad is 100% of one for 8 years and then 100% of the other for 8 years – over and over. In this case, one group would be constantly trying to thwart the efforts of the other. This represents political anarchy, and there can be no long-term policy. Then the population could not depend on their government nor could any other government local or foreign depend on it.

Another choice could be for there to be both at the same time. Once in living memory there were both at the same time. Some issues needed to be changed because they no longer served current society. The society recognized this and complained. The public was not goaded into it by individual rabble-rousers and trouble-makers who, with the help of a faceless media, were calling themselves "activists." Many of those people have personal issues, but their personal issues and sensitivities are not to be construed as being national concerns – but too often they are because they know to play to the media.

Now, their words are not even questioned! They are so sincere and so vocal. There are too many public forums and too much social media for them.

Today the word "activist" seems to imply something positive. As if the population is sitting around immobile but desiring to be activated. Before the current day, activists were known as "trouble-makers" upsetting the status quo. There was a time when such activists were told to shut up and sit down. And they knew to do so.

Liberals know there is no going back. Every change is then built on to create more changes. They believe that eventually they will have created the utopian world. There is no evidence that this is happening, but they will keep changing things and making new laws just the same.

Many activists/rabble-rousers/trouble-makers just have a heightened sense of self-importance and an over-abundance of self-righteousness. Again "self" is the operative modifier and may indicate some level of the IES spectrum.

It could be assumed that the Me Generation (Baby Boomers 1946 – 1965) would have had a lot of self-awareness. Being raised in a non-traditional manner, they were taught by example that they were special and this placed many of them on the IES spectrum. The teachings of 1946 have contributed in a significant manner to current liberal society.

But there was a time when the nation did have both Liberals and Conservatives working for the good of the nation at the same time. Back then the nation came first. The representatives of the two socioeconomic philosophies negotiated. They compromised. In any given case, one might give up a little of his opinion if the other would do the same. And a bill would be drafted which each could support. This was "moderated change." It was not sudden nor severe – it occurred in an almost seamless manner.

This required that there be cooperation of the two groups for the welfare of the nation and not for their respective political party. Liberalism and Conservatism can and have worked together and the nation was better for this. But this was a long time ago. Back then, they knew that one complemented the other.

*****

The recurring theme of this book is that there was a change in the adult after 1946. “Yield to me” could be one of the more latent lessons from the IES childhoods. The United States is still reaping the products of a little pocket book, and now its influence continues and has become the national driver.

Every politician out of office promises change and they rarely say what that change is. The voters do not ask and, as the politician knows, the voter assumes the changes will be good. Sometimes they are. But if it is not...too bad. It will just get changed some more. Not made better...just changed.

The most hated politician in the last two centuries promised change. He was going to destroy the old system in which the person’s last name was the guarantee of good employment and advancement. Should an individual not have the preferred heritage and geographical area of origin, then the citizen was locked into a near-medieval society.

He not only promised change, he delivered. He hired people based on capability and made sure that others did the same. Those who demonstrated good work ethics got promotions,

He increased the electrification of the nation and added rail mileage in the country as promised. He set up a good, high-speed roadway system, and he set about having the perfect car manufactured for the people at a price they could afford.

A new denomination of money was issued, and in 1930 there were 4.2 marks to a dollar. He and his political party, based on the will of the voters, legally rose to power in 1934. Then inflation was reduced and the exchange rate became to 2.6 marks to a dollar. This was a serious reduction in inflation. The economy was improving rapidly under his leadership...and this was during the Depression.

He promised that all the citizens would feel good about themselves and be proud of their nation, and for a while they were.

These are all liberal changes – and he was a Liberal – but many Liberals, once in office become very conservative so that they can maintain their desired status quo – should they ever recognize one.

At the time, he was one of four world leaders – three of them smoked constantly; he did not smoke – three drank alcohol constantly; he did not drink – three were gluttons; he was a <u>near-</u>vegetarian –

three were physically out of shape; he was in better condition – three were womanizers; he was not.

Of these four, Churchill, Roosevelt, Stalin, and Hitler, three were promising change and they were changing everything they could – only Churchill was conservative; he wanted to maintain the status quo. The Liberal who was delivering what he said he would was Adolph Hitler.

Not all Liberals are good.

Not all changes are good.

Not all Conservatives are good.

Some things need to be changed.

A United Kingdom politician said in a speech – "When it is not necessary to change, it is necessary to not change." This seems to be a conservative attitude. Things should change when necessary – and only if there is a fall-back position should the change not give the desired results. Additionally, the change should occur with the least disturbance of the population.

In a Democracy, the people determine what needs to be changed.

When thinking about the role of the activist in society it can be remembered that Demigods come in all forms.

Chapter 3 I Am Your Parent!

The greatest threat to the United States is ignorance and the American Dim Ages are well advanced now. The child's education is to start with the parent(s).

The first step in all education begins with reading ability. The definition of functional illiteracy has become so convoluted by introducing social considerations and Political Correctness that the very word "functional" may have several definitions for miscellaneous printed materials for various social groups. It would be better to establish criteria to identify it before trying to explain why it exists.

As an example, a usable criterion might be ... "Can the person read an OTC medicine bottle to determine the proper dose for himself and his child?"

This is a straightforward and expected requirement for any adult. The inability to do this would be dangerous. This information is not in code, but the reader must be able to connect several parameters at one time; age, maybe weight, number of pills per dose per unit time, and the like.

To introduce conditions such as vision impairment, or being foreign born, or any number of qualifiers is only listing the reasons for functional illiteracy. That is an attempt to make excuses for functional illiteracy. The reasons are irrelevant when attempting to identify the condition.

Functional illiteracy should be a yes/no consideration and if yes make use of the "spectrum" concept that has become so popular. One could be high on the spectrum while another might be low. Reading tests could easily be developed. But this would result in an evaluation and make someone feel badly about himself.

Social technicians can engage in rhetoric about the reasons for functional illiteracy once it is determined to exist in some individual. There are still those speculating on the method of determining functional illiteracy...but this will likely change because "illiteracy" has such a bad connotation. It will likely be reversed so that this will be a measurement (not evaluation) of functional literacy! In this manner the testing will not be determining how poorly someone can read, but how well they can read. (Blindness can become "limited vision.")

It is estimated that 14% of United States adults (42 million) are unable to perform simple, expected everyday activities which hinge on literacy – independently of what it is called.

It would be expected that the parents would be aware if they were raising a functionally illiterate child, and if they were, remedy this shortcoming. This is assuming (without confidence) that the parent(s) was (were) not functionally illiterate themselves.

A child can learn to read and perform simple math and never enter a school; consequently, a large educational institution should not be needed to learn such basic skills.

The parent and the teacher are the most important influences in the child's early life. These two significant people must communicate and the child should not think that he can "divide and conquer." The parent must maintain a good line of communication with the teacher. It would be more efficient for the parent to initiate this contact because the teacher, having many students would have to contact many parents, some of whom would be too busy or perhaps not even interested.

Today it is possible that the child, while still a fetus, can have access to the United States education system when his pregnant mother attends Early Head Start. The child can become a voter in national elections before leaving the United States' free education system – functionally illiterate/literate or not.

A good education is available anywhere in the United States when it is considered that all the knowledge in the world is available on most 10-year-old's ever-present phone. (Ten is the average age of the carrier having his first phone.) Yet some carriers do not access this world of information, just as there are some who do not access the information the teacher is offering. This is hardly the teacher's fault.

It may be that the young do not see the advantages of a good education and in many, many cases, there are none. The student with a 4.0 GPA and a Bachelor's degree specializing in Early Medieval Russian Poetry may have placed himself out of a general, commercial/profit-making market. However, he could perhaps get a meager job teaching Early Medieval Russian Poetry to other students.

If the student is independently wealthy then he can afford the luxury of studying anything his heart desires. However, if the student sees a future where he might need an income, he should review what his options and possibilities are before requesting student loans. (Early Medieval Russian Poetry may not be a good choice for a viable professional career.)

The basic question should be: "Will someone pay me money to exercise my degree?" This means other than teaching other naive young people how to do what cannot support them – other than by their teaching even more people the same thing. This seems to be an academic pyramid scheme.

The parent should be the child's first career counselor.

It could be expected that there are student loans being made to students to get an education in a field which could not provide enough income for them to even begin to pay back the loan. One might wonder why such loans would be granted with so little possibility of paying for them.

Hobbies and casual interests are entertaining and possibly a lot of fun to study, but even in 2018, good advice for some young people entering college might be: "Marry well" – as old fashioned and insulting as that sounds.

And for the high school student with no viable career in mind, there is always their first option – the military. This should not be considered their last resort. The advantages of the military are significant. However, this does require research, as any early job search should.

But the parent(s) is (are) to be the parent(s) and all that entails. Discussing unicorns, rainbows, and wishing on a star might hurt a lot more over time than it helps.

Raising a child in the old traditional manner (when the United States was great) would be difficult today when applying corporal punishment can get the parent arrested. Some political groups will pass laws forcing on others what that group thinks is constructive. It is inconceivable that a law could be repealed to give the parents rights to corporal punishment for their child. In some states the criterion is that the punishment cannot cause pain. Nor is this to be done when the parent is angry...the implication is that this should be administered with cold-blooded calculations.

The most important thing in a child's life is education. This is a fact. This includes all aspects of the human condition and this includes religious training. It does not matter what the child says is most important. He is a child with an immature brain. He is to be led and inspired; not coddled, humored, and elevated in a social structure based on entitlement.

A married couple who worked with young people wrote a book in which they related their experiences. From their own lives and observations they wrote, "Twelve Rules for Raising Gang Members and Drug Addicts."

1. Begin with infancy to give the child everything he wants. In this way he will grow up to believe the world owes him a living.

2. When he picks up bad words, laugh at him. This will make him think he is cute. It will also encourage him to pick up "cuter" phrases, that will blow off the top of your head later.

3. Never give him any spiritual training. Wait until he is 21 and let him decide for himself.

4. Avoid use of the word "wrong." It may develop a guilt complex. This will condition him to believe, after he is arrested for stealing a car, that society is against him, and he is being persecuted.

5. Pick up everything he leaves lying around - books, shoes, and clothing. Do everything for him so he will be experienced in throwing all responsibility on others.

6. Let him read any printed matter he can get his hands on. Be careful that the silverware and drinking glasses are sterilized, but let his mind feast on garbage.

7. Quarrel frequently in the presence of your children. In this way they will not be too shocked when the home is broken up later.

8. Give your child all the spending money he wants. Never let him earn his own. Why should he have things as tough as you had them?

9. Satisfy his every craving of food, drink, and comfort. See that every sensual desire is gratified. Denial may lead to harmful frustrations.

10. Take his part against neighbors, teachers, and policemen. They are all prejudiced against your child.

11. When he gets into real trouble, apologize for yourself by saying, "I never could do anything with him."

12. Prepare for a life of grief. You will surely have it.

*****

Educational options could include a private schooling. The parent could choose a conservative school, though it could be rather expensive. The conservative school could be a religious school. Evaluating a potential school with at least the same diligence as when choosing the next family car could provide a perfect match between child and school.

There could be no social media other than phone for verbal messages. (Flip Phone.)

The child should be taught to respect the parent and themselves – and other authorities having influence over the child. Such respect of parents would create a sense of parental authority.

It was taught at one time that the child should think of his parents as his best friends.

No.

The child should think of his parents as his parents. A child who does not respect his parents is not likely to respect his teacher – or anyone. The parent should strive to be worthy of respect. The parallel between a parent at home and a teacher at school is near one-to-one.

Establish simple ground rules that they understand; they do not have to like them.

And "no" means "NO!" and there should be no ultimatums from anyone – parent nor child. The child should trust the word of his parents. Favors are rewarded for proper behavior; punishment is rewarded for improper behavior. The child should understand both favors and punishment are his deserved rewards and this should not come as a surprise to him. He should know what is expected of him.

The child should have the opportunity to put forward his objections and desires – but only civilly, and certainly not loudly or continually.

The child as a recluse is possible. Home schooling permits this. There could be some loss in early social education and adaptation, but this is a double-edged sword. Peer review is powerful. Peer pressure has driven young people to suicide.

Chapter 4 Considerations of National Options

– Rejection of Intimidation

It is a legal offence to stalk or intimidate another person to the point that he feels fear of mental (or physical) harm. Intimidation is a social act which permits a person to dominate another person. The more timid or even the more polite a person is, the more easily he can be intimidated. In the middle of the word "intimidation" is the word "timid." The act of intimidation is to make the other person timid. It is to quieten him and make him feel inferior – to make him get out of the way. This is a tacit violation of the freedom of speech. The person can still speak but he would just rather not right then.

An example of political intimidation is Political Correctness. And there are people in various activist organizations who are coached on being proactive. The author has attended such "classes" in the government. There, it was taught that if someone does not speak up, they are also guilty of the offense. There are even activist signs: "Silence is Violence." That is very proactive. And it rhymes!

And it is also very silly. The sign carriers know that few people will think about it and ask themselves if it makes sense. But it will become another marching (shouting) slogan. With all in the march shouting it in unison, it would be hard to ignore.

Silence rarely causes violence!

The reverse is more likely the case.

Men learn that there are many times when it is best to just shut up and walk away. In this of many cases, silence discourages violence – or even it prevents violence.

But this logic makes little difference – "Silence is Violence" is a cute turn of a rhyming phrase and with an ignorant public, it works to arouse and generate more non-thinking followers. (Review Chicken Little's sky-falling incident on page 135.)

"If it doesn't fit – you must acquit!" This rhyme heavily influenced the outcome of a major, nationally publicized murder trial. No other thinking was required – such as, 'Did it fit before? Why doesn't it fit right now? Did it get wet with water – or blood – causing it to shrink? It is leather and leather does shrink when it gets wet and dries.' This does not matter now. It did not matter then. O.J. Simpson was free – for a while.

Ayn Rand, in her books on Objectivism, taught many people how to be objective and avoid the "argument of intimidation" which is more often than not, subjective. Avoiding intimidation is easy.

First, the act of intimidation must be recognized. It is as if there is a ball with "Intimidation" printed on it and it is being pushed at a person the intimidator is trying to silence. Even when the other person believes that he is correct, he does not respond. By this act, he is already intimidated. He might think that he is being polite. Intimidators rely on others having this thought. This is the intimidator's sloping battlefield and he has the high ground. He always has this advantage when someone avoids verbal discourse – "to be polite." The intimidator is not being polite; he is being proactive/aggressive. The intimidator should not be encouraged by permitting him to silence anyone.

A hypothetical example is in a simple conversation:

The first person makes a general comment on national conditions: "I do not see what all the fuss is about."

This is an honest observation about many things seen and read in the media today, but the activist can seize on most any opportunity.

Activist: "What?! What do you mean you do not see what the fuss is about?! How insensitive can you be?! Are you unaware of the many wrongs in society? Do you not feel any human sense of guilt or responsibility? Have you no compassion?! Or even empathy?"

Note – these are all questions. They are the tools of the intimidator. These questions are not invitations for the other person to contribute to the conversation. The questions are to intimidate the other person to silence.

This is classic intimidation. He believes that if he silences a person he has convinced him. And even better, any other listeners may think that silence is an admission of error or agreement. (Win-win for the intimidator.) The ball of intimidation has just been passed into the first speaker's hands.

The speaker needs to learn to not just stand there holding the ball, but to shove the ball back by replying: "Yes. I meant what I said. There is so much noise and discourse and nothing is explained in adequate detail. Perhaps you can enlighten me about the specifics of the wrongs that you imply are taking place. I could gain by your wisdom and I might understand it all better. Will you please list the wrongs?"

The speaker has just shoved the ball back into the intimidator's hands with a question.

If the intimidator then starts explaining them, pay close attention for parlor platitudes and generalities. Then (should he slow down while trying to hand the ball back) state, "I am hearing a lot of just generalities and platitudes in what you are saying. Can you be more specific? When? Where? Who?"

The last act of the failed intimidator might be rolling eyes and a shrug while saying, "Well, if you must ask that question, you would not understand the answer!" (The ball is shoved back.)

Reply: "That may be true, or it might be that you are just blowing smoke and cannot address the issue in detail. Are you just repeating some pamphlet? Are you someone's shill?"

The ball is back in the intimidator's hands.

The intimidator hates direct questions about anything he says. He will slyly change the subject, or he may put his intimidation ball away, or most likely look for an easier target. He cannot shut up. This energy and indignation is what fuels him.

It must be remembered that – "Whoever would overthrow the liberty of a nation must begin by subduing the freeness of speech." The public should not permit someone to subdue their freeness of speech – unless physical violence is imminent.

Stifling conversation and preventing the discussion of ideas is part of the purposes of Political Correctness, as is the arbitrary falling back to "against Community Standards." This means that the proactive can control the forum and topic – and more importantly, he will choose the very words and he will get to explain what the words really mean – to him.

Proactive Political Correctness is a social attack on an individual. Political Correctness is just the weapon of choice.

*****

A person becomes a willing victim of false premises and clever-sounding but meaningless terms when he fails in his responsibility to perpetuate the Renaissance. The Renaissance was not just some esoteric subject in school that was supposed to be read as some passing whim.

The Renaissance was the beginning of everyone using their brains in a contemplative manner and not accepting everything someone said. At the time the Roman Catholic Church possessed all knowledge.

Now it is the media.

The media is the new world church and more time is spent at their altar than at any church's.

The Renaissance was to be a work in progress. It was supposed to continue through the centuries with each person involving himself.

The citizen turns his back on his intellect when he does not question others by using his logic. Too many citizens rely on others to tell them the answer – Facebook, YouTube, Twitter, Wikipedia – anything – anybody.

Too many people demonstrate that they accept the Internet as the Oracle of Truth and the media as its spokesman. The citizen should consider all information with the question of the Renaissance: "Does this really make sense?"

The Renaissance is perpetuated by the question: not the answer. The answer will require effort; the question should be intuitive and immediate.

Statements are not correct just because they are offered with sincerity and imaginative expressions – even in rhyme.

Each citizen should ask of himself: 'Does this really make sense? Is it really science or just supposition based on philosophy and the hypothetical desire that the world should be the way someone wants to think it is – or will be?'

Too often the validity is considered without thought of the source of the information.

In law, there is the Latin term *Cui bono* – meaning "To whose advantage or to what end?" Even a cartoon character asked, "Who says I am supposed to drink three glasses of milk a day? The man who sells us milk?"

The Renaissance was not just the name of a defined, short-term, and now long-dead era. If it was, the same people who perpetuated it have killed it – the general public.

Many contrary statements are made on the assumption that they will not be questioned. But if they are questioned, then an attempt will be made to disqualify the person who asked the question and in this way any discussion of the statement's validity is avoided. All citizens should beware of "the argument of intimidation."

When someone stated "There is only one race – the human race," many people began to repeat it. It is only philosophical, cute, and appealing. When asking if it makes sense, it is simply in error. It is possible that the person saying it did not believe it either, but it is current, i.e. – Politically Correct.

– Political Process Improvements?

It is likely that there could be no effective new political party because they would have to combat or neutralize the media. A new political party would need their own 24-hour satellite media – their own TV stations and newspapers – maybe several of each. Additionally, it is unlikely that there could be any political change which could create an atmosphere of bipartisan cooperation.

The United States has a variety of ethnic organizations today and they are trying to cultivate both real and imagined disparity to maintain the different cultures' identities. They are just not yet recognized as formal political parties – though the Liberal party serves as a multicultural party and this will continue for a while.

Eventually, as with most multicultural countries, a multicultural party will develop internal competition and so this may shift into caucuses of individual ethnic groups. Again this would not apply to Caucasian, Christian, or the Southern regions.

The Democratic system can be used to eliminate the Democratic system.

This has an example in the Germany of the 1930s.

Old Yugoslavia is an example of multicultural conflict destroying one country and creating a bunch of smaller ones. Now each will need to do what they were trying to avoid: form coalitions with other countries for security and commerce.

Islam is a very conservative religion. They have their own laws, and the laws, being Holy, supersede the laws of petty nations. This seems obvious to those who would think about it. A Muslim Party might be problematic in that the Islamist religion is warrior-based and once in power (of even a city block) they want to change what is there to be like they want it. This is change but hardly a liberal one. This defines multicultural conflict. Those disagreeing are encouraged to leave.

It is an offense to Muslims, and justifiably so, that local laws are in diametric opposition to their religious laws. They do not appreciate having a local law tell them that they can turn their back on their religion/law. They respond to this offense. This, too, should not be surprising.

Liberals give the most to society once they have accumulated enough from the national producers. This does not mean the rich but rather the people who provide the government the most money – the middle class.

Other considerations could be to stop the presidential debates. The TV show "Who Wants To Be President" gets lots of viewers, but that is a personality contest and the public will then think that they are voting for a person rather than for a socioeconomic policy. When it comes to media persona, few can beat a trained actor or superb orator – or handsome Liberal.

It appears that once United States politicians are elected they go right into the next campaign with more fund-raising. Surely both parties would like to spend and campaign less for the same result.

Educating the public to break the habit of media binging would be constructive. The public's preferred source of information is the media which tells them what they want to hear. This is not enlightenment but the reinforcement of perceptions – right and wrong ones.

The public should be educated about female hysteria and anarchy and this issue would need to be heard in the Supreme Court. This female one-upwomanship has become the American French Revolution. After the revolution in France, the guillotine was a popular means for eliminating distractions. Most anyone could be accused of not being "faithful to the revolution" (whatever that meant) and then they had to prove (in some manner) that they were faithful. The accused was generally guilty by his lack of immediate proof to the contrary.

Today, it does not matter when, nor where, nor in what manner an act allegedly occurred, but any man can be accused of being disrespectful of women in many ways, and he must then prove to the public that he had not been. True or not, this is difficult to prove. His guilt is of little interest to the accuser; creating doubt is.

The basic issue is the question: If it were not true, why would she accuse him?

There could be several reasons. This applies to just a few charged offenses and there seems to be no limit in the passage of time.

Today, such an accusation is expected with any important appointment to political office.

Maybe it was as in the French Revolution – it was a politically-inspired charge. He had been politically incorrect before the word was fashionable. He had violated her civil rights before the civil rights amendment was ratified. All this makes little difference. The accusation is what is important. It is what it indicates to others and they can say what that is – for weeks. If the man is appointed to the position, strangely, the woman's charge cease. Redress is no longer an issue after his appointment or rejection.

The timing of these complaints is always noted. Candidates for the Supreme Court seem to have been great womanizers and the women are finally inspired to come forward at the most important time in the approval process. It would be fair if the Conservatives did a lot of this, as well, but in the case of the Liberal charged with being disrespectful of women, it would have little impact. There is a recent example of a high-office Liberal womanizing while in office and the Liberals were excused for it.

In many cases the trial of the accused is held in the public forum of the media. This is not even judgment by the accused's peers.

His charges of slander would be irrelevant. The accuser has nothing to lose, but gains free publicity. With the American's desire to be famous, this is payment enough for her services. If, indeed, that is all she was paid.

A woman today cannot be charged with having an abortion 40 years ago when it was illegal, but a man can be punished for doing something commonly done 40 years ago when it was not illegal. And at the most back then, it was rude and inconsiderate, and not always unsolicited. It could warrant a slap in the face (but generally did not) or a punch in the nose by the husband of said lady.

– Waiting for God

This option is the most passive and therefore has the most appeal to a Conservative. This is popular because it means one is to do nothing but retreat into a reclusive life style and wait to die. It might be advisable to move to a state that is known to be very conservative and one that has a low cost of living. Then this conservative person could just ignore the media and enjoy his books and art. He could leave the house to vote and then retreat back into his environmentally controlled chamber. He is hardly a threat to anyone...not even to his neighbors...whose names he does not know.

Chapter 5 Catastrophe!

If everyone recognized the national problems, much could be done about them, but they likely would not recognize them – or admit to cause.

The problem always goes back to basic Liberalism which generated fire making – and most likely put the sharp stone on the end of a stick – on up through the time of today and the 24-hour status quo. Many of those changes were not good, but human nature continued to look for and enjoy comfort. A lot of good things were left behind to be rediscovered later. History demonstrates this – and particularly in Europe between the Romano occupations and the Medieval period. Between those eras, much knowledge was lost during the Dark Ages.

Conservatives are generally political passivists. On occasion there are a few Conservatives who take up arms against Liberals, and when this happens, it is called Repression and this is considered in the media as being bad. When Liberals take up arms against Conservatives it is called Revolution and this is considered to be good. It is thought that the Conservative government most likely deserved it.

Not all revolutions involve war.

Once in power, the first thing the revolutionary leaders do is get rid of the revolutionaries. No government in power wants revolutionaries among the populace. Conservatism sets in to maintain all that the Liberal revolutionaries had acquired. The revolutionaries will also want to settle a few grudges.

Cuba was a good example of a revolution. I have it on good authority by one who was living in Cuba during some of their revolutions – including the last one – that Cuba often had scattered revolutions. It was almost seasonal entertainment. Then they had a big one financed by big money from overseas – not the United States – the Soviet Union.

Once the revolution was over, Cuba finally announced it was to be a Communist country and it became as conservative as the government which they had overthrown. After WWII, Russia became as tyranical in Eastern Europe as had been the Nazis. These are not isolated cases.

As Communists, conservative Cuba has sat in a virtual time lock for 60 years. This demonstrates the problem with excessive Conservatism.

The idea that a catastrophe is the only demonstrated means to reduce the liberal influences in a government is an old, but an uncontrolled one. It would need to be an act of nature to supersede party politics. It would need to be horrendous.

However, in the past, the United States was a God-fearing nation and "In God We Trust" was believed. This was important to the nation because then the United States citizen turned to the thought that maybe God was punishing them for their sinful ways.

Liberals and religion would be strange bedfellows. The idea that the United States today would rely on religion to define their problems and solutions is a little outdated.

However, this does not mean that someone else's religion could not inspire a catastrophe in the United States. It is assumed that the reason that some terrorist cell has not detonated a nuclear device in New York City or Washington, D.C., is simply because they do not have one. Yet.

The same opposing partisan factions that will shut down the government to "prove" how bad the sitting government is would exacerbate a pending catastrophic situation. First, each side would blame the other for the catastrophe and much time and energy would be lost instead of analyzing the threat.

"What did you know and when did you know it" would be tossed around night and day.

After each party had evaluated the situation, then they might see there would be nothing to gain for their party. If the United States was approaching financial ruin they might even see that the political parties need the nation and not the reverse. However, there would still be those in each party suggesting, "Let the United States collapse. This will show which political party was wrong!" This is not that hypothetical.

If such a catastrophe occurred in just the United States, China could call in their debts and foreclose. That is the easiest way for them to have their way in the United States – but then they might not even want to. They enjoy the United States as a market. But after a catastrophe, the United States would be a much smaller market.

This would need to be a world-wide catastrophe because if it happened to just the United States, there might be very few countries who would provide substantial assistance. Most every country is in competition with the United States, and even those who are not would get a quiet laugh up its national sleeve at a major United States catastrophe.

Those who depend on the United States would be sorry, but they are the ones who would least be able to help. One must choose his friends...and enemies...very carefully.

The world would need to be in the same planetary boat in the catastrophe.

A serious problem could become apocalyptic in a hurry. WWI was a family squabble that got out of hand. No one intended for there to be such bloodshed and loss; they were only trying to protect their pride and national borders or, with opportunity, increase them.

It is an interesting exercise to analyze the kinds of catastrophes which would change the mind-set of opposing political parties in the United States. This is assuming that there could be one.

Barring extra-planetary influences, there could be a major earthquake in the Western United States. A large earthquake in the Indian Ocean caused a tsunami that killed over a quarter million people. An earthquake in California could be anything from the loss of a few dishes to the loss of many square miles of heavily populated coast slipping into the Pacific.

Additionally, there are large, currently inactive volcanos which could become disturbed and erupt. There is a huge volcano in Yellowstone National Forest in Wyoming and it continues to expand. This would be many, many times larger than Mount St. Helens. Ash in the atmosphere can reduce sunlight at ground level and drop the world temperature – this would reduce world food production.

Some of these planetary catastrophes can be mutually triggered. A large earthquake in California could cause the volcano in Wyoming to erupt.

There are large volcanos in Mexico. Should there be a large eruption near Mexico City, the United States would continue to ignore its borders and the property gained from the Mexican-American war could be returned to their jurisdiction almost by default. This might not be avoidable. Mexicans coming into the United States are Mexican citizens. They do not suddenly develop an American psyche when they sneak in or race in.

Viruses and bacteria know no borders nor politics. These are the most democratic living influences on the planet.

The United States is being flooded by poor people from other countries and their health care and disease prevention is not nearly as thorough as that in the United States. Therefore, the potential threat that they offer should not be disregarded.

Additionally, in a global economy much of the world is mobile and at any given time there are 500,000 people in air transit. Considering flight distance and time-in-the-air, it is estimated that in each 24-hour day, there are 6,000,000 people flying somewhere.

The average flight length is three hours so a large number of these passengers will be on more than one aircraft during their journey.

Many diseases are airborne and transferred by breath, and the closed environment of an airliner cabin is an efficient space for spreading many of those diseases.

*****

A general review of known pathological threats follow.[17]

○ Smallpox

Smallpox is known to have been on the planet for 12,000 years and has killed 300-to-500-million people. It has destroyed cultures and reduced complete races to just small remnants. As many as 90% of native populations in the Americas died. This means South, Central, and North America. In just the 20th century alone, smallpox killed 300 million world-wide – 3 million per year. (The population of the United States is 327 million.)

Those who do recover from Smallpox are marred by skin lesions and are often blind.

It is erroneously assumed that Smallpox was eradicated world-wide, but there are two countries with known archives of the Smallpox virus: United States and Russia. There are questions about the archival security of the Russia and Siberian strains, and there is speculation that there are unknown archives elsewhere.

○ Ebola

Ebola in West Africa, which began in early 2014, is the largest and most complex outbreak of the disease to date. Ebola is in several places in Africa, and humans are globe-traveling animals. One strain of Ebola does not cause illness, while another strain has a 50% fatality rate, and another strain had a 71% fatality rate in the Sudan. There are cases where Ebola killed 90% of the infected.

A virus similar to Ebola is the Marburg virus and it was identified in 1967 when German laboratory workers were infected by monkeys from Uganda. Marburg is similar to Ebola in its bodily impact. In 1967 the mortality rate was 25% of those infected in the Congo, but in the 1998-2000 Marburg outbreak there and as well as in the 2005 outbreak in Angola, the mortality rate was 80%.

○ Human Immunodeficiency Virus (HIV/AIDS) –

HIV/AIDS has killed 36 million since 1981. There are as many as 35 million people with HIV and most are in Sub-Saharan Africa where 5% of the population is infected. This would be nearly 21

---

17 Much of the following information is from the World Health Organization (WHO) and the Center for Disease Control (CDC).

million people. In many cases, education and HIV/AIDS awareness along with new treatments have cut the death toll in half. One in twenty adults in Sub-Saharan Africa is HIV positive. This particular strain can mutate to something currently unknown.

○ Influenza –

Influenza is a threat that is here to stay. Its adaptability/ hybridization has no limits.

In a typical influenza season the deaths are 500,000 world-wide according to the World Health Organization (WHO), but new strains are always possible and the strain of 1918 is the most feared, even today. This is the H1N1 virus, having swine origin.

In 1918, it infected 3 out of 10 of the world's population and killed as many as 50 million people. It killed 25 million people in the first 25 weeks alone – a million a week. Strangely, it attacked the most hardy and healthy young adults. It seemed to leave children and the elderly alive – those with the weakest immune systems and those who were generally most vulnerable.

A natural modification of H1N1 produced H2N2 and H3N2. These were identified in mid-July, 1968, in Hong Kong. Seventeen days later the new strain was in Singapore and Vietnam, and in 90 days it was also in the Philippines, India, Australia, Europe, and the United States. About 15% of the Hong Kong population – nearly 500,000 – was infected. Though having a low mortality rate, it still killed nearly 2 million people. In the United States, the death toll was nearly 70,000.

No one knows what new strain may appear where and when – nor how dangerous it may be.

*****

○ Epidemic Bacteria

Bubonic plague killed 200 million from 1346 to 1353 in Europe and Asia. This is bacteriological rather than viral. The disease is well understood today. The last urban epidemic in the United States was in Los Angeles in 1924 and 1925. A diseased rat which was aboard a ship and was transported to the dock when the cargo was unloaded. The bacteria then spread from urban rats to rural rodents.

Consequently, there are currently bubonic plague centers in northern New Mexico, northern Arizona, southern Colorado,

California, southern Oregon, and western Nevada. Occasionally, these areas may have infected rodents.

Treatment for bubonic plague is effective once the disease is identified – and identifying it is easy once it is suspected. There is an average of 8 bubonic patients in the United States each year.

In the United States, the disease trail starts with the bacteria living in dark, dry tunnels in prairie dog towns. A prairie dog will ingest the bacteria into its blood while gnawing or cleaning itself in the tunnels. This will be through bleeding or sensitive gums. Then common fleas will feed on the prairie dog's contaminated blood. The infected fleas have difficulty feeding and are starving. In an attempt to feed, the fleas will bite again and again anything that might supply their food. Soon every prairie dog in the area, as well as all the fleas on them, will be infected.

The next animal bitten could be a human while he was feeding a wild prairie dog by hand or by merely walking through a prairie dog town. The fleas are very mobile.

When bubonic becomes pneumonic, which is statistically probable, then the disease can be spread between humans the same as the flu.

Bubonic (bacteria) is rodent/flea related, whereas another rodent-related threat is the serious Hanavirus; fortunately, it is only rodent (mouse) related. Hanavirus is very deadly according to the Centers for Disease Control and Prevention. In a large epidemic in the United States, the required medication might be too slow coming to the United States from friendly nations for it to do much good.

○ Malaria

The diseases carried by mosquitos are being discussed with the idea that as the planet warms, there will be more mosquitos. Mosquitos do not need a warm season. There are many mosquitos in Alaska, Canada, and Wisconsin, and these are areas which have a very cool climate. Mosquitos seem to be weather-proof and they are an efficient transfer system from ailing to healthy individuals.

Malaria is a parasitic disease that kills about 440,000 people a year and this is mostly in the tropical regions of Africa, particularly in the young, who have no resistence to the disease. It is uncommon in temperate climates. There is no vaccine to prevent malaria.

Many malaria parasites are unaffected by common drugs because they have, over time, become resistant to them.

The malaria-carrying mosquitos were known to exist in Texas in the 1930s, but the principal carrier of malaria is thought to have been removed from developed countries. It is not known to what extent mosquitos from tropic regions will migrate as the planet warms.

However, a person can be bitten by a disease-carrying mosquito and the parasites may travel to the liver and lie dormant there for as much as a year. The parasites end up infecting the red blood cells as they travel into the blood stream. Now a mosquito biting that person becomes a carrier and can pass the parasite to the next person it bites. Any one mosquito could bite many people.

In a global economy there is, by necessity, world travel, which can spread these diseases.

To consider other such diseases which could cause an epidemic catastrophe would be too speculative to address. However, this does not mean that there could not be one.

Chapter 6 Observations on the Political Evolution of the United States

Introduction

In the discussion of catastrophes it was necessary to consider the time element. By definition catastrophes are sudden, at least they are sudden in someone's judgment of life. This could be as little as a few seconds as in a nuclear event, or take a year or more in the case of a viral or bacteriological pandemic.

But it would be difficult to discuss "catastrophe" in the same terms as evolution. Evolution certainly takes longer. And this is its appeal. It is slow. A person can sometimes adapt to social evolution and keep pace with it.

– The Culmination of Political Parties

One might consider that the two socioeconomic philosophies which define the Liberals and Conservatives (by any party name), can be condensed into more understandable terms.

The Conservative:

Embraces and protects the acceptable status quo.

Resists change which is not guaranteed to improve the current situation.

But when Conservatism is perfected, it will be stagnant and resist all change.

This will continue until the citizens revolt to force change. This revolt is generally supported by another nation. The local "have nots" want what the "haves" have. The nation will become what the supporting nation wants it to be.

The Liberal:

Is for social change, immediately, by law or intimidation.

Enforces the individual's rights to supersede those of the general population.

In its perfected condition, this will convert a democracy into a socialist state. It will take a while for the name to actually change... and the name does not even have to change – a Democracy or a Socialist Democracy – they are both Democracies.

The name could become the Socialist Democracy of the United States of America or perhaps just the United Socialist States of America – USSA.

Whatever its name becomes, its policies will be liberal because the individual conservatives are so passive. A superb liberal orator promising change could create a Super Liberal government, and once that was done, it could be frozen in place by announcing it to be perfection and needing no more changes – thus, it becomes a Conservative government for the long-term. National Political Correctness/Community Standards would require re-education for those then wanting change.

When this has been done other places, it often fostered wars – some on a global scale.

As the citizen-producers – those who financially support the Socialist state – leave (if permitted to take their wealth with them), the state becomes poorer and it is safe from other countries because no one would want it. This will by necessity become a collective where all production capability is owned by the state. An elite party will elect someone to fill each office. This defines Communism but it could be called many things.

This condition will last much longer than the Conservative system. Should its natural resources be depleted – or if it does not have a tremendous population of poor to do repetitious cheap labor – it will become bankrupt with deepening recessions.

– Party Before Nation

In the following considerations it should always be remembered that the media controls the passion of the people.

The avid politician's and the public's inability to put the nation before the party and so eschew all thoughts of patriotism and nationalism would result in continued party animosity and polarization. From a review of history it can be seen that this will cause each party to become more extreme as they continue to attack the other party. They will also be spending effort to protect their party. The media is the vehicle for attack, as well as the fortress into which to withdraw for protection.

It might be advantageous to turn the attention back in history to a very early time when this nation was learning how to be a nation. The founders were not ignorant of political matters even though they were trying to organize a new nation. They had knowledge of, and sometimes first-hand experience with, the old political thinking of Britain.

It is difficult to read any political document from the founding fathers of this nation without recognizing that they were very smart people – some brilliant. Reading Washington's Farewell Address, which he wrote when he resigned from public service on September 19, 1796, one cannot fail to recognize his genius of thought. His warnings about political parties strikes a note of recognition today. His accurate assessment of political parties was that they turn the citizen's attention and loyalty from the best interests of the nation to those of a political party.

He wrote the same warnings for those who have their national pride diluted by local, geographic pride – as if regional pride could be separated from national pride. He was speaking of the "North, South,

East, and West," and though these regions were not as far apart as they are today, neither was the communication as immediate as now.

*****

"*Demogos*" (demogogue) in Greek meant a leader with superb oratory skills and only later did it mean one who would ignore logic and use only speaking skills to move people to do his bidding.

Even in 1716, it was written that "A plausible, insignificant word, in the mouth of an expert demogogue is a dangerous and dreadful weapon."

The Greek extreme of such a *demogos* was a *tryannos* (tyrant).

With the current party polarization, one party can eventually put up the *Demagos Tyrannos* as a candidate. He will be elected because of the growing public dissatisfaction with either or both parties. With no compromise, there is no cooperation and this increases partisan polarity.

This *Demagos Tyrannos* candidate will be different and someone so extreme that he can have a hidden agenda – the less detail that is discussed, the less opposition. Generalities will be assumed to be positive. No one would suggest unpopular change.

A cabal, which is hardly more than what the current two political parties' national committees are, will quietly dictate the action of the party. If either party is to function as they desire, it will eventually appear that it is necessary for the stronger party to eliminate the weaker. This can happen – and without a catastrophe, it cannot be avoided.

The political mechanics to do this peacefully did not exist in Germany when a similar situation occurred as that which presently exists in the United States.

The opposing German parties were the old Socialist Democratic Party (SPD) founded in 1874 (and very conservative), and the new party, the National Socialist German Worker's Party (NSDAP). The NSDAP was initially a mere labor organization but they gained the orator – *Demagos Tyrannos* – and then the party name, NSDAP, was shortened to be the Nazi Party. This was a liberal party promising wholesale changes.

An Enabling Act was put forward which meant that in times of national emergency, the "president" could invoke acts of his own creation and ignore precedence. Such acts are said to be necessary because it would take dangerously long to go through a "legislature."

The SPD, being conservative, opposed this act. The Nazis supported it because they had a plan and an organization geared for change – lots of changes – rapid ones. They were activists and they had an agenda. And they had a lot of marches to excite the undecided.

The SPD had gone from the controlling party in 1930 to having just 18% of the votes in 1933; whereas, the Nazis had gone from 18% in 1930 to 44% in 1933 and by then the Nazis had the majority in any multiple party vote. This turn-around was due to the speeches of the *Demagos Tyrannos*. He had only radio and film. (Any *Demagos Tyrannos* can do much more and do it faster with TV.)

The Enabling Act passed.

Then a fire in a public building was used by *Demagos Tyrannos* as the excuse to invoke the Enabling Act. The fire was blamed on a revolutionary group sponsored by a foreign government. This did not have to be true, but having it touted in the media had it believed.

Demagos Tyrannos now had full control of the country and this was done legally. He did this by promising change as a liberal and once this was gained, he then wanted to protect what he had established – his new status quo. Now, he was very conservative and restrictive in Germany, and being intense, he was also brutal to a new extreme.

As *Demagos Tyrannos,* Adolf Hitler used the Enabling Act to legally take control of Germany and dispense with the elected government representative body.

An American *Demagos Tyrannos* could use a similar act – the National Emergencies Act (the presidential emergency powers act).

In the United States, this National Emergencies Act has been used many times and many acts are still in force. This can cause one to wonder how long an emergency can last. Some of the acts do not seem to have even been a national emergency. This is a powerful tool if the president has his agenda established within his party.

Such a 1930s German-style legal revolution could occur in the United States. This time there would be many political factions with each being accused of evil deeds – in some manner. This would dilute any combined organized opposition – no compromise/ no cooperation.

The citizens can become as fanatical as organized political parties because the media empowers them. Even in 2018 long friendships have ended because of political party affiliation and alliances; indeed, families have to declare that there will be no political talk at family reunions, and there are many organizations who have similar rules. At first these were polite suggestions; now they are expected to be stated.

– The Human Paradox

The human animal is a complex system. He is said to be a creature of habit, and there is proof of this, yet at the same time he is the most adaptable animal – and there is proof of this – even on the lunar surface! Within minutes after first arriving on the moon, an astronaut is seen enjoying the 1/6th gravity of the moon by bounding like a kangaroo across the lunar surface. This <u>defines</u> and <u>demonstrates</u> adaptability.

Somewhere in these contradictory attributes there appears a paradox, and this, too, defines the human.

He is a Liberal in accepting change (adapting).

He is a Conservative when adapting and maintaining that change to become a habit.

He is both, seemingly at the same time, depending on the issue. The circumstances determine which he is at what time.

<u>This recognition is missing today in the United States.</u>

Consequently, the United States is a nation of paradoxical humans. The citizens must choose between changes all the time and this prevents adaptation/habit; or they can choose adaptation while knowing they are in a constantly changing world and this precludes expectation of recurring conditions... therefore, there can be no habit in a constantly changing world. This back and forth changing appears to have a 4- or 8-year cycle.

Discomfort exists when the human is unsuccessfully seeking comfort. After hundreds of thousands of years, the human still wants comfort and when this is not possible for him to attain, he feels disenfranchised and he behaves in irrational ways. He is forced back and forth between human and non-human.

It will take a lot of unnatural acts to force the realization on the Liberals and Conservatives that they need each other because apart they simply represent one-half of what humans are to be.

They each must be present and participate to maintain the environment which created the modern human – one who is liberal in one instance while being conservative in the next; or being both at one time but on different issues.

Democracies evolve, as well. Given the flexibility that democracy promises, the people desiring comfort will work hard to acquire their preferred life style, but later, why should they continue? If they do nothing, they will not go hungry. This is an important consideration.

So it comes to pass that humans are paradoxes in their acceptance of a new condition and then their adaptability. And each human is also desirous of comfort and when each gains some degree of satisfaction in his lifestyle, he will prefer that by habit and that, too, is part of his natural makeup.

To be the complete person that humans are to be, there must be a government that recognizes that people are never all one thing in all instances. There must be consideration of context and a working relationships between liberal and conservative politics – only in this way can the political system accommodate the nature of humans. Not doing this just frustrates and degrades all that humans can be.

The nation was intended to be a republic, but the idea of a democracy exists in the Preamble of the Constitution with "We, the people..." We were to be a nation of people dedicated to a common cause. We were not to be a divided nation of people dedicated exclusively to their disparate political parties.

Only by accepting the paradoxical nature of humans – that nature which brought humans from the lowest end of the food chain to the highest – will the political parties begin to put the unity of nation first and cooperate for the benefit of the complete human.

Finis

Epilogue

In my ten nonfiction books, I have had many concluding divisions. I have had addendums, bibliographies, glossaries, notes about the author, etc., but this is only the second epilogue.

In the first epilogue I explained how I ended that particular book: *Random Thoughts From A Veering Mind – A Journal of Whimsy.*

I had decided that I did not want to complete that book; I just wanted to stop it. With that book, "completing" it would have meant that I had died in the process of writing it and it would then be published posthumously. This was an option which I preferred to avoid. So I just quit writing it and explained why in the Epilogue.

In this epilogue, however, I want to reaffirm a few impressions in this book, *A Social History of the United States From 1945 to 2018 – With 20/20 Hindsight.*

After my near-two years of research and 90,000 words, the reader has every right to expect me to list a menu of solutions to the problems addressed in this book.

I am sorry, I cannot do this. I am sorry, truly, I am.

If I could see any bright way out of the current national situation, I would happily suggest it. I would be pleased to just know what it might be, whether I suggested it or not. All we can do is keep asking, "Does this really make sense?" And then vote for the socioeconomic philosophy that we think is the best way for people to be governed.

The United States has had 263 years of inertia to reach this point in its history. But a well-studied historian in Scotland said that a democracy (by that function; not name) has about 300 years to exist. Its end occurs when the voters demand more from the producers than the producers can or are willing to provide. With 37 more years to go and the rate the nation is changing, I think the Scot academician is correct.

Obviously, I am content with my life. (If aiming low enough, one can be a success early in life.) This contentment of mine, almost by definition, means I am not an activist. I have never been one. At one time I was for capitalism and free enterprise and this made me a

Conservative, but I was also then a Social Liberal. (I was also young, and in a world sense, unknowing.)

I was liberal on several issues, but now I am a Conservative about most everything. I have worked much of my 85 years to attain this life style and I would like for it to continue – until I die.

There has been but one wife – which in itself seems significant, but not to the two of us nor to our children. It just is. This all happened while we were not looking or counting the 65 years we have been married. Indeed, we have been together beginning as "steady daters," for 70 years. Perhaps this extreme degree of "status quo" makes me a real Conservative and one of the more rare sorts.

So I am Conservative, yet I am an unhappy one. I do not want more Conservatism. I do not want more Liberalism. At any given time, I think it takes both sides of the socioeconomic ideas to find the most appropriate and constructive path for our nation; indeed, for the paradoxical human – and this defines us all. And all political decisions should be <u>issue-dependent</u>. At the same time, one or the other philosophy should be applied, or they might each add a little, take out a little, and there be a consensus. This likely would be best in most all circumstances.

But today, we do not have a single national purpose and we do not have a united United States. I cannot imagine what could create a single sense of Americanism in the combined Legislature. The current one of combative political parties – parties which are often excessively petty in their squabbles and show no national concern. The socioeconomic philosophies should continue, but some effort could be made to accept that neither philosophy is to serve all the time and on every issue.

As a cultural anthropologist, if I were in a completely conservative society, I would spend my time trying to get out of it.

If I were in a completely liberal society, as I nearly am, I would try to get out of it, as well. The easiest way to do this would be to move to some conservative state, get a little house, and become a recluse. I would avoid most all media and submerge myself in the books, research, and arts I enjoy. I would show much care about who I wanted to be my friends. I know that in time there would be fewer and fewer of them, but that is not the result of political persuasion; it is just the fact of ageing.

Consequently, I thought this epilogue was necessary to assist the reader in the assimilation of what has been presented in this book.

This book is unlike any of my previous books and I cannot imagine my writing another like it. I am a little surprised that I completed it after becoming so discouraged so many times by my research. But I was convinced it should be written. And I still am. And it should be read. I am pleased with it and I think it is worthy of consideration and dissemination.

Someone, sometime in perhaps the year 2080 might read of the United States and its history through 1945 and wonder how it could have all gone so wrong. Such a 2080-person might find a dusty copy of this book or a text file on-line (or in whatever electronic archival system would be in use then). They then might wonder, 'Could they have not done something to perpetuate what they had?'

Certainly they could have.

They just did not.

Not so strangely, to cheer me somewhat, I started thinking about the next book while writing this book. The next book will be nonfiction, humourous, and with a good many grins in it – I hope.

In spite of the above, I enjoy my life. I have my personal English bar "The Windmill Free House" with Russian, Mexican, British, Carribean, Brazilian, etc., drinks.

I realized a while back that I was enjoying Colombian coffee from a cup made in China with a Route 66 logo on it, and I was setting it on a 1920 art nouveau table with an English ceramic top.

I was reading a book published in 1889 Victorian England, and as I read, the book was being illuminated by a 1930 art deco bridge lamp.

Playing in the background was music by 1927 crooners.

The chair I was sitting in was red velvet and of my own fabrication, style, and design, which I call "Mexican Mediterranean."

But this is a little less the result of multiculturism than it is the result of a Global Economy. This is all by choice. It is not required of me by law, nor is it likely to be replaced by market decree.

However, the computer system I am using for this manuscript has an old XP utility program and I will use it until it will no longer function. It was really good for a long time and I would like for it to continue. But I will have to replace it with something I do not want, do not need, will not understand, and when all these undesirable things occur, I will have to give a company a lot of money for it.

I do not know how long this new change will last before I will be forced to replace it yet again.

This is just more frivolous change I will have to accept in my life – no – it is not change; it is forced replacement.

About the Author

Ken Cashion is a prolific writer with biographies, histories, and travel journals in print. He has books about the engineering profession, and music, as well as those of general interests – all nonfiction. And now with *A Social History of the United States From 1945 to 2018 – With 20/20 Hindsight,* he has a book containing the results of his research and general observations on the many events and subjects that have helped shape the modern United States and will continue to do so into the distant future.

As a historian and Anglophile, he has traveled extensively in Britain and has written and taught three college courses on the social history of Britain from 500,000 BC through 1707 AD.

During his 37-year engineering career, the last 27 of which were with NASA, he has written myriad scientific papers and technical procedures. He had two significant patents awarded during the Apollo program.

He has also had nonfiction articles in the national press.

He continues his writing and research in a small, quiet south Mississippi town with his wife, Bettie, and cat brothers, William and Charlie.

Made in the USA
Coppell, TX
04 November 2019